Empowering Gifted Educators as Change Agents

Through an accessible, research-based program of professional learning, this critical resource empowers gifted educators to become change agents for equity in their classroom, school, or district.

Designed for practitioners seeking to increase the rate of identification and retention of underserved gifted populations, this book guides readers through the Four Zones of Equity-Driven Professional Learning Model, a practical set of tools specific to the field of gifted education. Readers will develop an all-inclusive professional learning plan specific to their teachers' understanding of cultural norms, guiding participants to gain insight into the characteristics of gifted marginalized students, coaching faculty in ways to increase classroom support, and equipping educators with the tools necessary to build effective partnerships with parents and communities.

Ideal for gifted educators, coordinators, and administrators, this playbook is packed with practical ideas, strategies, and activities to bring meaningful, equity-driven professional learning to life.

Katie D. Lewis is Associate Professor and Director of Secondary Education and Post-Baccalaureate Programs at York College of Pennsylvania, USA. She is also a Board Member of The Association for the Gifted (CEC-TAG).

Angela M. Novak is Assistant Professor and Academically and Intellectually Gifted Coordinator at East Carolina University, USA. She is also a Board Member of CEC-TAG and Co-Chair of the National Association for Gifted Children's Diversity and Equity Committee.

"The authors' approach toward equity-driven professional learning takes a comprehensive view toward creating systemic change in serving diverse gifted learners. Unlike 'piece-meal' approaches, this authentic resource takes a broad, overarching examination of the abundant obstacles that have prevented progress toward equity in gifted education. They then demonstrate, through numerous cases, scenarios, lessons, and activities, specific and practical actions school leaders and teachers can implement to overcome biases and obstacles inherent in our schools. Every teacher in the U.S. should have this book; I will be buying it for my teachers!"

Dina Brulles, Director of Gifted Education for Paradise Valley USD in Phoenix, Arizona, *USA*

"The Four Zones Equity-Driven Professional Learning Model (4ZEPL) has the power to restructure access to gifted and talented services in the classroom, at the school site, and district level. This guide offers a practical model that integrates culturally responsive professional development in response to the student's funds of knowledge. This book is a necessary addition to every district administrator, coordinator, or teacher's bookshelf who advocates for equitable access to gifted and talented services."

Julia Nyberg, Executive Director of California Association for the Gifted, *USA*

"The authors take a needed step in moving the equity in gifted education conversation to include the root causes and families and communities in the iterative process. Through the 4ZEPL framework and process, educators will address underrepresentation in their gifted services and mitigate attrition because of mismatched services or the absence of appropriate 'bridge' supports. This text will be instrumental in empowering and equipping gifted educators to exact positive changes in their schools and districts."

Monica Simonds, Director of Advanced Learning Programs and Services for Richardson ISD, Texas, *USA*

"Written with administrators and teacher educators in mind, *Empowering Gifted Educators as Change Agents* provides a fresh look at what equity-driven, research-based professional learning looks like. For those hoping to close the gap between best practices, identification and retention of under-served gifted learners, there can be no better playbook for change than the Four Zones Equity-Driven Professional Learning Model. The authors of this book have produced a game plan to achieve transformative change that empowers teachers to be the change while becoming advocates for antiracism not just in thoughts but also in practice."

Wendy A. Behrens, President-Elect of CEC-TAG, *USA*

"The need for greater inclusivity and culturally responsive practices in gifted education cannot be ignored. Dr. Lewis and Dr. Novak have presented a systematic approach to equity driven professional learning that will guide school faculty as they progress on their individual journeys toward diversity, equity, and inclusion in gifted services."

C. Matthew Fugate, University of Houston-Downtown, *USA*

"Finally, a book about engaging teachers of gifted in ongoing professional learning using data to determine needs! A bonus is the conversational tone emitted throughout. Reading it feels like I'm chatting with Angela and Katie over coffee. Powerful."

Jolene Teske, Advanced Learning Supervisor for Des Moines, *USA*

"Chock-full of creative ideas for quality professional learning activities, this playbook provides facilitators with fresh learning experiences to build awareness about equity in delivering gifted education services. By exploring their Four Zone Equity-Driven Professional Learning Model, the authors lead readers through understanding applicable research and theories relevant to delivering culturally responsive professional learning."

Bronwyn MacFarlane, Editor for *STEM Education for High Ability Learners* and *Specialized Schools for High Ability Learners: Designing and Implementing Programming, USA*

Empowering Gifted Educators as Change Agents

A Playbook for Equity-Driven Professional Learning

Katie D. Lewis and Angela M. Novak

NEW YORK AND LONDON

Cover image: Getty Images, Alexandr Vorontsov, Creative #: 1252589858

First published 2022
by Routledge
605 Third Avenue, New York, NY 10158

and by Routledge
4 Park Square, Milton Park, Abingdon, Oxon, OX14 4RN

Routledge is an imprint of the Taylor & Francis Group, an informa business

Library of Congress Cataloging-in-Publication Data
A catalog record for this title has been requested

ISBN: 9781032051383 (hbk)
ISBN: 9781032045689 (pbk)
ISBN: 9781003196204 (ebk)

DOI: 10.4324/9781003196204

Typeset in Palatino
by Deanta Global Publishing Services, Chennai, India

For those that came before and those that follow;
gifted minds and souls that raised us and inspire us.

In Memory of Ginny and Dick Hubbard, and Julia Novak

For John, Mom, and Dad

To our children:
Sean, Katie, Emma, Patrick
Izzy, Thomas, Jake

Contents

Acknowledgments

We gratefully acknowledge those coaches, athletes, teachers, and students whose stories have shaped this book. We could not have done this without our families, friends, and colleagues who have championed our dreams, encouraging and believing in us along the way. Whether it has been a word of wisdom or taking the kids so we can work, your support has been invaluable, thank you. We are humbled by the everlasting love of our parents; they have been our greatest fans. Thank you to all who helped make this book possible. We love and appreciate you.

Introduction

Olympic Sprinter Wilma Rudolph said, "Never underestimate the power of dreams and the influence of the human spirit. We are all the same in this notion: The potential for greatness lives within each of us."[1] We are teachers. We are frontline warriors during a national pandemic, and we go on teaching. We teach in classrooms with asbestos and leaky roofs, with 20-year-old books, or with no supplies at all, and nevertheless, we persist. We've practiced tornado drills, nuclear drills, and active shooter drills, and yet, we educate. We teach. We lead. We inspire.

The "Trouble" with Professional Development

But when it comes to attending a professional learning (PL) session after school on a Wednesday afternoon… well… We have all been there, whether you are a first-year teacher or a veteran teacher, stuck in yet another professional development session where a presenter is droning on and on. Perhaps you are a daydreamer, a multi-tasker, or a doodler but as we all know, teachers can be the worst students. Often, we are guilty of all the off-task behaviors our students routinely demonstrate—which drive us nuts! Yet, at the same time, hopefully, you have also experienced professional development (PD) done better, as an actively engaged and motivated learner, excited to take new ideas back to your classroom, sharing and listening with colleagues. Too often though, these feelings of renewed energy quickly fade after the PD when teachers return to their own classrooms and are not provided the support or follow-up necessary to make lasting changes.

The good news is that the field of education recognized these struggles with professional development workshops and responded with a change to PL best practices. Professional learning—with a purposeful shift in terminology from development to learning—is based in adult learning theory.[2]

How do adults learn? After all, how we teach students is based on what we know about student development theory, though that comes with a caveat: traditional student learning theory is based on developmental, moral, and behavioral psychological theorists that studied predominantly, if not exclusively, White subjects, e.g., Piaget, Skinner, Vygotsky, Erickson, and Kohlberg;[3]

DOI: 10.4324/9781003196204-1

thus, it is not culturally responsive or relevant. Professional Learning at its core definition suffers the same caveat, but we'll get to that in Chapter 3.

Professional learning which focuses on all things gifted faces all the same struggles, but often these struggles are amplified due to the limited amounts of PL focused on the nature and needs of gifted education. Requirements for gifted and talented programs vary state by state, and this inconsistency directly impacts the frequency and quality of PL focused on the gifted and talented. For example, in Pennsylvania, there is a mandate to serve and identify gifted students, yet there is not a mandate for PL for teachers of the gifted. In contrast, Texas mandates gifted programs identify and serve gifted students, as well as requiring 30 hours of PD focused on the nature and needs of gifted learners and an annual update of 6 hours of professional development for teachers of the gifted. Pennsylvania's gifted programs may need to sneak in their PL sessions for gifted teachers, while in Texas, the struggle becomes how to effectively use the 6 hours of required training. These two states highlight the struggles of implementing effective PL targeting all things gifted. We are preaching to the choir, right? This is where this book comes in—providing a structured (yet flexible) approach to delivering equity-driven PL for educators of the gifted. A colleague of Angela's, Dr. Loni Crumb, said in a book club discussion of *Me and White Supremacy*, "It's okay if we're preaching to the choir sometimes… the choir needs practice too."[4] Let's start by looking at the current trends and best practices in professional learning.

Shifting to Professional Learning

The shift to professional learning encompasses the need for data-driven training: why are we sitting around this table after school? This gets to one of Angela's favorite questions in gifted education, professional learning, and just to ask in general, "So what?" What's the purpose, what's the meaning, how does this connect to our students' lives, as learners, as practicing members of the discipline? What about this is culturally relevant? What about this is driving equity? Professional learning at its core is driven by data; and by data, we're not talking about test scores! Information about needed professional learning comes from many sources: teachers' needs assessments (self-report), teacher and administrative surveys (reliable and valid outside scales), teacher observations scales completed by self, peers, and/or administration, analysis of evaluation tools, reliable and valid surveys of: students, families, and community members, and outside evaluations of the district. And yes, test scores may be part of the equation—as long as that data source helps provide guidance to selecting the appropriate topics of professional learning. Does this sound a little like using a pre-assessment to determine what students know before starting in on a new unit? Just like with your students, this data-driven process comes in steps: carefully and intentionally plan and administer the assessment, conscientiously collect and analyze the data (Angela tells her assessment classes that disaggregation is their best friend!), and then create an equitable plan for "what's next."

The shift to professional learning from professional development has a lot to do with "what's next": learning is a lifelong process; it is not over once you complete an hour-long workshop on Thursday afternoon. Ongoing and sustained are key components of professional learning. Ongoing is typically temporal: how long is the professional learning sequence going to last? Sustained is similar, but tends to have more of a trainer/trainee contact-hours reference: how long will you have continued access to the trainer for support? Realistically, you may see these terms (like many in education) used interchangeably, but for the purposes of this book, we will use the definitions above. Ideally, effective professional learning is multiple sessions over an extended time with prolonged engagement with the facilitator or trainer. Timing is an integral component to successful professional learning, and what deviates the term from development. So too, is the content.

Authentic learning is a research-based best practice in teaching; in professional learning, facilitators don't need to reach far to come up with authentic situations, their students come to class with ready-made theory-to-practice environments, ripe for exploration. Different authors or researchers may refer to this aspect of professional learning as job-embeddedness, contextualization, theory-to-practice connections, coherent, or transferable. While each has its own individual connotation, the overall gist is the ability for the participant to make relevant meaning of the content and concepts of the professional learning by integrating it into their work experiences. This means that if the professional learning is for elementary teachers, the content should be relevant at that level, and include examples and relevant contextualization for all specialists and administrators that are attending the professional learning sessions: what does this look like in first grade as compared to fourth, in PE, or in a 3–5 Resource class? Two additional aspects of content included in the professional learning shift are collaboration and reflection. While professional development in the past may have included one or both of these aspects, both collaboration and reflection are essential components to effective professional learning. Ideally, facilitators encourage collaborative work, a time for collaborative reflection for the group, as well as time and space for individual processing and reflection.

We also know, as teachers, not to get buried in eduspeak, the meaningful (or sometimes not-so-meaningful!) jargon used by educators. Or, as Angela prefers to welcome college students yearly to what she describes as the "joy that is *The Princess Bride*"; she quotes Inigo Montoya, artfully played by Mandy Patankin, to illustrate eduspeak: "You keep using that word, I do not think it means what you think it means." For the purposes of this book, we will use the term professional learning, or PL, to refer to professional learning as described above, meeting the requirements of ongoing, sustained, collaborative, job-embedded, reflective, data-supported, and intensive. When we are referring to more traditional teacher training, we will use the term professional development, or PD. We will explicitly note any exceptions to this terminology, which will likely be when we are using direct quotations from outside sources.

ESSA

This change was cemented in 2015 by the Every Student Succeeds Act (ESSA)[5] which revised its definition of the term professional development to mean all activities should be created with the purpose of providing "educators (including teachers, principals, other school leaders, specialized instructional support personnel, paraprofessionals, and as applicable, early childhood educators with the knowledge and skills necessary to enable students to succeed in a well-rounded education,"[6] including being sustained, intensive, collaborative, job-embedded, data-driven, and classroom-focused (Section 8101(42)). While the legislation kept the term professional development, the definition clearly aligns with the research supporting professional learning best practices. ESSA guidelines encouraged districts to move away from one-day PD workshops in which topics are briefly covered to ongoing PL sessions where one topic may be explored in depth with classroom applications using collaboration between grade level teams. As teachers, this makes sense—we know from our own classrooms that students retain more information, make changes, and see growth when learning is a recursive process.

Tight budgets are a reality in schools, and COVID guidelines have only added to the constraints. You may be asking yourself, this PL sounds great, but how in the world am I going to be able to pay for this out of my budget (or be able to convince my administrator to add this to the budget line)? Good news is that teachers are resourceful—we know how to do a lot on a shoestring budget, but there is some federal funding available, which we can tap into for our gifted programs. ESSA specifically included gifted and talented students in both Title I and Title II funding.[7]

Title I funding provides federal funding to districts/schools where a high percentage of the students are identified as children from low-income families. Title I funds are designed to be used to provide academic support and services (purchasing of curriculum, personnel to deliver instruction and other academic opportunities) to students who are at risk of failing based on their socioeconomic status. ESSA specifically identifies that gifted and talented students are included in Title I funding, and that funds may be used to identify and serve gifted students.

Title II funds are earmarked for professional learning which is focused on increasing student achievement through developing the content knowledge and skill of the educators (including the administrators!). Title II funds are awarded when districts have developed professional learning plans which identify the students' needs, and how the PL will target these skills for the educators. Districts may specify that the funds will be used to provide PL focused on gifted education pedagogy.

Accessing funds will require some advocacy to your administration and school district, but for the first time, the law does specifically include gifted and talented education. To find out more about how to apply, go to the US Department of Education website or the National Association for Gifted Children, Advocate for Gifted Children webpage.[8]

Standards in Professional Learning

While the word *standards* may make you cringe thinking of standardizing tests and test pressure, don't let it scare you off! Standards in PL, much like academic standards, are designed to ensure that educators, like students, are receiving high-quality learning experiences which translate into student growth. Evolved over time, current equity-driven professional learning standards reflect the tenets of ESSA; effective PL is systematic, continuous, embeds time for reflection and feedback, as well as being grounded in practical applications to the classroom. Understanding a little bit of the history of the standards is useful knowledge for you, as you develop PL for your districts. The first thing to note is that equity-driven gifted PL standards are composed of several sets of PL standards. In order to truly address the depth and complexity of equity-driven PL, one must pull from several sets of standards, beginning with the professional learning set of seven standards developed by Learning Forward.[9] These seven standards are supported by research, resources for monitoring and assessing the effectiveness of the PL, and are a great starting point. The first standard is *Learning Communities* which emphasizes that communities where learning is continuous, and responsibility is shared and aligned to goals, results in increased educator effectiveness. *Resources,* the second standard, recognizes that it is important to work collaboratively to ensure resources are prioritized, shared throughout districts so that the goal of increasing educator effectiveness is met. The third standard, *Learning Designs,* states that PL should incorporate multiple research-based theories and approaches to creating PL in order to increase educator effectiveness. Next, the standard of *Outcomes,* which addresses the alignment of PL goals with student academic achievement. *Leadership* is the sixth standard, which focuses on the role of the leaders to carefully develop, advocate, and implement PL. *Implementation*: PL must focus on long-term benefits and teacher change, rather than one-shot workshops. The final standard, *Data,* recognizes that effective PL must be monitored and assessed through data collection.[10]

While the Learning Forward standards set the stage for highly effective PL, they do not address diversity, equity, or cultural awareness in PL—or even the unique needs in gifted education. This is where the National Association for Gifted Children (NAGC) Standards and the Council for Exceptional Children-The Association for the Gifted (CEC-TAG) come into play. NAGC, revised its standards for gifted programming in 2019 with the purpose of increasing its focus on equity as well as aligning the PL learning outcomes to student outcomes—this alignment makes sense, right? If the PL is successful, then teachers experience a change in their practice, which results in a change in student learning. Remember, while teachers are not graded on PL, there must be a process in place to evaluate the effectiveness of the PL—with the intention of being able to increase teacher effectiveness—but not to penalize the teachers (or facilitators!). NAGC gifted programming standards provide a minimum of practices, but are not enough to do justice to equity, inclusion, diversity, or culturally responsive pedagogy in PL (see Chapter 3 for a discussion on the NAGC standards that address equity). To understand best practices in equity PL, we turn first to the National Education Association (NEA) which recognizes five basic cultural competence areas for educators. First, *valuing diversity;* educators and systems must work toward accepting differences and then move from acceptance to respecting cultural differences. This enables educators to reflect and become *culturally self-aware*; a truly critical piece to equity is the ability to know one's self in order to understand others. Understanding one's own experiences, beliefs, and values enables one to paint a clearer picture of their sense of self, which, in turn, may impact how they fit within their school and community dynamics. *Dynamics of difference* is a key skill area which addresses potential understanding miscommunications and ways to react to these challenges. *Knowledge of students' culture* recognizes that teachers must learn about the nature and needs of the students in their classrooms in order to effectively meet their needs. The last skill set is *institutionalizing cultural knowledge and adapting to diversity*, at which point, educators are culturally competent and are equipped with the skills to serve the population at large and work toward institutionalizing the understanding. We will take a closer look at culturally responsive professional learning, the impact of culturally responsive training, and the need for equity literacy in Chapter 3.

Research-Based Best Practices in the Field of Professional Learning

We've covered the shift from PD to PL, ESSA and its corresponding funding, and the standards related to PL. Next comes one of the more important decisions you will need to make as you embark on your PL journey. What PL format best fits the needs of your teachers, your school/district, your time constraints, and your budget? This decision must not be made lightly, as it plays a significant role in the successful implementation of your PL. Consider your classroom instruction—if you do not take into consideration the needs of your learners, even a well-written lesson plan may fall flat. Let's take a look at two research-based best practice PL models: the professional learning community (PLC) and the cohort model.

Professional Learning Community

First, the professional learning community (PLC). A PLC is a school-wide approach to PL, where educators engage in a cyclical process of reflection, learning about instructional practices, collaboration with colleagues, and evaluating the impact on student outcomes. A key component of a PLC is that educators identify a need, a desired area of study based on what is happening in their classrooms or at their school. Sometimes in implementation, PLCs can tend toward more administratively led topic choices; it is ideal if the educators recognize the need and are invested in the subject.

Action research is often implemented as part of a PLC, with a focus on growing as a team. Educators are encouraged to collaborate—not only sharing what works, but also asking questions. PLCs encourage educators to take new ideas back to the classroom where they are implemented and/or modeled by a peer, analyze the results, and begin the cycle again with the goal of continuous student growth. Because of the cyclical nature, a PLC is naturally ongoing, typically lasting for a semester or a year. Meetings can vary in structure, ideally biweekly, though some schools enable weekly meeting times for PLCs, while others are not able to meet more than once per month. A PLC should meet at least monthly to be effective, though more often is ideal; the ongoing aspect is key to the work. Sustained leadership is also essential, though PLCs are often internally led rather than by an external facilitator.

Strengths of this model include: the potential for collaboration amongst educators where ideas of what works (or doesn't work) can be shared within the context of community; the opportunities for reflection (both individual and group) are built in; it is adaptable for the online learning environment; it is an environment that fosters relationships amongst educators through the development of mutual respect and trust; and it is a platform that keeps educators informed of current educational research.[11] When implemented with fidelity, PLCs result in positive student outcomes. A challenge to a PLC can be the facilitation; while it is sustained, often due to leadership through an internal facilitator (often a grade-level chair), that individual may not have the appropriate training in the pedagogy of the topic. Additionally, if the teachers are not able to implement the practices discussed in the PLC, the action-research cycle can be halted: the administration must be fully on board! Not just the administration, but all members of the PLC should be open to change, and the members of the PLC must be valued within their community as teachers, as scholars, as humans. The attitudes and the culture of the members and the school and community are integral to the success of the PLC, the professional learning that occurs within, and the impact that PL has on the children.

Cohort

A second commonly used PL approach is the cohort model. Several of the elements will seem similar as the model is presented: a group of educators move through an intensive, reflective, sustained, ongoing, collaborative, job-embedded, data-driven series of professional learning experiences as a unit. Didn't we just talk about that? A principal difference between a PLC and a cohort is the makeup of the membership. While a PLC generally comes from within a school building, a cohort is generally pulled from a district, but across schools. The group may have grade or school level in common (all elementary or 3rd grade) or perhaps the same subject area (all language arts or all gifted) but a distinction found in cohorts is the ability to network and share ideas across schools, bringing the new knowledge "back to the building."

Similar to PLCs, cohorts are a shared learning experience, and their effectiveness is largely dependent upon the culture established within the cohort, the ability to implement the learning in the classroom/school, and reflect and collaborate with the cohort in that cyclical process.[12] Cohorts are more likely to be led by outside facilitators; as groups from different buildings gather in a central location, a single facilitator leads the group. While this can be an internal facilitator within the school district, it can also be a contracted individual or group. Cohorts may take the form of a local certification program offered by the district, or formal coursework offered by college or university. Because of the gathering aspect of a cohort, they are likely to meet less often than a PLC; more likely on a monthly basis. The virtual learning environment strengthened by the physical school closures of 2019–2021 provide new insight into online professional learning options, and how PLCs and cohorts can be supported in this modality.

Supporting PLCs and Cohorts Online

A few years ago, if you'd asked us about online professional learning options, we'd have talked to you about webinars, online communities, listservs, and online classes. In the wake of the COVID-19 pandemic and the world's shift to online learning, online working, online conferences, online socializing, online... everything... well, now we have a slightly different perspective! There have been aspects of professional learning, and in particular components of PLCs and cohorts, that have been able to be completed in an online format, just like we have had online classes at universities since Angela earned her Master's degree (that was 15 years ago!). Throughout this book, we will be presenting the Four Zones Equity-Driven Professional Learning (4ZEPL) as a cohort model, with the understanding that moving forward, we are using the term cohort *interchangeably* with PLC: the activities themselves that we are describing could be done with either model. In each chapter, we will also offer suggestions, as appropriate, for how best to support the use of the 4ZEPL through online modalities. As a general rule, we offer these suggestions:

- **Incorporate multiple modalities.**
  - Do not depend on "readings" alone. Use TED Talks, videos, webinars, podcasts, songs, and poetry.
  - Vary the readings—use chapters, articles, books, and KidLit.
  - Incorporate all voices. Black voices. Brown voices. Queer voices. Disabled voices. Student voices. Parent voices. Teacher voices. Admin voices. But in particular, seek out voices at the intersections. Black Queer voices. Brown Disabled voices. Thrice-exceptional student voices.
- **Find an appropriate platform.**
  - You may have an online platform already through your district; it is ideal to use a learning management system, or LMS, that educators are already familiar with, rather than branching out into something new for the purposes of professional learning. It may be what you use for e-learning, or where you house curriculum resources.
  - Consider the activities that you will engage in; can your LMS:
    - Host online meetings?
      - With breakout rooms?
      - With polling?
      - With annotation or other interactive features?
    - Hold synchronous or asynchronous discussion boards?
    - Host file sharing or a wiki page for members to contribute ideas and resources?
    - Provide static content pages on which a facilitator can post materials?
    - Be accessible from a variety of points (apps and web access?)
- **Maintain a connection.**
  - Online doesn't mean invisible! Facilitators need to engage with their participants actively and intentionally.
  - Collaboration is still an essential best practice—even though online the methods of collaboration may differ. This is why there are look-fors such as break out rooms, online meetings, wiki-pages, and file sharing in the LMS platforms.
  - Relationship-building is just as, if not more, important in an online community. Facilitators can post videos to introduce themselves

and encourage (but not require) participants to do the same. Also consider:

- Coffee Shop or Happy Hour nights (online meetings), where the hour meetup is a more informal debrief/social space rather than a formal discussion about content. This can also be an open-ended discussion board.
- Resource-sharing/book-talk discussion board, where participants are encouraged to post about what they are reading (on or off topic—or create one board for each!)
- Encourage the use of video and audio submissions rather than written submissions.
- Interest survey (potentially tagged on to the needs assessment—more about that in Chapter 2). Create one or two optional discussion boards throughout the sessions that tie in to participants' interests.
- One-on-one meetups via video or phone, conducted between the facilitator and each participant at the start of the session, midsession (when possible, based on the length of the session), and end of the session.
- Check-in on life. Angela regularly has a *how's life* check-in as a class assignment for both her graduate and undergraduate students. The grade is Complete or Excused, so students don't feel pressured to add one more thing to their overflowing plates. But it gives her the opportunity to take the pulse of her students, not just academically, but affectively and holistically (see the Check-In Assignment below—an example that Angela uses in her online classes).

Check-In Assignment

Note: Full Credit for Completion! This is marked "Complete/Excused"—so if you don't have time, no stress—it's excused if you don't do it.

My grandfather, who we affectionately call Grandpa Doc, lives in Wake Forest about two miles from me, and for as long as I could remember, when asked "How are you?" he'd say: *"As well as can be expected under the present circumstances, whatever they may be."* He was a college professor too—Niagara University in New York (Chemistry). He's in his late 90s now and has dementia, so he doesn't say it as often. Every once in a while, he says part of the phrase… It brings a happy tear to my eye to hear the pieces that he remembers! This is Grandma and Grandpa Doc at their 70th Anniversary Party, a few years ago.

For this assignment, I'd like to hear how you are doing. If all you have the time, energy, or desire to do is copy and paste *"As well as can be expected under the present circumstances, whatever they may be."* that's fine—I know you're out there, and that you're, well, as okay as you can be. And well, I like to hear the phrase every once in a while. :)

But if you'd like to tell me more—please do!

- If you've been writing a blog to process your feelings—you can share that
- If you'd like to share a video of yourself, talking directly to me—feel free
- If you'd like to draw a cartoon of your emotions—that works
- If you want to find the five memes that best sum up your feelings from day to day—sounds fun
- If you want to send me pictures of pets, kids, or siblings and use the "My coworker..." description that's trending on The Twitter (I call it "The Twitter" so y'all know I'm old and don't know what I'm doing…)—works for me
- If you need to talk—let me know, we'll schedule a time to Zoom, Webex, or use that ol' fashioned phone
- If you want to tell me you've FINALLY watched *The Princess Bride*, or *The Farewell*, or some other movie I've gone on and on about—definitely let me know and give me your review
- Really—ANYTHING GOES. Well, PG-13, or "lite R" rating please, let's keep the professor/student relationship intact

To sum up: HOW ARE YOU?

Yours in handwashing, mask-wearing, and antiracism,
Doc
And just for fun, the obligatory "describe your pet as a coworker" post:

I took my 15 minute break and my coworker would NOT get out of my face the entire time. NO boundaries. UGH.

- **Set yourself (the facilitator) and your participants up for success.**
  - Model best practices.
    - Pause and give space to reflect, for the information to sit with people, and for your message to absorb. Wait-time and think-time are not just for kids!
    - Follow up with participants, through discussion boards, email, continuous chat platforms. Be accessible.
    - Use a profile picture—of you. In the digital age and in online schooling we welcome students to provide a multitude of online images to represent their personalities; this is an equitable practice. As the facilitator, it is important that the participants see the leader with whom they will be interacting over the next days, weeks, or months. You can share avatars and bitmojis in a variety of different ways, but your main profile picture should be a clear, recent photograph of your engaging self.

    - Have an agenda and a clear purpose—and share it! What's your purpose, what's your goal? What are we here for, anyway? A long time ago, we sat in a workshop about how to give a workshop (meta, right?) and the presenter said that you should do three things: tell them what you're going to tell them, then tell them those things, then tell them what you just told them. That's kind of simplified, but, well, it's also kind of… true!
    - Have ground rules, expectations, norms… we'll get into this a lot more in Chapter 2, but what you establish as a norm in person may be different than your norms online. Such as:
        - Mute if you're not currently speaking.
        - Use a profile photo or avatar to create community.
        - Use the in-software reactions to join the conversation.
- Model and encourage self-care. This is so important, it should be number one!
    - Have a comfortable setting—whether it is a standing desk, your kitchen table, your office (with a great ergonomic chair). Be where you can work and be comfortable.
    - Have water or another beverage close by! Have this as a ground rule or encourage participants to do the same.
    - Take breaks, while at the same time reinforcing to participants "if you need one, take one!"
    - When life happens, address it. Katie and Angela, we've been teachers—elementary, middle, or college teachers—*the morning after*: the morning after 9-11, the morning after George Floyd, the morning after Trayvon Martin, the morning after Sandy Hook. During one of your professional learning facilitations, you too may have a morning after. Take time for acknowledgment, for the expressions of feelings rather than pushing them away; allow your group to be a haven of processing and reflecting. You don't need to know the answers, but provide time, space, and place.

Before the novel coronavirus changed life immeasurably in 2019, best practices in online teaching were already established. Online education has made numerous gains since, and the translation to professional learning is significant. While for many, face-to-face PL is still ideal, online is not out of the question, and for some, it may be the preferred method. Blended, hybrid, or hy-flex options are becoming more common and may be the wave of the future.

About this Book

We developed this research-based model, the Four Zones Equity-Driven Professional Learning Model (4ZEPL), because there is a gap between best practices, identification, and retention of underserved gifted learners. While there is research focused on improving each area of need, these solutions operate in silos—but as we know, learning does not. Professional learning is the most effective way to reach educators, change mindsets, and provide new knowledge and skill sets. 4ZEPL is designed to work with educators in their zone of proximal development, providing the necessary scaffolding to ensure the learner is successful in creating new understandings. This book is intended to be used as a playbook for equity-driven professional learning through the Four Zones Equity-Driven Professional Learning Model. The professional learning facilitator, or the coach should use the playbook as the game strategy for developing and providing high quality PL for gifted educators.

Planning with the end in mind, just as you would if you were coaching a soccer team, this book is strategically designed to provide the necessary skill and knowledge base necessary for individual and group growth. Keeping in line with the coaching metaphor there are some key phrases to look for. At the beginning of the 4ZEPL Chapters, the *What's the Play* will explain the zone with a brief explanation of the research base, followed by the *Put it in Play* where teacher/administrator-orientated strategies for facilitating the PL will be shared along with the steps for effective implementation; *Cautions and Caveats* highlights key considerations or what could go wrong when moving through the particular zone; finally the chapters end with *Professional Learning Playbook*, resources, and examples of differentiated PL activities.

We hope you find this book a useful tool to guide the development of your professional learning on your campus. We are all in this together, championing for our marginalized students, and developing quality professional learning which leads to positive and meaningful changes within our gifted and talented programs.

Coach Katie and Coach Angela

Notes

1 Naden, C. J., & Blue, R. (2004). *Wilma Rudolph*. Raintree, p. 7.
2 Gilson, C. (2018). Moving toward differentiated professional learning for teachers learning to differentiate for gifted students. In A. M. Novak & C. L. Weber (Eds.), *Best practices in professional learning and teacher preparation: Methods and strategies for gifted professional development* (Vol. 1, pp. 93–120). Prufrock Press.

3 Love, B. L. (2019). *We want to do more than survive: Abolitionist teaching and the pursuit of educational freedom.* Beacon. https://www.nagc.org/get-involved/advocate-gifted-children
4 L. Crumb (personal communication, March 31, 2021).
5 Every Student Succeeds Act, 20 U.S.C.§ 6301 (2015). https://www.congress.gov/bill/114th-congress/senate-bill/1177
6 Ibid.
7 National Association for Gifted Children. (n.d.). Questions and answers about the Every Student Succeeds Act (ESSA). https://www.nagc.org/sites/default/files/Advocacy/Q+A%20on%20ESSA%20(web).pdf
8 Advocate for Gifted Children. https://www.nagc.org/get-involved/advocate-gifted-children
9 Learning Forward. (2017). Standards for professional learning. School-based professional learning for implementing the Common Core. https://learningforward.org/wp-content/uploads/2017/09/school-based-professional-learning-unit-4-packet.pdf
10 Ibid.
11 Servisis, J. (2020, September 16). *4 benefits of an active professional learning community.* International Society for Technology in Education. https://www.iste.org/explore/4-benefits-active-professional-learning-community
12 Browne-Ferrigno, T., & Maughan, B. D. (2014). *Cohort development: A guide for faculty and program developers.* Carnegie Project on the Education Doctorate. http://c.ymcdn.com/sites/www.cpedinitiative.org/resource/resmgr/Literature/cped_cohort_development_guid.pdf

1

The Need for Equity-Driven Professional Learning

Michael Bennett, a football defensive end and author, shares his thoughts on the importance of activism:

> If you don't ask why, you'll never be attacked or criticized. No one is going to go after you or your family. But if you don't ask why, nothing, not a damn thing, is ever going to change. I think that's the difference between philanthropy and activism. Philanthropy is this kind of life-saving work. Activism is when you ask why this work needs to be done in the first place.[1]

Why start with a quote on activism? Why are we writing a book about equity-driven professional learning? What is going on in gifted education that this is even necessary? From its inception as a field, gifted education has not been equitable; but for every step forward we've taken, how many steps have we taken back?

Underrepresentation in Gifted Education

It is no secret that marginalized groups are often underrepresented in gifted education. In 2017–18, the Office of Civil Rights reported that there were 3,255,040 identified gifted learners enrolled in gifted programming across the United States. Digging deeper into the numbers, it quickly becomes apparent

DOI: 10.4324/9781003196204-2

that marginalized student populations are missing from the report. This concept of missingness refers to the "students who could/should have been identified, based on the percentages identified in each state on average (lower boundary) and at the higher rate of identification in non-Title I schools (upper boundary)."[2] The causes of missingness stem from two areas: first, a student attends a school which does not identify any gifted students; or second, the student belongs to a marginalized population. The question that remains is: Why? Why are about 40% to 50% of US public school students missing from gifted identification? The answer is complicated.

Barriers

Access is the first barrier. Lack of access is due to a myriad of reasons. First, roughly one-third of US children attend a school district that does not identify *any* gifted students.[3] In this situation, the lack of access impacts *all* gifted learners. Another factor is the socioeconomic status of the school district. Wealthier schools identify more students than Title I schools. Ethnicity factors into access as well, since children who are Asian or White are significantly more likely to be identified for gifted and talented programs than students who are identified as American Indian/Alaska Native American, Black, Latinx, Native Hawaiian/Pacific Islander, or two or more races.

Issues in Identification

Within the school, identification measures have long been recognized as a problem zone. Are the tests valid and reliable? For all student populations? Do the tests paint a true picture of the students or just a snapshot in time? Teachers, themselves, are often a barrier to access. (Wait, teachers? I know, right?) Classroom teachers are often the first point of contact during the initial referral process in gifted services. These issues in identification are a substantial barrier to achieving proportionality—equity—in gifted programs.

Standardized Assessments

Standardized assessments, in theory, offer an objective measure of student academic intelligence which can be compared across students of similar age or grade-level groups. While standardized tests are viewed as valuable for this objectivity, too often they result in biased test scores for students of lower socioeconomic status, English language learners, or students from minoritized groups. The causes of these lower test scores are often tied to culture and background knowledge and based on the personal biases of the test creators.

Not all students have had the same exposure to daily life experiences, travel, cultural experiences, reading materials, or academic coaching as either the test creators or the children for whom the test creators are designing the test. Without these same experiences or the opportunity to learn about the phenomenon that may be on the instrument, some children enter the assessment with an advantage purely based on who they are, not their innate ability or aptitude. Others have a corresponding disadvantage and are less prepared to take the standardized assessment. For example, if an assessment shows a picture of a spinning toy and asks the student to identify it, some students may not recognize it as a top, never having been exposed to this type of toy, whether due to culture, economics, or place. The item could be specifically culturally biased, such as a test question asking a student to identify the month that we celebrate New Year's Day, which can have varying correct answers depending on the students' culture.

Which Answer Would You Choose?

Q: When do we celebrate New Year's Day?

A. October
B. January
C. February
D. March

What Is Biased About New Year's Day?

Chinese New Year is typically celebrated in February, but it can occur between January 21 and February 20. So, either B or C could be correct. Anyone still following the Early Roman calendar (Et tu, Brute?) holds their New Year's festivities on March 1, and those of Wiccan faith gather and share blessings on Samhain, October 31. Not only do people celebrate New Year's Day on different days, not everybody (note the "we") celebrates holidays (Jehovah's Witnesses, for example); the same with date changes and events such as Independence Day, Memorial Day, and Thanksgiving. Specificity and clarity are important in assessment, rather than the assumption of "White Christian holiday of…," but even more crucial is the deletion of these biased questions.

Nonverbal assessments were espoused as the answer to discrimination. There's no reading! There's nothing for students to have to muddle through; it's a level playing field! However, there is no culture-free or bias-free assessment. Assessments have creators, and humans are not culture-free or bias-free. If a nonverbal assessment shows a picture of a nut, grass, a worm, and a fish, a picture of a squirrel, and then a directional arrow pointing to the squirrel's mouth, the test is nonverbal. The intention is clear: these are four food choices; which one does the squirrel eat? If I, Angela, looked at this test item, I would think: easy-peasy, no bias. A squirrel is obviously a cute little woodland critter. Squirrels climb trees, they eat nuts, that seems reasonable. But then I remember a story Katie told me, of when she and her family moved from the Mexico/Texas border to Pennsylvania. And her kids (12 weeks, 2, 4, and 5) saw a squirrel for the first time in their lives and the eldest asked "Mom what *is* that thing?" I've clearly forgotten my formative years on the Oklahoma plains and become a full-fledged East-Coaster... who needs to check that East Coast bias! (Next time you see Katie, ask her about her eldest's first writing prompt after moving from TX to PA in December and starting school in January—*How to Build a Snowman!*) Even nonverbal assessments, such as the Cognitive Abilities Test nonverbal subscale (CogAT-Nv) and the Naglieri Nonverbal Abilities Test (NNAT) may result in score differences. These tests are often the go-to identification choice for districts and it should be no surprise then, that underrepresentation is often an outcome. Thus, these assessment tools may not be as valid or reliable when evaluating underrepresented student populations.

Teachers as Gatekeepers

Teachers are asked to complete a checklist of gifted characteristics, rating the student on their level of gifted behaviors. These standardized checklists are composed of the typically recognized gifted behaviors such as an independent learner, question asker, eager participant in class. But what happens when the teacher doesn't recognize the nontraditional (read: non-White) characteristics of gifted students? What if the student prefers to work in groups or doesn't seek out leadership roles in the classroom? What if the teacher sees a bilingual student's language learning as a deficit, rather than their ability to learn in two languages being the asset it is? More often than not, the student simply isn't referred. Students who come from culturally diverse backgrounds often present giftedness through what teachers view as nontraditional ways.

These checklists—teacher, parent, or student—offer one checkpoint in the identification process, and it is important to remember that it is just one point (assuming we are following best practices). The goal of these checklists is often to serve as the initial checkpoint: the referral. A referral or nomination indicates that the teacher feels there may be *something there* or a child may be showing signs that may indicate giftedness. With a referral, the teacher is opening the door for a student to be evaluated for gifted programming. You may have heard the terms referral and recommendation used interchangeably. It is important to note that a recommendation is different from a referral. After the identification process is completed and the student has been fully evaluated, then the gifted education team makes a recommendation for services. At this point, the recommendation serves as the official decision of the gifted education team. A teacher could potentially still act as the gatekeeper, but at this later point in the identification process there are several data items versus a referral, which is often only the teacher's checklist.

While there are some standardized gifted characteristic checklists available, districts may opt to create their own checklist or evaluation tool. District-created tools can be a pragmatic approach for creating effective identification tools for marginalized students. By creating a localized instrument, districts can account for their student demographics and apply localized norms. However, just as when you create an assessment for your own classroom, one must be cognizant of the validity, reliability, and fairness of the assessment. It is *very* easy to create an assessment that doesn't measure what you think it will measure. Validity answers the question: Does this assessment measure the concepts and competencies from the unit? In this case, the validity of the district-created tool would measure the characteristics of giftedness grounded in gifted education literature. Validity can easily miss the mark if the questions are not based on the research. Reliability refers to the consistency of the results—consider when the test is administered, are students performing at the same level or are there questions that the majority of the class misses? Think about Chick-fil-A: every time you go through the drive-through, the sweet tea, the fries, and the nuggets are always the same—this is reliability. Fairness takes into consideration the content and context of the assessment and the students, and whether there are potential biases that would impact the outcomes of the instrument. An effective assessment is valid, reliable, and fair—but just like shooting at a target, it is very easy to miss the mark—creating an assessment that is either valid, fair, or reliable. Keep working, keep practicing, until you hit the bullseye; all are essential. District-created tools need to be evaluated for fairness, reliability, and validity before being depended upon as a measure for student identification.

This brings us to the ultimate question, which educators wrestle with: Is there a perfect tool for identifying gifted learners? Unfortunately, there's not a perfect tool. There are too many movable parts to be considered when selecting the perfect tool to have a one-size-fits-all approach. Districts have tried this—and the end result? Underrepresentation. Instead, you must select the tools which best meet the needs of your student population in your district. Factors to consider include the demographics of your district, availability of resources to administer and evaluate the assessments, as well as what kinds of services are available for identified students. Consider short-term and long-term goals, as well as take an honest look at your current identification process for areas of strengths and needs improvements. Teachers are great at networking and sharing what works—identification shouldn't be any different—ask your colleagues, and go to conferences to learn about new tools. But, always keep your district's specific needs in mind. Remember, you shouldn't be afraid to make changes to the identification process already in place—just because we have always done something one way doesn't mean that's the best or only way.

Issues in Programming

Beyond the identification stage, missingness of gifted students continues to plague gifted programming in retention as well. Once students are identified for gifted programming, why don't they stay? Let's take a look at some of the factors impacting retention of gifted learners. Ideally, we should adjust our identification process to allow for more students to enter the gifted program; yet, as a practice, gifted education hasn't yet moved toward making adjustments to accommodate these same learners in the gifted program. Rather than fixing the problem, we have, in essence, kicked the can down the road.

Programmatic Match to Identification Methods

"They" say to write what you know... two of Angela's kiddos are 2e, or twice-exceptional, children. To protect their anonymity (not only current but future) we'll use they/their pronouns and a pseudonym of Jay to tell this story. Jay is highly gifted, with coexisting exceptionalities of ADHD, or as Dr. Matt Fugate terms it, ADHG;[4] they qualify for speech services and occupational therapy for motor skills, and were diagnosed with social anxiety disorder. Jay was identified in one state as gifted in English, then moved to another state, where they were identified in Math, then moved to another district within the same state, where the district took the identification from both the previous state and district and identified and served Jay in both Math and English. In this new district the identification methods included a standardized ability test score at the 98th percentile to qualify in both areas or above, *or* the 95th percentile or above on that same test with corresponding state test scores at the highly proficient rate and teacher rating forms to qualify in individual areas. The ability test and state tests had verbal and quantitative sections; the ability test also had a nonverbal section. Jay enjoyed the gifted pullout class at first, always loved the Math pullout class, but then suddenly shut down in the English pullout class. They refused to do the work, they didn't want to go, and the teacher was emailing Angela with concerns, so Angela asked what they were doing. The teacher shared that the district had a required gifted curriculum that each teacher followed, though it should be noted at this point that Jay was the only student pulled for gifted English at that time. They were writing a required five-paragraph essay. Jay was comparatively weaker in readiness in terms of writing, had challenges in motor skills pertaining to handwriting for which they went to occupational therapy, and, frankly, was an "obstinate headstrong fool" in the words of Jane Austen. Angela explained the barriers and asked for differentiation and a change in lessons, especially given the one-person class, but was told that there was no possible detour in the curriculum. From that point on, Jay has believed that they are not gifted in English, does not understand why they are in "those classes," and has refused to participate.

Jay's story sets up what occurs frequently in gifted programs: a mismatch from identification methods to programming. Dr. Sally Reis calls this internal consistency, and it is one measure of a solid gifted program. And concurrently, it is what drives students out of programs. In the previous section, we described the need for more equitable identification measures in gifted education. There are potential solutions—these are described in the next section—that's a positive! However, often that is where the solution stops. More work needs to be done to ensure that there is a match between the identification model and the programmatic model.

Equitable, Reflective Programming

Beyond having the identification methods match the programming, there is a need for gifted programming to be both equitable for learners and reflective of the community and the students in the program. Equitable programming means that resources, whether human, material, or financial, need to be distributed equally across gifted education programs. Beyond the resources, equitable programming also recognizes good teaching practices—not all gifted learners learn the same way! Equitable programming acknowledges and modifies curriculum and instructional practices to meet the needs of the learners. Just as Angela shared above, where the program model did not match the learner, here the programming is not equitable for the learner due to the standardized approach to the gifted curriculum. As we know, culture plays a role in how giftedness manifests in students; yet, after identification, many gifted programs do not account for these differences in the curriculum or program delivery. All aspects of gifted programming should be reflective of the diversity within the community as well as the students.

Specific Solutions to Specific Barriers

Researchers and districts have worked together to implement potential solutions to the aforementioned barriers to gifted programming accessibility. The solutions presented below are divided into identification and programmatic categories, though some have interwoven threads. They are all individual strategies designed to fix an issue at hand: see a problem, find a solution, place a repair patch: this is on-the-field injury triage.

Identification Solutions

Recognizing that marginalized students may not have the same opportunities to develop critical inquiry skills or cultural experiences, frontloading curricula provides these students with scaffolded educational experiences before the initial screening process. Frontloading is a purposeful plan to develop foundational knowledge and skills which will enable the student to perform higher-level tasks; for example, an objective may be to provide scaffolded learning opportunities for students to develop inquiry-based skills. Frontloading is often grounded in real-world tasks with the teacher modeling the process of thinking through a problem and searching for solutions. Collaborative learning plays a large role in frontloading, and content vocabulary is pre-taught along with any necessary background knowledge so that the students are prepared to tackle the problem.

Frontloading gifted curricula begins in kindergarten where students are exposed to problem-based learning and deep dive into curriculum topics. For gifted education, frontloading builds a bridge for marginalized students to have access to enrichment experiences which may be otherwise lacking. Schools who provide this bridge to gifted programming find that when they implement grade-level screening with their second graders, they are identifying more diverse gifted learners. Frontloading gifted curricula is a practical, cost-effective solution that increases identification of marginalized students and equity within gifted programs.

Another practical solution to breaking down barriers is changing the identification process to include more equitable measures. Best practices in identifying gifted and talented students move beyond a single measure of giftedness and instead view the whole child through a portfolio. Within this portfolio, measures may include a standardized instrument such as a CogAT, as well as teacher and parent checklists, samples of student work, and classroom observations. Within the evaluation process, another strategy for increasing equitable identification is to blind the review process. While not always possible, the benefit of a blind review is that it removes some teacher bias. Similarly, having a team of educators evaluating each application increases the reliability of the identification process.

Within the portfolio, adjustments can also be made when selecting testing instruments, specifically when utilizing a standardized instrument with nationally normed scores. Instead of using a nationally normed cut-off score, districts may implement a policy to use localized norms for the cut-off scores.[5] Localized norms acknowledge that within one school building there are high-performing students compared to other students within the same student population. Why does this matter? It matters because students are likely pulled into the school through neighborhood zones and attend classes with their friends; there is no reason for them to be identified for gifted programs based on national norms rather than their proximal peers. This aligns with the US Department of Education's National Excellence report, which suggests that gifted students should be identified by comparing their abilities "with others of their age, experience, or environment."[6] Localized norms are shown to increase equity in identification.

Another option is to create a bridge program, which operates under the same principles of frontloading. Within these programs, marginalized students who may not qualify for gifted programming, but who still show gifted potential are placed into an enrichment or "pre-gifted" program. This bridge program continues to work on developing the critical thinking and learning skills fostering the gifted characteristics and the student is reevaluated at a future point. Within this accelerated learning environment, with appropriate levels of scaffolding, marginalized students grow as learners—academically and social-emotionally. This is an excellent program model for nurturing student potential. Some districts do not identify students for gifted programming until third or fourth grade and offer this enrichment model to selected K-2 students, or in some cases, all K-2 students.

In this primary model, however, there are threads of inequity. Is this a frontloading option that offers *some* students—based on parental support, teacher gatekeeping, identification from a previous state, or early reading ability—preparation in critical and creative thinking, and as a bonus, test preparation for the school-wide administered CogAT test for gifted screening (in Coach Angela's personal experience)? Or is this an opportunity for all students to receive that same enrichment, critical and creative thinking instruction, support, and test question awareness in advance of the universal screening?

Programmatic Solutions

While identification and programming are often lumped together when talking about gifted education, it is important to pull them apart when looking for ways to increase underrepresented students' participation in gifted programs. Often, school districts focus on changing the identification process—which is a necessary step, but that is only half of the puzzle. Think about it: if your district can increase the number of underrepresented student populations being identified for gifted programs, what happens when these students start participating in the program? Too often, these kids don't stick with the program—they drop out for a myriad of reasons. Often this is because the gifted program delivery hasn't changed at all to support these students. For example, a gifted English language learner (ELL) student may not be successful in an accelerated program without scaffolding for language acquisition. Frontloading and bridge programs are great examples of modifying gifted programs for identification purposes for underrepresented populations, but we need to look for ways to differentiate gifted education for identified learners.

This requires districts and teachers of the gifted to examine their gifted curriculum and program model. Providing scaffolding for gifted learners within their gifted seminar courses is necessary for student success. Just as the bridge and frontloading programs provided opportunities for students to engage in critical thinking and problem-solving with supports, the same measures need to be in place for the identified learners. Consider the ELL gifted learner who is still developing language proficiency who comes to seminar but is unsuccessful due to a language barrier. Would this child get the same enrichment, the same joy out of the lesson or would this student feel like they don't belong? Instead, imagine the powerful experience this ELL gifted and talented (GT) student would have if the gifted resource teacher collaborated with the English as a Second Language (ESL) specialist.

These scaffolding strategies also apply to the creation of culturally relevant curriculum for gifted learners. Culturally relevant curriculum empowers learners to engage in a learning environment where diversity amongst learners is valued, explored, and viewed as a strength. Learners in this environment grow socially, emotionally, intellectually, and are empowered to develop their own voice. Along with a culturally relevant curriculum, gifted programming should also seek out mentors for gifted learners—both peers (same age or older) and professionals from outside of school. Mentorship is a powerful tool in fostering learning and the success of marginalized gifted learners.

So far, we have spent a lot of time exploring what doesn't work and what needs to change, but now let's focus on the vehicles which can propel us toward change. Change starts small. Maybe sparked by reviewing the district data, or new district initiatives or the voice of the faculty. However, this piecemeal approach for achieving equity in gifted education is not enough, true, and lasting change recognizes a need for overall awareness of the systems of oppression that have historically omitted students of color from gifted programs. Equity-driven gifted professional learning provides a holistic approach to systemic change—just as the portfolio provides a clearer picture of the gifted learner, equity-driven gifted professional learning provides education to support learner growth, self-reflection, application to the classroom, and scaffolded support for educators throughout the change process.

Systemic Change

Systemic change recognizes that all the parts of the gifted education system need to be examined and modified to affect long-term change. Otherwise, we are approaching change with the patchwork or on-the-field triage approach. Rather than looking for the root of the problem we are applying temporary solutions in the hopes of impacting change. Yet—we know this doesn't work—consider a life lesson we teach our children, that we ourselves learned as little ones. When told to clean your room, did you sweep your mess under the bed or shove it into a closet? And did you pass the initial inspection, only to have your dreams of playing outside with friends collapse upon closer inspection? There are many facets of gifted education that are problematic that have potential solutions—but if we are hoping to enact lasting change, we must enact systemic change.

We know that the long-term issues in gifted education revolve around disproportionality and representation in programs: who is identified, who is served? This is not unique to gifted education. We intentionally termed the four-zone professional learning model "equity-driven" rather than culturally responsive because it is grounded in equity literacy as a framework. While culturally relevant pedagogy is part of this work, it is operationalized as a "both/and," not as an "either/or" choice; it is fundamental to contextualize the work we will be doing together as equity work.

Equity is part of a broader set of concepts that work in tandem—abbreviated in a variety of orders by different people and organizations (e.g., DEI, DEJI, DEI-J, BEDJ) but are generally comprised of the following.

Diversity

Historically, the definition of diversity has been "different" or "other" than me, or the dominant group, which translates to "not White." While grading a series of lesson plans one day, Angela commiserated that she wanted a rubric category for "Diversity does not mean 'not White'" just to solidify this point (she didn't do it!). Diversity is a variety of groups or social identities represented in a space. Diversity is not limited to racial or ethnic groups, but includes all ways that individuals identify, such as gender, class, ability/(dis) ability, sexuality, religion, and others.

Inclusion or Belonging

Words matter. Angela has never jived with "culturally responsive," though she uses it because that's the recognized term in the field; she's always questioned, why should we just be responsive? Wouldn't it be better if we weren't creating the trauma first? (She likes "cultural agility," if you're curious, but recognizes that's also not a perfect term!) There are debates around inclusion as a term *vs.* belonging/belongingness, with members of the field preferring one over the other. Diversity is ensuring that there is representation at the table. Inclusion at its base is seen as everyone being welcomed. Inclusion should also be the outcome of a welcoming environment with all members *expressing their truths and being their authentic selves.* Establishing common meaning of terms can be an important tool in equity work, as the first definition of inclusion is markedly different from the second. Belonging/ness is an environment that ensures that diversity is not tokenism, that every voice is not just tolerated but extolled, and that membership is mutually beneficial. Words and actions matter.

Equity

In understanding equity, it can be helpful to break down *inequity*: material (healthcare, housing, computers, books) and nonmaterial access (institutional culture, policy, biases) and opportunities are unfairly distributed, resulting in predictably different outcomes (grades, graduation rates, policing arrests/deaths, school-to-prison pipeline) and experiences (microaggressions, belongingness, bias-free work/school environments) by identity groups (e.g., race/ethnicity, socioeconomic status, gender, language, (dis) ability). Equity, then, is fair access for full participation for all. As defined by the Equity Literacy Institute,[7] equity has two essential aspects: a commitment to action and a way of being. Equity *is a process,* it is work. Through equity work, we strive to redistribute fair and just access and opportunities for all. Equity *is also an outcome,* a way of being on a personal level and a societal level: anti-bias, antidiscrimination, antiracist, anti–identity-predictable outcomes, and experiences.

Social Justice

Like equity, social justice is both a *process and an ulterior goal.* While equity's work of fair distribution is one of access and opportunity, social justice is broader, as it analyzes, actively works toward, and has an outcome of a fair distribution of power, privilege, and resources with respect to those same social identities identified earlier. Social justice has an ultimate goal of a society in which members of all identity groups have equitably distributed resources, live within a vision that is mutually beneficial for all identity groups, and in which all identity groups are (not just feel, but are) both physically and psychologically safe and secure.[8]

Anti-Bias and Antiracism

Another subset of more targeted work within equity is ABAR work: Anti-bias, Antiracism work. There are four goals in anti-bias education, which are used as a framework for teachers and students, as they develop as critical thinkers and champions of equity. We love how there is a goal for the teacher as well as the student—highlighting the need for the teacher's outcomes to be tied to change in the student. The four goals are as follows:

Goal 1: Identity
- Teachers will nurture each child's construction of knowledgeable, confident, individual personal and social identities.
- Each child demonstrates self-awareness, confidence, family pride, and positive social identities.

Goal 2: Diversity
- Teachers will promote each child's comfortable, empathetic interaction with people from diverse backgrounds.
- Each child will express comfort and joy with human diversity; accurate language for human differences; and deep, caring human connections

Goal 3: Justice
- Teachers will foster each child's capacity to critically identify bias and will nurture each child's empathy for the hurt bias causes.
- Each child will increasingly recognize unfairness, have language to describe unfairness, and understand that unfairness hurts.

Goal 4: Activism
- Teachers will cultivate each child's ability and confidence to stand up for oneself and for others in the face of bias.
- Each child will demonstrate empowerment and the skills to act, with others or alone, against prejudice and/or discriminatory actions.[9]

These anti-bias goals not only look inward at who I am as an individual, as well as recognizing and valuing diversity, but take the next critical steps of working toward justice and activism. Learning to identify bias, developing the skills to act, are necessary if there is to be systemic change. As educators, this means looking for the causes of inequities in gifted education, but more importantly, taking action to change the system. Equity-driven professional learning and the 4ZEPL can be a systemic change within the building or district (depending on who is participating).

Antiracism is not a new concept, though it has been brought into the limelight with books such as Ibram X. Kendi's *How to Be an Antiracist* and Tiffany M. Jewell's *This Book is Anti-Racist*. The concept of antiracism is action-oriented, it is intentional, rather than the passive—"I'm not a racist." An analogy that Beverly Daniels Tatum uses to describe antiracism is the walking escalators at the airport. You know the ones you can walk alongside, but hey, might as well take the ride, right? Get to your gate just a little faster? Now, once you are on the people-mover, you have a few choices. You can stand and just let it move you from your starting point to your destination. Or you can make up some extra time and get those steps in, while on the mechanical grates! Think about standing and going along for the ride as "I'm not a racist"; you're not actively doing or saying anything racist, but you're also not intentionally combating racism, either. If you're clocking time on your Fitbit, well, that's the analogy for active racism; you are intentionally engaging in racism actions or words. Notice that either way you travel—resting, and doing nothing, or striding forward with intentionality—you will step off and emerge at racism's gate. Antiracists walk in the opposite direction of the people-mover; they recognize the mechanism for what it is—the structure, the grates—and they actively use their bodies and their minds to work against it, walking backward until they step off at the start.

Spheres of Influence

Throughout this book, we will integrate aspects of diversity, equity, inclusion, belongingness, and social justice. We will have strategies that emphasize anti-bias and antiracism. We will discuss the research frameworks that undergird the four-zone model, including culturally relevant professional learning, the funds of knowledge framework, and equity literacy. At the forefront, this is a book on professional learning in gifted education, but it is grounded in equity, and these are all parts of equity. To be successful in equity endeavors, it is crucial to focus not on just individual approaches that address small parts of the inequity issues in gifted education, but to have an overall awareness of anti-Blackness, White supremacy, and the systems of oppression that have historically omitted students of color from gifted programs. This is what equity-driven gifted professional learning truly is. The zones (we'll dive into those in the next chapter!) are designed to have a greater systemic effect—the school and community as a system. True systemic change can be broader than this system, impacting the larger school system rather than the individual school; valued readers at the administrative level may be prepared to lead systemic change at this level. As we write the book and offer the four zones, we acknowledge that this is still one piece toward systemic change, and a smaller piece toward structural change, a grossly needed step. Structural change is broader—governmental, beyond one school or one district. The Four Zone Equity-Driven Professional Learning Model is designed to push for systemic change through the building or district—within *your sphere of influence.*

Paul Gorski and Marceline DuBose of the Equity Literacy Institute[10] describe a set of concentric ovals as the spheres of equity control and equity influence. Your sphere of equity control is your personal ideology; what are your beliefs? In your position at your school or organization, over what do you have control: is it your homework policy, your grading policy, your classroom environment (management)? This is what you can change, on your own. Your sphere of influence is outside of your direct control, but you may be in a position to enact change by advocating, organizing, or educating; you can still influence the situation! This could be sitting on a committee to change an organizational policy or a hiring decision or educating others through professional learning.

With turnkey training and grassroots activism, this sphere of influence can create a ripple effect outside of the building. But it does not replace advocacy at different levels. It does not replace everyday antiracism. It does not replace the need for abolitionist teachers, doing the work, every day. In the Resources section for Chapter 3, when we discuss the theoretical framework, you'll find some books, articles, and websites that are helpful for this work that, while essential, is beyond the scope of this book. We encourage you to explore these resources with the words of Ella Baker in mind: "You didn't see me on television, you didn't see news stories about me. The kind of role that I tried to play was to pick up pieces or put together pieces out of which I hoped organization might come. My theory is, strong people don't need strong leaders."

Challenges for Equity Work in Gifted Programs

Equity work is an ongoing process, which often seems an uphill battle, where two steps forward lead to one step backward. As teachers, we know that every student comes to us with their own unique stories filled with triumphs and struggles. We have seen firsthand how students' lives are impacted when they are dealing with negative life experiences. And at the same time, we have also seen the effect of positive interventions on the student's academic and social-emotional learning! Every day, educators with boots on the ground work hard to level the playing field for these students. Yet, our impact as individual educators can only go so far, as many of these negative life experiences can be tied back to inequities in America. Gifted and talented programs have approached inequities by targeting specific areas in isolation—for example, assessment or identification. Resulting in temporary wins in the battle for equity. However, for meaningful change within gifted education, we need to approach the access and opportunities gaps from multiple angles and levels. This is a large ask—one that will involve stakeholders from the building, district, state, and federal levels. Yet, it is a worthy task, beginning with identifying short-term goals, which are easily achieved along with longer-term goals which can be simultaneously initiated. For example, a short-term goal could be setting up a program to bridge the opportunity gap for underrepresented students. At the same time, stakeholders can begin the progress of advocating for gifted-education policy and program changes.

As a coach, one identifies the short-term and long-term training goals and working backward from there creates solid workouts to position the team to be in the best position to win the championship. We too, the gifted coordinators, specialists, and program directors can create a solid training program, using the 4ZEPL, to prepare our gifted educators to champion for our underrepresented gifted students. Go Team!

Notes

1 Bennett, M., & Zirin, D. (2018). *Things that make white people uncomfortable.* Haymarket Books.
2 Gentry, M., Gray, A., Whiting, G. W., Maeda, Y., & Pereira, N. (2019). *Systems failure: Access denied.* https://www.dropbox.com/s/0lxzznnyh5u0jj1/Access%20Denied.pdf (para 6).
3 Ibid.
4 Fugate, C. M. (2020). To be gifted and ADHD: Understanding their unique challenges. In C. M. Fugate, W. A. Behrens & C. Boswell (Eds.), *Understanding twice-exceptional learners: Connecting research to practice.* Prufrock Academic Press.
5 Peters, S., Rambo-Hernandez, K., Makel, M., Matthews, M., & Plucker, J. (2019, May 14). *Local norms improve equity in gifted identification.* National Association for Gifted Children. https://www.nagc.org/blog/local-norms-improve-equity-gifted-identification
6 U.S. Department of Education. (1993). *National excellence: A case for developing America's talent.* Washington, DC: Office of Educational Research and Improvement.
7 Gorski, P. C. (2020). *Equity literacy principles.* EdChange and the Equity Literacy Institute. http:/edchange.org/handouts/Equity-Literacy-Principles.pdf
8 Bell, L. (2013). Theoretical foundations. In M. Adams, W. J. Blumenfeld, C. Castañeda, H. W. Hackman, M. L. Petrs, & X. Zúñiga. (Eds.), *Readings for diversity and social justice.* Routledge.
9 Derman-Sparks, L., & Edwards, J. (2020). *Anti-bias education for young children and ourselves* (2nd edition). The National Association for Education of Young Children. p. 5.
10 Gorski, P.C., & DuBose, M. (2021). *Learning to be a threat to inequity: Intro to equity literacy.* [Online course]. Equity Literacy Institute. https://www.equitylearn.com/courses/the-equity-literacy-framework

2

Introduction to the Four Zone Equity-Driven Professional Learning Model

By introducing the Four Zone Equity-Driven Professional Learning Model (4ZEPL) we present a research-based, systematic, and systemic method of disrupting inequities in gifted and talented programs by promoting teacher professional learning around culture and equity, increasing student supports before, during, and after identification, and encouraging family and community relationships. We draw words of wisdom from Gwen Berry, Olympic athlete in the hammer throw, who said, "My purpose and my mission is bigger than sports, I'm here to represent those… who died due to systemic racism. That's the important part. That's why I'm going. That's why I'm here today."[1] Our overall goal is to disrupt systemic racism and systemic oppression. This takes more than small fixes; it takes transformative change. In the end, our goal is to foster learning and growth, empowering change agents in the field of gifted education.

An Overview of the Four Zone Equity-Driven Professional Learning Model

In research, we start with a framework; this can serve as a guide or a lens to undergird our work. The Four Zones Equity-Driven Professional Learning Model (4ZEPL) was developed because we saw a clear disparity in gifted education, and a need to change the system of disproportionality of gifted Black and Brown kids. We started by exploring identification and teacher

DOI: 10.4324/9781003196204-3

observation checklists. I'm sure you are nodding along, yes, yes, those are problematic; you probably even have your own story to share of identification going wrong. But, after our first research study, when we explored the use of teacher observation checklists with gifted learners in a city on the southwest border, we knew that looking at identification methods only would not fix the problem. It was applying a brace around an ankle to get through the game, but that alone wasn't replacing true medical care; it wasn't a full-season solution, a cure for the player's injury.

In our first study, we surveyed a group of Hispanic bilingual teachers teaching in a school district where the majority of the students were bilingual and Hispanic. We were astounded to find that even with a group of teachers with similar cultural background and experiences, there was a misconception of what it means to be gifted.[2] It would take professional learning for the teachers to start changing their mindsets before the students would even be considered for identification. As we continued to study this issue, we also saw a desperate need for culturally responsive gifted education materials, curriculum, and support systems for both the teacher and the students. Yet, if we were going to be able to accomplish true and lasting change, we would also need support and buy-in from the community. Thus, the final zone of the 4ZEPL, which focuses on the parent and community.

As we engaged with the communities during our research and deeply reviewed the literature on professional learning, equity, and gifted education, we grounded our work in several theoretical frameworks, as lenses through which to analyze data, and ways to understand the pieces of the model that we were constructing, testing, implementing, and revising; similar to when you have a great idea for a classroom setting but need to try it out to be sure it really works before shouting your awesome lesson plan to the world!

The Four Zone Equity-Driven Professional Learning Model (see Figure 2.1),[3] not only answers the call for equity in gifted education, but it is also a practical model for PL, adaptable to your district, and when implemented with fidelity, results in positive changes in teacher mindsets, student outcomes, and a positive school culture. Zone 1: Increasing Educators' Understanding of Cultural Norms and Equity, provides professional learning that focuses on raising awareness of inequities across student populations. Equity work begins with self-reflection and understanding who I am, the community, and the school system. From here, PL continues with Zone 2: Increasing Educators' Understanding of Characteristics of Gifted Marginalized Students. PL continues the conversations about inequities but now emphasizes understanding how these inequities impact the manifestation of gifted characteristics and their educational experiences.

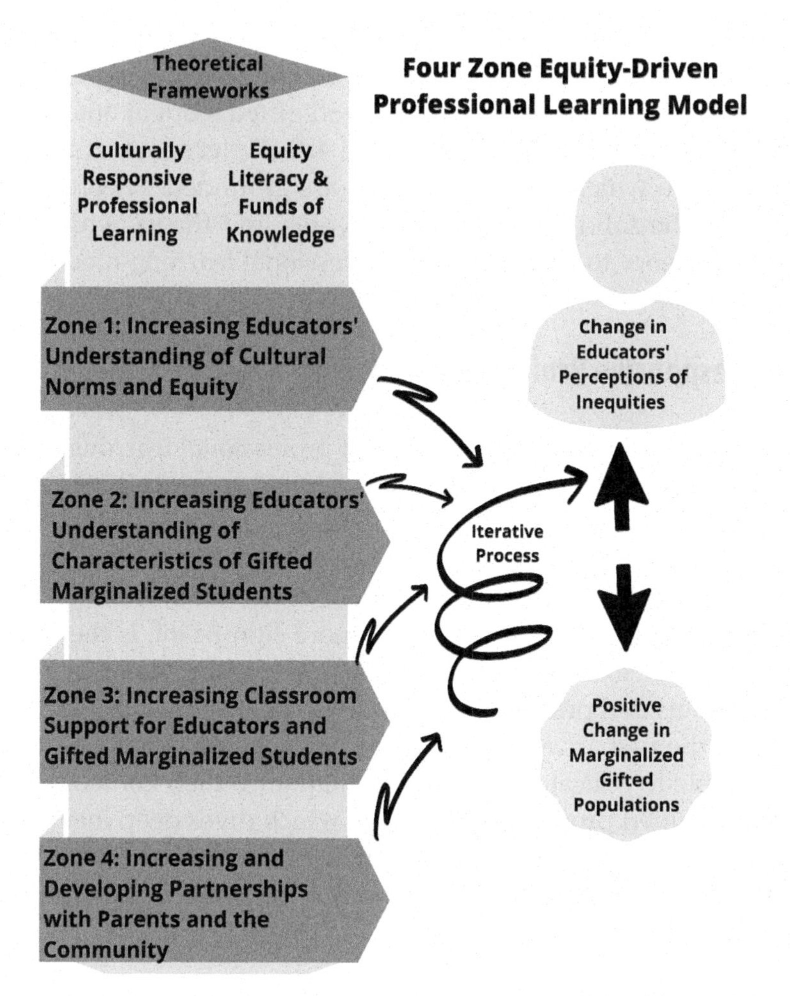

Figure 2.1 Four Zone Equity-Driven Professional Learning Model. Note: Novak and Lewis, 2021; reprinted with permission from the authors.

With a greater understanding of gifted marginalized students, the 4ZEPL turns its attention to providing students and teachers with the support, strategies, and resources they need to be successful beyond the identification process. Zone 3: Increasing Classroom Support for Educators and Gifted Marginalized Students is an important piece to puzzle as many programs focus the majority of their efforts on the identification process, forgetting to provide the much-needed support to retain students and foster their growth. Finally, Zone 4: Increasing and Developing Partnerships with Parents and the Community, engages the participants in PL focused on creating meaningful partnerships with families and communities. The zones are meant to be moved through in an iterative process, supporting the teachers' need for additional PL in various topics. As educators experience the ongoing 4ZEPL support system, they experience a positive change in their perceptions of inequities along with improved marginalized gifted student outcomes.[4]

Now that you have an overview of the 4ZEPL, let's look at the theoretical frameworks in which each of the zones are grounded. Theoretical frameworks provide the solid foundation of research and theory which is drawn upon to apply theory to practice in the professional learning models.

Culturally Responsive Professional Learning

We have already discussed the evolution of professional learning from workshops to data-driven, ongoing sessions developed specifically for a group of educators. Currently, K-12 education policy is regulated by the Every Student Succeeds Act (ESSA). ESSA acknowledges the critical role of professional learning, especially as it connects to student outcomes and achieving equity and inclusivity within schools. But, even more significant, is the recognition within the federal legislation about the role of professional learning in changing teacher beliefs and practices in all aspects of K-12 education. In Chapter 1, we discussed the vast array of professional learning environments and experiences available to educators to grow and enhance their content knowledge and skills. Sustained professional learning which dives deep into a topic creates the opportunity for educators to learn, implement the new strategies, reflect on the effectiveness, make modifications, and begin the learning cycle again.

Why and When Teachers Change

You may be familiar with Thomas Guskey,[5] either from your college days or perhaps from professional learning. He explored how professional learning could impact teachers' beliefs and practices in the classroom. Teacher change occurs when one realizes a change in student behavior or academic achievement after attending a PL session. After the PL session the teacher goes back into the classroom energized about a new teaching strategy, tries it out, and sees positive student outcomes; then the teacher will experience a change in their beliefs and practices. We're sure you can probably recall an instance when you experienced a change in your own teaching practices as a result of PL. However, if there is not an opportunity to implement the new idea, or when the new idea is tried out but doesn't work well… then there is a negative impact on the teacher's beliefs, and the teacher is less motivated to change practices or perhaps even to try the new strategy again. If, as facilitators, we want to change teacher beliefs and practices, then we must consider two factors. First, what is the teacher's motivation for attending the PL? Second, how does the change in attitude and beliefs occur? Guskey flipped the idea that you must be motivated to change to see positive outcomes, to seeing student outcomes as the motivation to change. This simple reversal is essential to understanding that while we know that not every teacher will want to attend an equity-driven PL session that includes hard questions and reflections, if we can help the teacher experience positive student outcomes after the PL, then there is an opportunity to change teacher beliefs. Yes, buy-in is important, but buy-in sometimes takes time. Thinking about our own kids, how often are they convinced they will *hate* whatever we are having for dinner simply because it is new or looks different? But if we can just get them to take a few bites, most of the time they come around and are flabbergasted that it is actually good. The same is true with equity-driven PL; we may need to drag our faculty to the PL session, but if the participants can just buy into a few small bites of the PL, often this is enough to start the ball rolling and the process of changing mindsets.

Characteristics of Successful PL

PL must embed opportunities for educators to practice the new concepts learned during the session. The facilitators need to recognize that change is a slow process and can be difficult for people to move through. Second, it is important that there are opportunities for regular feedback on their application of the new ideas. As the facilitator, be sure to provide a space to ask questions, model, supply encouragement, and be willing to apply some pressure as needed. Some tension and discomfort in engaging with new ideas is important for a reluctant learner, but often results in positive outcomes. Applying pressure to shift mindsets must be balanced—too little results in minimal change, while too much can result in polarizing faculty. PL is an ongoing process, not an event. Therefore, ongoing support and continued follow-up are key factors. The 4ZEPL is set up to allow for this ongoing support, scaffolded opportunities to change practices, movement between zones to refine understandings, as well as opportunities to celebrate positive learning outcomes.

Professional learning where attendees have continued support throughout the learning process results in the greatest return. This support system entails space for demonstration teaching, coaching, as well as brainstorming opportunities. Without this network, teachers are less likely to experience positive student outcomes. We want to keep in mind our best practices from the classroom! Don't you find it a little ironic that educators who understand how to effectively engage students in learning through differentiation are often still being taught during PL with outdated instructional practices? ESSA as well as NAGC have set the new standard for effective PL, and it is up to us to now implement it effectively. The NAGC *Pre-K-Grade 12 Gifted Education Programming Standards* were recently revised based on best practices, theory, and gifted research. NAGC identified five key areas for teachers of gifted learners: characteristics and behaviors of underrepresented populations, cultural awareness, twice-exceptional characteristics, fostering positive peer culture, and unbiased identification assessments.[6] Professional learning is an opportunity to expand teachers' understanding of culture and equity as measured through student outcomes. This is especially true in the field of gifted education, which unfortunately is not an accurate reflection of the total student population in schools.

Culturally responsive PL addresses the need for teachers to be culturally agile in instructional strategies by understanding the cultural capital and assets that students bring with them, as well as how these assets are interwoven in the classroom environment, student–teacher interactions, and the learning process. Culturally responsive professional learning is "grounded in the research on teacher learning that is mindful of the role culture plays in the knowledge that educators bring to their practice, as well as how educators learn and make sense of their daily practice."[7] Equity-driven professional learning within the field of gifted education needs to be infused with cultural agility, understanding, and reflection; we developed the Seven Guiding Principles for Developing Equity-Driven Professional Learning[8] in order to meet this need.

Learning about gifted learners and curriculum to enrich their content knowledge is only one piece of the puzzle. PL needs to focus on how to interweave this deep understanding of content with the cultural nature of learning. We, as teachers, need space to explore our own understandings of culture through both our personal and professional cultural identities, so that we are aware of possible unintentional messages and biases we may bring into the classroom. A cornerstone of PL for educators of the gifted should be a balance of exploration of their own cultural identities with the needs and strengths of students from various cultural backgrounds.

Equity Context and the 4ZEPL

The 4ZEPL is centered around two principal theories: equity literacy and funds of knowledge. These theories offer a different view to many of the current theories in the field of gifted education which are centered around the concept of deficit thinking. Deficit thinking places the burden of change on the student, suggesting that it is the student who needs to change or do more to thrive. Yet, in a non-deficit view or a strengths-based view, the burden of change lies on the school to support the student through the creation of support systems or systemic change.

Equity Literacy Theoretical Framework

Equity literacy provides specific principles to counter deficit thinking. Focused on achieving equity, these principles bring equity to the center of the diversity conversation. Social justice seeks to fix a broken educational system, not just patch repair it. Gorski and Swalwell developed the equity literacy framework which is supported by guiding principles and abilities. The abilities are Recognize, Respond, Redress, and Cultivate and Sustain. In *Recognize,* the goal is to be aware of when you or others are stepping over the line when it comes to bias, oppression, inequity, inequality, or discrimination. This requires training and ongoing personal education of self and others; it is not easy, but it is important. You need to understand when you see something, hear something, do something; and when these things happen, you need to be able to *respond.* In airports across the country, a loudspeaker reminds us that if you see something, say something. *Respond* is the ability to move beyond the recognition and thoughtfully and equitably address these forms of bias, discrimination oppression, inequity, or inequality that we have seen, heard, or enacted. *Redress* moves beyond response into advocacy, looking at positive social changes in one's personal spheres of influence. Finally, *Cultivate and Sustain* are abilities that encourage individuals to proactively take steps toward creating communities that are equitable, bias-free, discrimination-free, and anti-oppressive.[9] Note, that these are all abilities, and by their very nature, abilities require knowledge to foster and intentionality to maintain.

In addition to the centering abilities, equity literacy has seven principles that align the work and center the focus on social justice. These principles are: Direct Confrontation, Equity Ideology, Prioritization, Redistribution, Fix Injustice Not Kids, One Size Fits Few, and Evidence-Informed Equity.[10]

The Direct Confrontation principles highlight that our first role in equity work is to state when and where racism is occurring. We first must name and confront the racism, in any iteration, that is at play in the organization. This racism or oppression could be cultural, interpersonal, institutional, or structural, but if there is any debate that racism is occurring, the organization is not ready to begin the equity work. The Equity Ideology principle refers to the fact that equity is a lens or a framework. It is not a task to complete, it is not the opening discussion in the meeting before you move on; rather, it is embedded in the work of the organization. It is a commitment.

The Prioritization and Redistribution principles often go hand in hand. Prioritization means putting the needs of students and families that have too often been marginalized and minoritized first and asking how the new policies will impact the marginalized and minoritized families, asking what impact this new policy will have on the marginalized and minoritized families. Redistribution considers opportunity and cultural, material, and social access. Actively changing inequitable practices and policies is necessary to redistribute the oppressive culture that currently exists and create equitable opportunity and access. In gifted education, this is likely identification at first glance, but it goes much deeper, into recruitment and retention.

Angela's favorite principle is #FixInjusticeNotKids (yes, it's a hashtag too!). She lives and breathes this principle, and it's one that her undergrads know by heart by the end of their time with her! Injustice is the priority, not restorative practices, not grit, not resilience, not social emotional learning, not cultural responsiveness, not gifted programs… (say *what*??). Isn't that the opposite of what you've been saying? Being understanding of a student's cultural background and responding to their cultural needs, while they are important steps (and part of the 4ZEPL!), they (alone) are narrow in focus. We want to look at the bigger picture, and by widening the lens we can focus on social justice. The idea here is that the system is what needs changing, not the kids. The kids did not create the world that they are living in, so… why are we putting the impetus for change on them? The *burden* for change on them?

The final two principles also flow together since they are grounded in the One Size Fits Few and Evidence-Informed Equity research principles. With One Size Fits Few, consider the general idea behind research. We gather data to generalize back to the larger, representative population. But in reality, within your school and your community, we say: do as we say, not as we do (sorry!). Don't generalize! Take what the research says, yes; but then learn about your communities, the people in your place and in your space. No two groups are alike in learning, in values, or in communication. One single research-based cultural framework is not the answer to working effectively with a community since it will be grounded in assumptions, not equity. Evidence-informed equity is two-fold; yes, scholarly articles are important, so too is research based in listening and responding to the community: students, families, and community stakeholders. These are data-informed, evidence-based best practices, not just what is in the research articles.

Equity literacy requires a paradigm shift of justice before harmony, the recognition that rising up to engage in social justice work is more important than cultivating successful conflict resolution or promoting a peaceful learning environment. This framework is based heavily on understanding the students and the community. It is deeply entrenched in the rejection of deficit thinking ideology. The community focus and the repudiation of deficit thinking are central to the second theoretical framework: the funds of knowledge (FoK).

Funds of Knowledge Theoretical Framework

The Funds of Knowledge Theoretical framework developed out of a pilot study of ten teachers in 1990. In schools, our instructional practices and interactions are often tied to larger issues of social class and power. This theoretical framework, developed in collaboration with teachers, recognizes the knowledge which families and communities bring to schools. These funds of knowledge, when assessed by educators, provide resources and support for learning.

The FoK model begins with building social relationships with parents and families. Through the development of relationships, teachers realize and utilize the funds of knowledge, support from the community, which families can bring into the classroom, as well as understanding how these funds are seen in the students' homes. Understanding the family culture and everyday practices within a household can help teachers understand how the child learns in schools. The FoK method brings families and communities into the classroom through a strengths-based view, looking for the support and knowledge children already have when they come to school.

Funds of knowledge are revealed through the development of relationships between the teacher and the parent. This enables the teacher to involve the parent in the learning process by engaging them in sharing examples relevant to the class or inviting family members to share their work. "You can know the academic standards inside and out, and write the most creative lesson plans, but if positive, affirming, and mutually respectful relationships are not the norm in our classrooms, no learning will take place."[11] As a teacher, you probably already know the power that a positive relationship with families can have in the learning process. These connections are essential to FoK.

Teammates in Education

Katie always admired coaches; they seem to be able to motivate a group of kids to work together and push their limits in ways that classroom teachers rarely can do. Her admiration went so far that her first master's degree is in sports leadership (that's code for coaching). As a high school rowing coach, Katie has memories of challenging a group of kids to compete for a fun-size bag of M&Ms—and, wow, did the kids get competitive! Maybe you are thinking, yeah, but with athletes you have a selected group of more motivated students compared to a classroom teacher who may have a more mixed group of students. This is a fair statement, but it is worth noting that the high school kids that Katie coached were not all top athletes. Some joined the team because they were cut from another team, others joined because their parents told them they had to do an extracurricular. Katie also experienced this same phenomenon coaching U8 and U10 soccer teams.

The ability to unite an entire team around a common goal, motivate them to achieve their personal best as well as team goals, and inspire a sincere commitment to train toward achieving these goals is what we wanted to harness in our professional learning model. So, the question remains, what is the secret that coaches possess?

Coaches follow several key guidelines in achieving their success:

1. **Planning with the End in Mind:** Coaches work backward when developing their training plans, creating a training plan so that the athletes hit their peak performance for the championship games. Sound familiar? We do this as teachers in the classroom when we use backward planning to develop lesson plans. But how often do we apply this to professional learning?
2. **Celebrating Little (and *Big*) Wins:** We have always known that sports celebrate their victory in big ways. But what is often less apparent to the fans, is how coaches also celebrate the little wins along the way. When a player hits a personal record, there's cause to celebrate, and when the team hits a staggered goal, there's recognition and praise for this accomplishment. We do this in the classroom to some extent, but we could probably be better at it. In professional learning, we recognize those teachers who stand out, but how often have you heard the facilitators recognizing and celebrating individual progress toward goals? And when the progress is recognized, is it truly celebrated or more for show?
3. **You Are Only as Strong as the Weakest Link:** This mentality of coaches helps to drive strategic training plans as well as build community within the team. Recognizing that there is *no I in team* and encouraging the teammates to support each other is a secret of coaching magic. Fostering a sense of community is essential to the success of the team. Classroom teachers vary dramatically in their community-building success, but, if we look at professional learning, there are very few authentic methods through which community is developed and fostered.
4. **Individualized Training Programs:** Coaches supplement players' training with individualized programs. Here the coaches are acknowledging that different players are at different levels of fitness or ability; yet, if the training is adjusted for the athlete while still targeting the same end goal, then greater positive outcomes are yielded. Yes, teachers do this all the time! Professional learning is moving in that direction, but we are still mostly in the one-size-fits-all model.
5. **Establishing a Sense of Unity:** Coaches spend time on team-building exercises, fostering a sense of unity and commitment to each other.

This sense of *we are all in this together* attitude becomes a common thread that keeps players united. This unity becomes the backbone of the team when things don't go as planned, or when there's cause to celebrate. Unity is created through shared experiences—the tough practices, the bus ride to a game, the shared joy or disappointment in a game. In the classroom, we can develop a sense of unity, but many teachers struggle with creating an authentic feel to the unity for a variety of reasons. Sometimes it is a lack of buy-in from the students, the classroom climate, or a lack of a sense of shared things in common. Professional learning rarely inspires a sense of unity during one-day workshops or mandatory faculty meetings (unless you count a mutual feeling of being disgruntled).

6. **Motivation:** Motivation is the secret weapon of coaches. When working with the athletes, coaches can motivate the athlete to work toward personal goals while at the same time working toward achieving the team goals. We try to do this in the classroom, but it often is unsuccessful because of the lack of buy-in from the students and/or the lack of unity. Rarely do you experience this unity in professional learning. Everyone is attending the PL because it's mandated, but how often are all the participants truly excited to be there? The closest we get to this is perhaps during annual conferences where you get to gather with other gifted specialists who are all passionate about the same topic.

It is these lessons learned in coaching that we wanted to embed into our 4ZEPL. We strongly feel that these core principles of coaching when applied to professional learning create an environment where educators can grow as individuals but also as a faculty. We all want our students to do well, but often we must first break down our barriers that we build as adults to accomplish our goals. As we move through this book, we will refer to you, the facilitator, as the coach of your team. As the coach, your role is to prepare your teachers to meet the equity-driven PL goals.

What's the Play, Coach?

First things first, you will need to develop your training plan, working backward—just as a coach prepares for the championship game. Equity work is an ongoing process, so it may seem difficult to pinpoint an end point or championship game. However, without a point in time to work toward, it is easy to put off the PL or become sidetracked. Instead, we recommend first identifying your learning goals and the amount of time you realistically have available to provide the PL, being sure to factor in the synchronous as well as asynchronous learning time.

Second, you must consider who is on your team. Assess the participants who will need to partake in the PL, just as a coach would evaluate his players, consider their strengths and areas to grow related to gifted education and equity. You are not evaluating your colleagues to cut them from the team (sorry friends, everyone makes the team!), but rather you are assessing them to implement the most effective training method which will yield the greatest end results.

Third, scope out your training facilities and resources. Picking the PLC that is the best fit for your teachers, and the readily available resources at your school, is important.

Why Zones?

In sports, the zone refers to the mindset of the player who is performing at their peak performance, and truly embracing and enjoying the moment of top productivity. A zone also refers to the area or region of a field in which a player is responsible for covering or playing. We purposefully selected the word zone for this PL model because we believe that each of these four zones is a fluid space that teachers should move through and between without restriction. Sometimes it will be necessary to move backward through a previous zone when facilitating the PL, because equity work is hard work.

Some professional learning programs use the word *stage* or *level*, but this suggests that when a participant completes the training at a required level, they no longer need to revisit the topic. However, in equity-driven professional learning, we believe that each zone contains pertinent information for all learners, and much like Webb's Depths of Knowledge[12] participants can dive deeper into understanding within each zone. Webb's Depths of Knowledge provides four levels of depth within which a concept could be explored in depth. At the lowest level, the concept is explored simply in terms of recall and reproduction (Do you know the dates of the American Revolution? Who was the 35th President of the United States? Can you identify the characteristics of a gifted learner?). The most complex, deepest dive into understanding occurs at Level 4, extended thinking. Here the learner wrestles with understanding through a more in-depth analysis which often extends over a period of time. For example, the students might evaluate the relevancy and accuracy of historical accounts of the American Revolution from multiple sources or compares and contracts conflicting policies from Supreme Court decisions or critiques the historical impact of gifted education policies. In the 4ZEPL, participants can dive deeper into understandings within each PL zone, making each zone relevant and applicable to all participants. Therefore, fluid movement between zones is necessary as one's knowledge base grows. For example, someone may begin with learning the basics of a cultural group during a first visit to Zone 1, and later be ready to go back and dive deeper in, necessitating a second visit to the zone.

Defense? Offense? Cover Your Bases?

Developing highly effective, equity-driven PL requires the coach to think flexibly and understand that not everyone will be ready for every zone at the same time, and there may be several different tracks for the participants within each zone. While this may seem daunting at first, realistically the PL could run similarly to flexible groups in the classroom. Figure 2.2 walks through the 4ZEPL in action, after taking the participants' pulse through a targeted pre-assessment and planning adjusted zones into three groups based on that data. Throughout the PL, the facilitator should incorporate time for self-reflective journaling prompts, discussions, and debriefs. Each zone has embedded within it the seven guiding principles for equity-driven professional learning (discussed in detail in Chapter 3).[13]

A change in teacher beliefs most often comes after a teacher has seen a change in a student's achievement. As the coach, you are guiding the participants through this journey of change. You will help the participants develop both their defense and offense skills through the 4ZEPL. As a coach, we believe that the best defense is a strong offense. To this end, the players learn how to put on the pressure to score points. In gifted PL, we are putting on the pressure to identify and serve underrepresented gifted learners in our schools. To put it a different way, we are looking for how participants can enact change in their own spheres of influence. Each of the zones helps the adult learner to examine not only how giftedness presents in various cultural groups, but also to look inward to reflect on the role that their own personal beliefs play in the education of gifted learners.

The 4ZEPL also develops a strong defense strategy by developing the knowledge and skills of the participants to champion for marginalized student populations and advocate for these gifted learners. What other spheres of influence do teachers hold beyond classroom referrals and recommendations? Change won't happen piecemeal, but by working to fix the broken system. In the summer of 2020, Angela attended an online seminar by Black Minds Matter author Dr. J. Luke Wood; one of the guests was a high school student that belonged to a student advocacy group. Her student organization ended their meetings by repeating the words of Assata Shakur, first in a whisper, and ending in a thunderous chorus: "It is our duty to fight for our freedom. It is our duty to win. We must love and support each other. We have nothing to lose but our chains."

Coaches whose teams are most successful develop strategies for both defense and offense as well as a few signature plays to pull out in tense moments. We believe the 4ZEPL does just this for professional learning. As we move through the rest of the book, we will follow the coaching metaphor, sharing a training plan and strategies for developing and maintaining motivation.

	PLC 1 Growth Group	PLC 2 Proficient Group	PLC 3 Extension Group
	Little to no cultural & equity awareness: misconceptions related to gifted characteristics in traditionally marginalized gifted groups in the community	Average cultural & equity awareness: misconceptions related to gifted characteristics in traditionally marginalized gifted groups in the community	Culturally & equity aware: recognizes gifted characteristics in traditionally marginalized gifted groups in the community
Zone 1	**-Understanding the self is the first step of the journey: the group first unpacks culture and Whiteness, discussing the ways the participants' culture influences their teaching and their** classroom. -PLC discusses the ways in which systems of oppression and bias are seen in the school and community and how these impact gifted students and families. The facilitator should be prepared to offer scaffolding or examples to start the conversation, as the group may not have immediate recognition or awareness of examples. -Facilitators provide background knowledge through multiple modalities about the traditionally marginalized gifted students groups in general, providing a global understanding of the ethnic group and then narrowing to those found within the district, community, and school. Facilitators should emphasize the importance of not generalizing but knowing the community and students. -Facilitators guide discussion through the common misconceptions and stereotypes of the traditionally marginalized gifted students group(s) in the school, district, and community.	-Based on the pre-assessment, this group likely has an initial understanding of self and culture; Understanding the **self is the always the first step of the journey, and unpack**ing culture and unpacking Whiteness, while discussing the **ways the participants' culture influences their teaching and their classroom is still the first step. However the discussion** may go deeper, focusing on privilege, on intersectionality, and/or focusing on upstander vs. bystander. -Again, it is important for the facilitators to situate the discussion in how racism, oppression and bias operates in this place and space. This group, based on the pre-assessment, should have more detailed and/or realistic examples and may need less scaffolding to think of them. **-Facilitators provide specific deep knowledge through mul**tiple modalities on traditionally marginalized groups found within the district, community, and school. -Facilitators introduce the FoK Framework.	-Primary Facilitators introduce the Funds of Knowledge Framework (FoK) in a train the trainer model. -PLC shares the Zone 1 facilitation role with support from the main facilitator. -Primary Facilitator provides supplemental knowledge to PLC through multiple modalities to extend knowledge on giftedness, equity, and/or traditionally marginalized gifted students groups based on the pre-assessment; debriefs with PLC in small groups or one-on-one depending on numbers. -It is important to ensure that while PLC is taking on a leading role in facilitating PLCs 1 & 2 with the Lead Facilitator, that they are also engaging in new content with the Lead Facilitator; just like gifted kiddos they have the right to learn something new every day.
	Throughout, provide time for self-reflective journaling prompts, discussions, and debriefs.		
Zone 2	In this example, based on the pre-assessment, neither PLC 1 or 2 has a solid understanding of giftedness in the targeted gifted population. Therefore, the activities in Zone 2 are the same: -Discuss the impact of systemic inequities from Zone 1 on the students' educational experience. Relate that to gifted education. -Presentation through multiple modalities and discussion of: ---**What does giftedness look like in this specific culture? Who is considered gifted? What kinds of gifts are recognized or** valued? ---How may giftedness present differently in the classroom from other gifted children? **-Using case studies and scenarios, facilitators should present information and have participants reflect on real-word examples,** making connections to students in the classroom. Provide time for discussion and sharing opportunities. -Facilitators should provide opportunities for job-embedded operationalization of the professional learning: have PLC 1 & 2 **educators to discuss their current students' profiles, and make connections to the Zone 1 & 2 content.** *Differentiation for Zone 2 is based on the level of cultural awareness and equity knowledge the PLCs demonstrated after Zone 1. For example, the facilitator differentiates the case studies, scenarios, discussion questions, and reflective prompts, mirroring the appropriate level of proximal development of the educators, allowing for their growth.*		-Group members share the Zone 2 facilitation role with support from the main facilitator. -Primary Facilitator provides supplemental knowledge through multiple modalities to extend PLC members' knowledge on giftedness, equity, and/or traditionally marginalized gifted populations based on the pre-assessment. PLC debriefs with facilitator in small groups or one-on-one depending on numbers. -Primary facilitator provides opportunities for PLC 3 educators **to discuss their current students' profiles, and make connec**tions to the Zone 3 content to ensure they are connecting with new content and extending their knowledge.
	Throughout, provide time for self-reflective journaling prompts, discussions, and debriefs		

Figure 2.2 Zones in action: Sample planning chart for differentiated groups. Note: Adapted from Novak and Lewis, 2021.

Zone 3	-Facilitators present through multiple modalities and engage PLC in discussion of the teacher supports that exist in the district to help provide equity in the gifted classroom and/or for gifted learners. -Educators will engage in guided exploration of practical and actionable resources that can support traditionally marginalized gifted learners and have an opportunity to put resources to use in their lesson planning with the guidance of the facilitator and in collaboration with their PLC members. -Educators will be asked to try lessons using the supports, then **reflect and report back at the next PLC meeting.** -Educators learn information about and engage in discussion regarding non-instructional supports (e.g., mentorships, affiliate groups) for minoritized gifted learners. -Educators identify human resources available within their district who can support gifted programming- for example the ESL teacher may have strategies to support second language acquisition.	-Facilitators present through multiple modalities and engage PLC in discussion of the teacher supports that exist in the district that help to provide equity in the classroom and/or for gifted learners. -Facilitators present through multiple modalities different tools that support equity in gifted curriculum. -Facilitators provide an example of inequitable curriculum from the district. Educators discuss ways to modify it for equity and identify practical, actional ways to provide resources in the classroom to support minoritized gifted students. -Educators discuss instructional (frontloading and talent development) and non instructional supports available for gifted learners and identify practices in their districts that are commensurate practices. -Educators identify human resources available within their district who can support gifted programming- for example the ESL teacher may have strategies to support second language acquisition.	-Facilitators present through multiple modalities a variety of tools that support equity in gifted curriculum. -PLC conducts a review of school and district gifted curriculum for equity/inequity; discuss ways to modify the curriculum for equity and identify practical, actional ways to provide resources in the classroom to support minoritized gifted learners. -PLC discusses the concept of reparations and what/how this looks like in gifted education. **-PLC identifies human resources available within the districts** who can support gifted programming- for example the ESL teacher may have strategies to support second language acquisition. -Facilitators provide opportunities for educators to plan together, share ideas, and for demonstration teaching.
	Throughout, provide time for self-reflective journaling prompts, discussions, and debriefs.		
Zone 4	-Facilitators present in multiple modalities the basic tenets of FoK, primarily focusing on strengths/assets based viewpoints and cultural capital. -As part of ongoing and sustained work, PLC 3 received training to continue to support PLC 1 in this role (see Zone 1). -PLC members attend events within the school community. -Facilitators support PLC as they review current parent and community engagement opportunities focused on gifted programming assessing for level of impact and quality of engagement. -Facilitators and PLC members explore avenues to involve the local members of the historically minoritized communities in gifted programming. -PLC creates a plan to welcome parents and community to the school and/or a community space for information sessions about the program; PLC works with the planning committee to ensure that there is a panel of speakers that can address any concerns that arise about the gifted programming.	-Facilitators train PLC to conduct home visits and build asset-based relationships with families and the community, per the FoK framework. -PLC works with facilitators to review current parent and community engagement opportunities focused on gifted programming assessing for level of impact and quality of engagement. -PLC works with facilitators to explore avenues to involve local members of the historically minoritized communities in gifted programming. -PLC plans information sessions for parents and community; researches expert speakers to invite that will provide culturally relevant input on the gifted programming.	-PLC members conduct home visits and build asset-based relationships with families and the community, per the FoK framework; mentor PLC 2 with this work. -PLC begins to work with administration to revise current parent and community engagement opportunities focused on gifted programming assessing for level of impact and quality of engagement. -PLC creates an action plan with at least two local community members input to involve local members of the historically minoritized communities in gifted programming. -PLC plans and conducts information sessions for parents and the community, serving as the expert speakers.
	Throughout, provide time for self-reflective journaling prompts, discussions, and debriefs.		
Embedded Equity Driven Professional Learning Principles *Taking a Pulse, Individualizing Professional Learning Plans, Establishing a Safe Zone, Going Beyond the Tip of the Iceberg, Bridging the Gap between School and Home, Engaging in Courageous Conversations, Identifying Grows and Glows*			

Figure 2.2 (Continued)

Resources

Books

- *How to Be an Antiracist* by Ibram X Kendi
- *This Book is Anti-Racist* by Tiffany M. Jewell
- *Coaching for Equity* by Elena Aguilar
- *Solving Disproportionality and Achieving Equity* by Edward Fergus
- *We Want to Do More than Survive* by Bettina Love

Websites

- Being Antiracist, National Museum of African American History and Culture, https://nmaahc.si.edu/learn/talking-about-race/topics/being-antiracist
- Equity Literacy Institute, https://www.equityliteracy.org/
- EdChange, http://www.edchange.org/
- Approaches toward Equity, https://www.equityliteracy.org/approaches-to-educational-equity

Articles

- "The Urgent Need for Antiracist Education" by Christina Torres, https://www.edweek.org/leadership/opinion-the-urgent-need-for-anti-racist-education/2019/08
- "Equity Literacy for All" by Paul Gorski and Katy Swalwell, http://edchange.org/publications/Equity-Literacy-for-All.pdf
- "Avoiding Racial Equity Detours" by Paul Gorski, http://edchange.org/publications/Avoiding-Racial-Equity-Detours-Gorski.pdf

Notes

1 Brito, C. (2021, June 29). *Olympic hammer thrower Gwen Berry responds to backlash after she turns away from U.S. flag during national anthem.* https://www.cbsnews.com/news/gwen-berry-olympics-national-anthem-flag/

2 Lewis, K. D., Novak, A. M., & Coronado, J. (2015). Teachers' perceptions of characteristics of gifted Hispanic bilingual students: Perspectives from the border. *Texas Forum of Teacher Education*, *5*(1), 71–91. doi: 10.1177/1076217520915743

3 Novak, A. M., & Lewis, K. D. (2021, March 8–13). *Four zones of professional learning: Fostering equity in gifted programs.* [Conference session]. Council for Exceptional Children Convention. Virtual. glance

4 Novak, A. M., & Lewis, K. D. (2022). A methodological approach to designing a theory: The journey of the four zone professional learning model. *Roeper Review*, *44*(1), 49–62. https://doi.org/10.1080/02783193.2021.2005206

5 Guskey, T. R. (2016). Gauge impact with 5 levels of data. *Learning Forward*, *37*(1), 32–37.

6 National Association for Gifted Children. (2019). *Pre-K-Grade 12 gifted programming standards.* http://www.nagc.org/sites/default/files/ standards/Intro%202019%20Programming%20Standards.pdf National Association for Gifted Children and Council for Exceptional.
7 King, K. A., Artiles, A. J., & Kozleski, E. B. (2009). *Professional learning for culturally responsive teaching.* Equity Alliance at ASU, p. 5. _Culturally_Responsive_Teaching%20%281%29.pdf
8 Novak, A. M., Lewis, K. D., & Weber, C. L. (2020). Guiding principles in developing equity-driven professional learning for educators of gifted students. *Gifted Child Today, 43*(3), 169–183. doi: 10.1177/1076217520915743 (see Chapter 2).
9 Gorski, P. C., & Swalwell, K. (2015). Equity literacy for all. *Educational Leadership, 72*(6), 34–40
10 Gorski, P. C. (2020). *Equity literacy principles.* EdChange and the Equity Literacy Institute.
11 Amanti, C. (2005). Beyond a beads and feathers approach. In N. González, L. C. Moll, C. Amanti (Eds.), *Funds of knowledge: Theorizing practices in households, communities, and classrooms* (pp. 131–142). Routledge.
12 Webb, N. (1997). *Research Monograph Number 6: Criteria for alignment of expectations and assessments on mathematics and science education.* Washington, DC: CCSSO.
13 Novak, A. M., & Lewis, K. D. (2022). A methodological approach to designing a theory: The journey of the four zone professional learning model. *Roeper Review, 44*(1), 49–62. https://doi.org/10.1080/02783193.2021.2005206

3

Seven Guiding Principles for Equity Driven Professional Learning

Katie and Angela are honored to count among their fellow doctoral alums Arthur Ashe, a gifted professional tennis player who said, "True heroism is remarkably sober, very undramatic. It is not the urge to surpass all others at whatever cost, but the urge to serve others at whatever cost."[1] This quote has added meaning; framed and propped up against a mug given to Angela during her second year of teaching. It's a little weathered from a few moves, with some of the vellum peeling away, but you can still read, "Not all heroes wear capes. Some are teachers."

In thinking about equity, effective teaching, and professional learning, we know there are best practices for each of these separate topics. Yet, when we reviewed the literature, we felt a lack in a concrete direction on how these three areas all intersect. In an article for *Tempo*, Katie first outlined guidelines for a culturally responsive classroom.[2] Since then, we've refined these guidelines over time, crafting them into the Guiding Principles for Equity Driven Professional Learning,[3] embedding them in practice using case studies,[4] and within the 4ZEPL.[5] These principles are:

1) Taking a Pulse
2) Individualizing Professional Learning Plans 
3) Establishing a Safe Zone 
4) Going Beyond the Tip of the Iceberg 

DOI: 10.4324/9781003196204-4

5) Engaging in Courageous Conversations

6) Bridging the Gap between School and Home 

7) Identifying Grows and Glows 

Connecting to the Research: Standards and Outcomes

Each principle is grounded in research-based best practices in professional learning, culturally responsive teaching, and equity. There are standards that undergird the principles in general, as well as underlying bodies of research that inform the practices. This section will go into the research-based standards and outcomes support behind the general principles. It is important to note that except for professional learning standards, which are based in adult learning theory and already applicable to our situation, the research focuses on teachers and students, which we then apply to the professional learning context. If an outcome states "in the classroom," this classroom is interpreted for our use as the PL setting, the curriculum as the PL content, the teacher is the PL facilitator, and the students, you guessed it, the PL participants! Each of the following sections of Your Guide to the Principles will have an inset of Connecting to the Research to share how each guiding principle is informed by research-based best practices, as well as which of the discussed standards and outcomes best connects to the principle. (Angela could likely draw you a flow chart and talk circles about how many, many more connect! But it was important to cut her off at some point!)

Standards: Professional Learning and Gifted

In the introductory chapter, we discussed the Learning Forward standards for professional learning as a basis for the professional learning informed research aspect of the model. The same standards inform the equity-driven principles for professional learning. The seven Learning Forward standards are based on research and are intended to substantiate educators' skills in working toward school improvement goals. Successful professional learning involves:

- **Learning Communities:** Professional learning that increases educator effectiveness and results for all students occurs within learning communities committed to continuous improvement, collective responsibility, and goal alignment.

- **Resources:** Professional learning that increases educator effectiveness and results for all students requires prioritizing, monitoring, and coordinating resources for educator learning.
- **Learning Designs:** Professional learning that increases educator effectiveness and results for all students integrates theories, research, and models of human learning to achieve its intended outcomes.
- **Outcomes:** Professional learning that increases educator effectiveness and results for all students aligns its outcomes with educator performance and student curriculum standards.
- **Leadership:** Professional learning that increases educator effectiveness and results for all students requires skillful leaders who develop capacity, advocate, and create support systems for professional learning.
- **Data:** Professional learning that increases educator effectiveness and results for all students uses a variety of sources and types of student, educator, and system data to plan, assess, and evaluate professional learning.
- **Implementation:** Professional learning that increases educator effectiveness and results for all students applies research on change and sustains support for implementation of professional learning for long-term change.[6]

The principles are based on blanket best practices in professional learning; none of the Learning Forward standards speak specifically to equity, though they are currently in the process of revision. And while they are research-based, a question we should always ask ourselves is, based on what research? As we mentioned earlier, the traditional learning theory that many educational systems base their instructional philosophies on is steeped in research conducted by White male scientists, with samples that were likely all White, middle to upper class, without any students that had moderate to severe learning, neurodiverse, or emotional exceptionalities. What can be said about professional learning research? Are the studies based on a diverse sample of teachers? We know that, nationwide, the majority of US teachers are White, resting around 80% according to the National Center for Educational Statistics (2018 data),[7] but that's not true of every district, every school. We shared in Chapter 2 that we started the 4ZEPL journey because of the results of one of our research studies—a PL study in which teachers with similar ethnicities and cultural identities to the students were not successful at recognizing and identifying gifted characteristics. The language in the standards is specific to "all students"; however, when working with equity in mind, prioritization is an important principle, as is naming the need for equity distribution and redistribution (see Chapter 2 for the equity literacy principles and—spoiler alert!—later in this chapter as well). Thus, these standards alone are not enough to guide effective equity-driven professional learning. Moreover, these standards are not specific to gifted education.

But wait... ask and you shall receive! There are standards in gifted education. The National Association for Gifted Children (NAGC) has Programming Standards that underwent a recent 2019 revision process; these revised standards have a greater focus on equity than the original. The programming standards have evidence-based teacher practices that align with student outcomes. Standard 6 is the Professional Development standard, and 6.3 is the equity and inclusion student outcome, which reads, "All students with gifts and talents are able to develop their abilities as a result of educators who are committed to removing barriers to access and creating inclusive gifted education communities."[8] There are three teacher practices that correspond to this student outcome:

- **6.3.1.** Educators participate in professional learning focused on curriculum and pedagogy that are responsive to diversity for individuals with gifts and talents.
- **6.3.2.** Educators recognize their biases, develop philosophies responsive to diversity, commit themselves to removing barriers, and create inclusive learning environments that meet the educational interests, strengths, and needs of diverse students with gifts and talents.
- **6.3.3.** Educators understand how knowledge, perspectives, and historical and current issues influence professional practice and the education and treatment of individuals with gifts and talents both in school and society.[9]

Select NAGC Programming Standards that address equity are included in the Resources section of this chapter.

Programming is only one aspect of addressing equity in the greater system; teachers are significant gatekeepers (you are reading this book after all). NAGC and the Talented and Gifted (TAG) division of the Council for Exceptional Children (CEC) collaborated to create the NAGC and CEC-TAG Teacher Preparation Standards and the Advanced Standards in Gifted Education Teacher Preparation. These are included in the same Appendix A document, aligned categorically with the programming standards for ease of use. Of note in the professional learning and advocacy heading: "Beginning gifted education professionals model respect for diversity, understanding that it is an integral part of society's institutions and impacts learning of individuals with gifts and talents in the delivery of gifted education services"[10] and "Gifted education specialists use culturally responsive practices to enhance collaboration."[11] In addition to the culturally responsive, diversity-focused, and/or equity-framed gifted programming standards, the guiding principles are steeped in research-based outcomes from multicultural, culturally competent, and equity literature.

Outcomes: Multicultural, Culturally Responsive, Cultural Competence, Equity... Both/And not Either/Or

A significant research base to the equity-driven guiding principles is the work in equity, culturally responsive teaching, and multicultural education. Are these synonyms? No. Don't we all just want the same thing? In some ways, yes. But the definitions of each vary, and the goals of each depend on who you are talking to and in what context. Recall the definition of equity in Chapter 1: *fair access for full participation for all.* In educational contexts we sometimes use these terms interchangeably, while a detour to equity is a reliance on cultural competence alone as a framework for professional learning. Paul Gorski writes "Cultural competence is important. But by itself, it's no threat to racism."[12] The guiding principles are based in both/and, not either/or, domains of research; just as our work must be to transform the field.

The National Association for Multicultural Education, or NAME[13] has a mission to advance and advocate for social justice and equity. The organization has an extensive definition of multicultural education, describing it as a philosophical concept, encompassing multiple ideals: freedom, equality, equity, justice, and human dignity. NAME acknowledges multicultural education as a process; recall back in Chapter 1 as we distinguished equity and diversity work as either process or outcome/goal (or both). As part of the process of multicultural education, NAME advocates for the centrality of students and their life experiences in the teaching process, and actively prepares students to work toward advocating for structural equality in their spheres of influence. Thus, to the fullest extent possible, the curriculum used should be antiracist, anti-bias, and anti-discriminatory, with teachers and students critically analyzing issues of oppression and power.

Likewise, as much as possible, an environment that supports multicultural education has a staff that is both culturally, ethnically, and linguistically diverse, and is culturally competent. Like we said—we love their extensive definition; read the full definition on their website.[14] While they don't have standards, they have five outcomes for students, each connected to research based on teaching and learning. These outcomes are:

- **Positive Academic Identities:** Students recognize themselves individually and as members of their identity groups as academically and intellectually capable. Students utilize inquiry and communication skills as appropriate and participate in knowledge construction, leading to developing social justice.
- **Positive Social Identities:** Social identity is not limited to ethnic or racial identity, but encompasses religion, gender, sexuality, economics or class, geography/place, language, nationality, culture (dis) ability or exceptionality, and age. Students can affirm, through accurate language and knowledge, belongingness in multiple identity groups and how these identities, theirs and others, interact. A crucial component of this student outcome is students' ability to express confidence and pride in their identities without devaluing others' identities.
- **Respectful Engagement with Diverse People:** "Mama, Miss Amy's skin is so dark!" one of Angela's children exclaimed at three years old, as Angela's hand rested next to her neighbor Amy's, as they chatted together on the front stoop. Was this cause for embarrassment? Censure? Ignore, uncomfortable laugh, and move on? None of the above. Students, children of all ages, should be able to use language to describe similarities and differences between themselves and others. Students should express curiosity, and engage in open-minded exploration of ideas, perspectives and beliefs that differ from theirs, or those that emerge from their social identities, and in particular the dominant social identity. The ability to engage in respectful, empathetic critical conversation is an important outcome of a multicultural education.

In Chapter 1, we defined social justice as both a process and a goal. NAME's multicultural student outcomes have social justice divided into two behaviors, consciousness and action.

- **Social Justice Consciousness:** Students can recognize what is justice and injustice, fair and unfair. In this outcome, students analyze the impact of the injustice and its repercussions on both self and others. NAME indicates that in this outcome, students "link their own well-being with that of people who differ from themselves and understand that one's well-being may result from the marginalization of others."[15] Students can identify relevant information pertaining to the issue as well as recognize multiple viewpoints.

- **Social Justice Action:** This outcome moves students and teachers from thinking to doing. Students are challenged to "recognize their own responsibility to resist exclusion, prejudice and injustice in their everyday lives, despite pressure from others to do otherwise or displeasure from those around them who may thwart their efforts for social justice."[16] Students engage in participatory democratic activism and evaluate the effectiveness of their strategies. Teachers also engage in their own activism.

NAME conceptualizes multicultural learning through how teachers and students interact and how their relationship impacts these outcomes through four dimensions: curriculum, assessment, pedagogy, and intellectual challenge (see Figure 3.1).[17]

Teachers frame their actions through considering what they can do in their own classes or schools, or in the words we use in this book (Gorski's and DuBose's words): spheres of influence.

Culturally responsive teaching is slowly becoming the standard across the country. As we shared in the introduction chapter, the National Education Association,[18] identified five areas of cultural competence in which both educators and the larger educational systems should continually grow. They are fully described on pages 6–7, but in short, are:

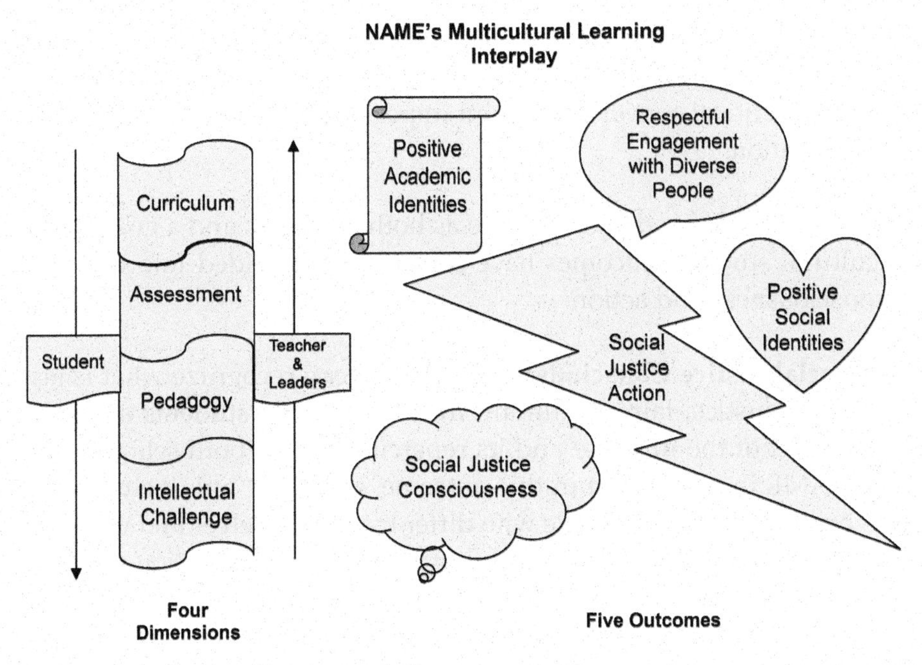

Figure 3.1 NAME's multicultural learning interplay.

- **Valuing Diversity:** Individuals move from acceptance to respect of cultural differences
- **Culturally Self-Aware:** Understand and reflect upon oneself, impacting the school and community
- **Dynamics of Difference:** Individuals understand challenges in communication and plan proactively
- **Knowledge of Students' Culture:** Individuals understand and respect who they serve in the community
- **Institutionalize Cultural Knowledge and Adapting to Diversity:** Individuals within the system institutionalize their cultural competency knowledge to serve the population at large

In addition, a 2019 report from New America[19] shared the results of a study investigating the standards across 50 states, delving into the presence or lack of cultural competence or cultural responsiveness within individual state teaching standards. Eight competencies for culturally responsive teaching (see Figure 3.2) emerged from the study, drawn from a review of the research, and used as a guide to facilitate the study of the state standards. These teacher-focused strategies can be viewed through a professional learning lens as tools to add to the teachers' repertoires during a PL training, and as strategies.[20]

In Chapter 2, we took a deep dive into research when we discussed the framework for the 4ZEPL. We've revisited the definition of equity already in this chapter, which is integral to the guiding principles; so too, is the equity literacy framework.[21] In particular, the equity-driven guiding principles for professional learning are grounded in the following equity literacy principles discussed in more detail in pages 39–40 of Chapter 2:

- **Direct Confrontation Principle:** Acknowledge that racism exists and name where and when it is seen and heard in the organization.
- **Redistribution Principle:** Review processes, policies, and practices, examining how they marginalize students and reform or transform them. Identification is a great place to start.
- **Prioritization Principle:** Place needed emphasis on (prioritize) historically minoritized and marginalized students, on their interests and needs.
- **Equity Ideology Principle:** Equity should be embedded in everything we do; it is an ideological approach, not piecemeal strategies.
- **#FixInjusticeNotKids Principle:** Children didn't cause the broken system; they don't need fixing! Fix the system by addressing the issues of bias, discrimination, and racism in the structure of the schools,

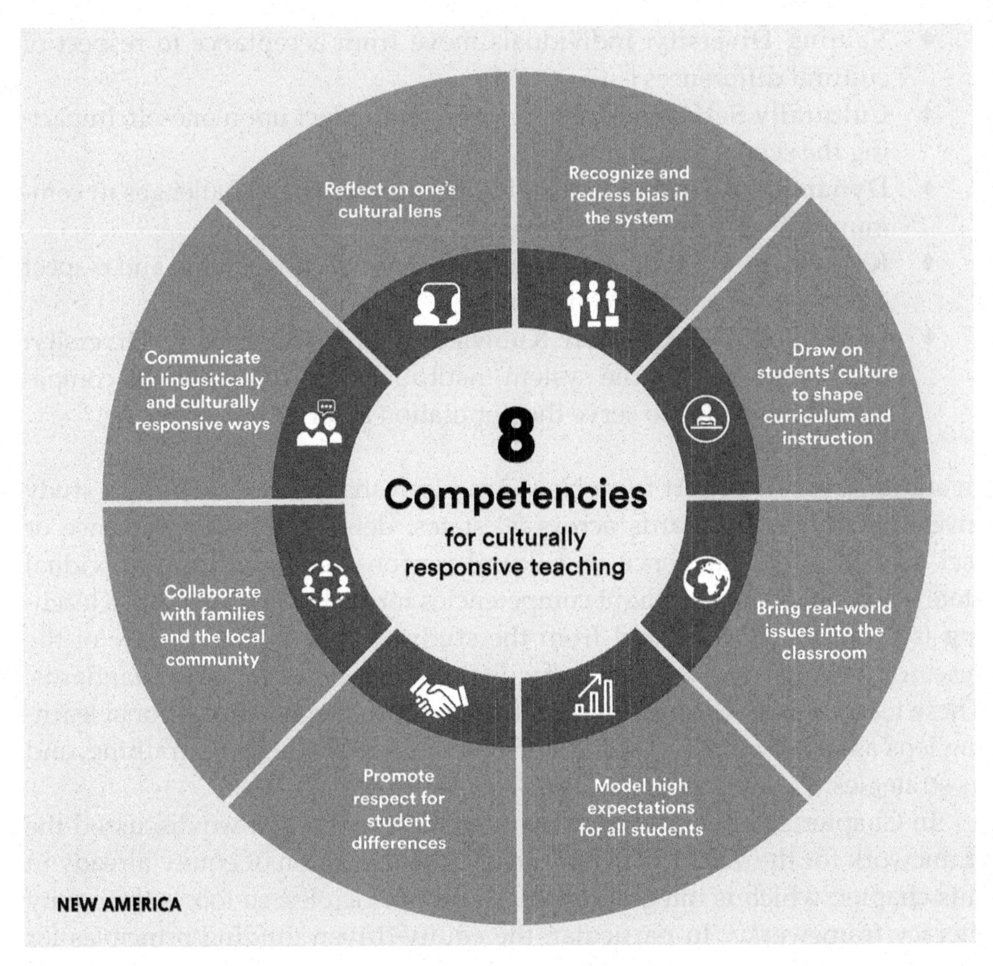

Figure 3.2 Eight competencies for culturally responsive teaching. Note: Muñiz, 2019; The New America Report carries a Creative Commons Attribution 4.0 International License. www .newamerica.org

rather than trying to alter the kids to fit into the biased, discriminatory, racist system.

- **One Size Fits Few:** Learn about the community in which you work; basing equity work in one cultural framework will be grounded in assumptions, not equity.
- **Evidence-Informed Equity:** Base equity work in both scholarly research and in the community: student and parent voices are essential to the process.

Equity literacy is centered by the four abilities: Recognizing when you or others are exhibiting bias; responding to that bias; redressing or advocating for positive change; and cultivating and sustaining that advocacy into creating communities that are equitable, discrimination-free, anti-oppressive, and bias-free.

At the beginning of this section, we wrote: "Are these synonyms? No. Don't we all just want the same thing? In some ways, yes." Take a moment to process and reflect on the themes you noted throughout the section. And note the differences as well. Reflect on the quote, "Cultural competence is important. But by itself, it's no threat to racism" as we move into the guiding principles for equity driven professional learning.

Your Guide to the Principles

There are seven guiding principles for developing equity-driven PL. These guiding principles were developed by the authors, grounded in the literature for professional learning, equity-literacy. These principles should guide all PL sessions, interwoven throughout the sessions —rather than addressed in isolation. In the following section, we walk through each of these principles along with alignment to the research and standards. Additionally, each principle has an icon which will appear throughout the subsequent chapters to indicate where/how it would be applied within and across the 4ZEPL.

Taking a Pulse

Consider your classroom, as you begin a new unit of study, what should be the first thing that you do? Hopefully, you immediately answered: Pre-assessment! Effective instruction begins and ends with assessing a student's understanding. Why? To inform your instruction and to ensure that all learners are learning in the zone of proximal development (ZPD), that happy place where there's the push and pull of challenge. Not too easy (Boring!), not too hard (Frustrating!), but just right. The Goldilocks Principle of teaching! Without the formative assessment, the lesson's effectiveness is likely to dip. The same principle applies to professional learning (PL). If we want our participants to get the most out of the PL, then we need to know their prior levels of knowledge. For example, the facilitator should use pre-assessments or pre-screenings as a tool for gauging the participants' cultural knowledge and skills going into the PL as well as throughout the PL. There are many options for cultural awareness surveys, which can be found online, as well as an example in the resources section of Chapter 4.

Equity-focused PL, while it may cover any topic within gifted, is at its core focused on being culturally aware. Therefore, it is necessary for individuals to recognize their own cultural experiences, knowledge, and ideas across cultural domains. Because of the personal nature of these PL sessions, confidentiality is essential. As a facilitator, you set the tone for the PL; begin by ensuring all participants that their pre-survey reflections will be kept confidential and not be used to evaluate their performance. This is not a *gotcha*, but a personal reflection, an opportunity to establish growth points, and a piece of data-gathering to make the PL meaningful and effective.

But, like pulse monitoring during exercise, the pre-assessment shouldn't be a one and done. Rather, the facilitator should regularly monitor the pulse of the participants for learning growth as well as frustration/confusion levels. Collecting several data points over the course of the PL sessions as well as following the sessions enables the facilitator to continue monitoring the targeted areas of growth and future professional learning needs.

Connecting to the Research

What we think and feel as individuals matters. Not just to us (though of course that's true), but who we are as people influences how we teach. Educators' personal beliefs have such a strong influence on their instructional delivery, that these beliefs can overpower professional knowledge.[22] These beliefs can be related to instructional practices or the students themselves, from the way teachers think that students learn to their social characteristics.[23] While these complex systems of beliefs are developed over time, with new experiences and understandings of the world as contributing factors, deep-rooted assumptions and biases may still exist.[24,25] Because these beliefs have the potential to negatively impact teachers' views and interactions with students, and professional learning has been shown to positively impact teachers beliefs,[26] establishing a baseline pulse in which teachers explore their own potential biases and preconceived notions of culture[27] and continuing to monitor that pulse is an important strategy throughout professional learning.

Competencies Alignment	Standards Alignment
• NAME Multicultural Learning: Assessment • NEA Skill Areas: Valuing diversity; Being culturally self-aware • Cultural Competencies: Reflecting on one's cultural lens; Recognize bias in the system • Equity Literacy: Recognize; Direct confrontation	• Learning Forward: Data • NAGC Programming Standards: 3.1.4* Curriculum Planning • CEC-TAG Standards: 2.3A* Curricular Content Knowledge *NAGC and CEC-TAG Advanced curriculum standards (3.1.4, 2.3A) refer to the use of pre-assessments and/or differentiated curricula with students; we apply their use to PL

Individualizing Professional Learning Plans

We know our gifted students do not all learn the same way, so why is that when it comes to professional learning, we assume teachers all learn the same way and are all joining with the same knowledge and skills? If we have taken the pulse of our teachers coupled with district data, it makes sense to design individualized professional learning. Individualizing PL allows facilitators to address areas of weakness before the PL begins, either through providing enrichment materials or frontloading the curriculum, purposefully grouping participants, or accelerating the PL process—sounds familiar? These are all effective teaching strategies we use with our gifted kiddos! We differentiate our instruction for our students, and we *should* differentiate for gifted teachers. Growing as a learner depends on working within your ZPD, and professional learning is no different (think back to all the PL days you may have zoned out in or felt completely out of water!). It is even more important that during PL focused on cultural competency, we differentiate because within one building, levels of cultural competency may vary drastically.

Let's say our results from *taking the pulse* show we have three groups; those who would benefit from exploring what is systemic bias and basic levels of cultural competencies; another who are ready to explore the ways giftedness presents across cultural groups; and a third group who perhaps has a solid understanding of the first two areas, but would benefit from diving into different ways of identifying gifted learners across all groups. *Individualizing the professional learning plans* would enable each of these groups to grow as learners. This example also highlights the need to be flexible with your professional learning delivery model—here a PLC may work better than an all-faculty PL session.

Connecting to the Research

In researching professional learning, Gilson[28] uses the lens of adult education. We often say to think of PL as you think of teaching students, and in many ways, there are distinct similarities, but teacher brains and teacher needs are quite distinct. Gilson advocates for differentiated PL that meets the varied needs of the adult learners on staff. As mentioned in *taking a pulse*, research tells us that quality PL has an impact on teacher beliefs.[29] Specifically, research has shown correlations between targeted professional learning and positive changes in teacher attitudes, beliefs, perceptions, and understandings.[30] In particular, using a needs assessment, such as those suggested in Chapter 4, provides the professional learning facilitator an opportunity to use data to prioritize topics; this is positively correlated with positive changes in teacher outcomes.

Competencies Alignment	Standards Alignment
NAME Multicultural Learning: Pedagogy, Intellectual Challenge, Positive Academic Identities NEA Skill Areas: Dynamics of difference; Knowledge of students' culture Cultural Competencies: Bring real-world issues into the classroom; Draw on students' culture to shape curriculum and instruction Equity Literacy: Recognize, Respond, Equity Ideology, One Size Fits Few	Learning Forward: Learning Communities; Learning Designs NAGC Programming Standards: 3.1.4* Curriculum Planning CEC-TAG Standards: 2.3A* Curricular Content Knowledge *NAGC and CEC-TAG Advanced curriculum standards (3.1.4, 2.3A) refer to the use of pre-assessments and/or differentiated curricula with students; we apply their use to PL

Establishing a Safe Zone

Perhaps this is the hardest, yet most important, principle to establish during equity-driven PL. Picture a classroom which you've walked into and can feel the excitement for learning and the positive vibes; now picture that classroom where students are still learning but the air is tense with student unease. In both classrooms, the learning environment—the intangible tone set by the teacher and students—directly impacted the trust—or lack thereof—between people. In equity-driven PL, there will be challenging and often uncomfortable (the elephant in the room) conversations which need to be had—but which, without mutual trust and respect, will fall flat. Administrators, teachers, paraprofessionals, and all stakeholders need to know that the PL is a safe space to ask questions and share their experiences—without fear of judgment or being reprimanded. This does not mean that participants have a hall pass to say or do anything—we know words hurt. Boundaries and rules for engagement need to be established and followed by all parties. And, when necessary, it is the facilitator's role to step in and acknowledge potentially harmful or misguided statements with the approach of 'this is a teachable moment, let's talk about this now." Consider this in terms of calling out versus calling in.

The term calling someone out is not new—from our early days as students in elementary school ourselves, that was the term for jeers for a missed kick on the playground or a wrong answer in class. In PL, calling out has its time: if there is harm being caused by a participant's words or deeds in that moment, or you need to let a participant know that their words or actions are not acceptable and will not be tolerated in this place and space, it is appropriate to call out. In most cases, however, calling in is a better approach. In 2019, former President Barack Obama called out the call-out culture as a misrepresentation of activism, saying that pointing out that others are doing something or saying something racist, then sitting back and using that call-out as a symbol of your wokeness—that alone is not activism. Calling in allows for dialogue, bringing individuals into the discussion and listening to their perspective, making a connection, and sharing your perspective and making connections to effect change. The great Dr. Mary Frazier, a pioneer in gifted education shared the advice with her students—I didn't change anyone's mind by making them mad at me first.[31] Calling in focuses on the reflective, rather than reactive, process and brings the full room into the dialogue, rather than alienating individuals or groups.

Similarly, there is conversation in equity spaces about the terms safe *vs.* brave places—what is it we are looking for? We are using the term safe zone, but as we've talked about in previous chapters, it is important to define this terminology—we've mentioned that this is a place for safety in sharing, but also in pushing dialogue: that you are safe to be your authentic self, but that sharing is guided by rules of common understanding toward a goal of antiracism, anti-bias, and equity. This is not an environment where someone can a racial slur and follow it up with "but you said it is a safe space." Not that kind of safe zone. Defining the terms is crucial. The line between safe and brave spaces is often that safe zones are comfort-laden for sharing, whereas brave zones push beyond the comfort through dialogue—often into discomfort. We recognize that it is in the disequilibrium, the discomfort, the dissonance—that's where the growth is likely to happen. Our safe zone encourages safety in sharing, but also embraces the pedagogy of discomfort.[32]

One last aspect of the safe zone to guard against is the "not ready yet" crowd. The safe zone does not provide a pass to say "it's not yet time for this talk." The school, district, and community has made a commitment to equity.

That's why this professional learning is taking place. That's why you are here with us, reading this book. Paul Gorski puts it so perfectly, we are sharing his words:

> The hard truth is, racial equity cannot be achieved with an obsessive commitment to "meeting people where they are" when "where they are" is fraught with racial bias and privilege. Students, families, and educators experiencing racism cannot afford to wait for us to saunter toward a more serious racial equity vision. They cannot afford to wait, in particular, for all white educators to ease into racial equity commitments at a pace of our choosing while they suffer the consequences of our casualness.[33]

Connecting to the Research

Scharf[34] identified five components of shared inquiry and dialogue that participants should engage in, which align with the structure of the safe zones. The first is listening, which is different from hearing. We know when someone is actively listening to our conversation by verbal and nonverbal cues (think about the conversation you had with someone who was still looking at their phone). Listening entails thinking about the words being said and the meaning, experiences, context, and emotion behind what is not said. Respect is the second component—and a term which we frequently use, but often have a hard time defining. Respect, in this context, means that each member has a right to their own thoughts and opinions *and* can share opposing views without risk. This is a powerful notion. Thirdly, humility, recognizing that the opinions of others are just that—opinions—ideas shared from one perspective, based on the individual's lived experiences and there are other views which may not have been heard yet—from within or outside of the group. Next, voice: each member of the group has the responsibility to ask questions for clarification and to share their perspective with the goal of seeking truth. Finally, but most importantly, trust. Trust that when conflicts arise—because they will arise—they can be worked through together as a unit.

In a seminal 1999 book, *Feeling Power: Emotions and Education,* Megan Boler described the pedagogy of discomfort as a critical inquiry, inviting educators to "recognize how emotions define how and what one chooses to see, and conversely, not to see."[35] A subsequent model of professional learning centralizes the pedagogy of discomfort within the context of professional practice, prior knowledge experience, and identities, and trust and collegiality.[36] Nolan and Molla's model positions transformative professional learning as a reflective practice, involving three interrelated processes: the creation of disjuncture, the trigger of deliberation, and then the transformation of professional dispositions. As noted earlier, this disjuncture, or disequilibrium, is where growth and learning sparks, hence the connection to the brave zone. Other aspects of this professional learning model are seen in other components of the guiding principles.

Competencies Alignment	Standards Alignment
• NAME Multicultural Learning: Respective engagement with diverse people • NEA Skill Areas: Valuing diversity; Dynamics of difference • Cultural Competencies: Promote respect for student differences; Model high expectations for all students • Equity Literacy: Recognize, Respond; Evidence-informed equity; Equity ideology; Direct confrontation	• Learning Forward: Learning Designs • NAGC Pre-K-Grade 12 Programming Standards: 6.3 Equity and Inclusion; 6.4 Lifelong Learning • CEC-TAG Standards: 6.3T Professional Learning and Ethical Practice; 7.1A Collaboration

Going Beyond the Tip of the Iceberg

Katie will always think of the *Titanic* when she hears the word iceberg; the assumptions made by the leaders on the ship based on the visible portion of the iceberg resulted in horrific casualties. An iceberg is an inverted triangle of ice, with the largest mass below the surface—understanding someone's culture is the same. In schools, we tend to celebrate the very tip of the iceberg—there are monthly school lunches celebrating various cultures or a come dressed up as X culture day, or projects which gloss over cultural celebrations or songs. Yes, these are easy ways to celebrate and include diversity. Yet, the heart of the cultural group is below the surface—this is where we need to focus when expanding our understanding.

This principle focuses on just that—diving deep into cultural understandings, learning how culture impacts students' learning and manifestations of giftedness. When the PL *goes beyond the tip of the iceberg*, the learner experiences growth which may result in a change in practice and student outcomes. Moving beyond the tip of the iceberg requires deliberate planning—and often the facilitator may need to invest time in strategically identifying culturally relevant materials that are relevant to the community at hand (don't worry, we will help you with that!)

Connecting to the Research

In 2020, the members of the Council for Exceptional Children-Talented and Gifted division (CEC-TAG, or simply TAG) updated and reissued, for the second time since 2001, *A Call to Action: Supporting Equity, Diversity, and Access for Gifted Students,*[37] emphasizing a need for accountability to racially, culturally, ethnically, and linguistically diverse (RCELD) gifted students that are underrepresented in gifted and talented programs and advanced courses. Two points of emphasis in the report are the need for professional learning and culturally responsive curriculum and instruction, both with the same undercurrent: know your students—know them with depth, know them with breadth. Use this knowledge to inform your practice.

Going beyond the tip of the iceberg is supported in research in gifted education that focuses on the value of educators building meaningful understanding of their students, specifically of their cultural characteristics and gifted manifestations.[38,39] Researchers have gathered lists of culturally-informed characteristics, sometimes labeled 'non-traditional gifted characteristics' which may have otherwise been overlooked by teachers in the identification process.[40] However, even when presented with these characteristics, teachers are not always adept at recognizing these characteristics of gifted students;[41] thus the importance of equity-driven professional learning that *goes beyond the tip of the iceberg.* [42, 43]

Competencies Alignment	Standards Alignment
• NAME Multicultural Learning: Positive academic identities; Positive social identities; Respectful engagement with diverse people • NEA Skill Areas: Knowledge of students' culture; Institutionalizing cultural knowledge and adapting to diversity • Cultural Competencies: Promote respect for student differences; Reflect on one's cultural lens; Draw on students' culture to shape curriculum and instruction • Equity Literacy: Recognize; Respond; Redress; One Size Fits Few; Evidence-informed equity	• Learning Forward: Learning Designs • NAGC Programming Standards: 6.3 Equity and Inclusion; 6.4 Lifelong Learning • CEC-TAG Standards: 1.1T Learner Development and Individual Learning Differences; 3.2A Program, Services, and Outcomes

Engaging in Courageous Conversations

Picture a scene of some older gentlemen sitting around a porch playing checkers and having a lively conversation; they jokingly claim they are solving all the world's problems around a cup of joe. This isn't completely wrong; many misunderstandings can be clarified through conversations where both parties are actively listening, sharing ideas, and learning from each other. Educators who participate in PL should be afforded the opportunity to engage in critical debate, ask questions, and reflect on new understandings as part of the learning process. Criticality is an essential component—connecting back to the ideas in *safe zone*, in particular, the pedagogy of discomfort is imperative in courageous conversations.

> Pedagogy of discomfort urges students as well as educators to move outside of their comfort zones. Pedagogy of discomfort invites critical inquiry regarding cherished beliefs and assumptions; and calls for students and educators to take responsibility and even action in the collective struggle for social justice.[44]

Part of criticality is in questioning: both how and when we ask critical thinking questions.

If we investigate the K-12 classroom where we utilize Webb's Depth of Knowledge and Hess' Cognitive Rigor Matrix, we can see the path in which critical thinking is developed. Webb's Depth of Knowledge builds off the familiar Bloom's Taxonomy but contends within each level of Bloom's Taxonomy that thinking exists at various depths. For example, we often ask students to create a model as a culminating project. Consider the model of the life cycle of an animal or the mobile of the solar system. Does the creation of a model demonstrate the highest levels of understanding, or would asking the students to consider the life cycle of an animal and create a new species of an animal who follows similar stages of the life cycle demonstrate a deeper level of understanding? We always tell teacher candidates that it is easy to come up with questions on the fly to ask students, but it is difficult to create higher-order thinking questions on the spot. The same principle rings true in the PL sessions if the facilitator is relying on questions on the fly; most likely, these questions will use lower-level thinking skills and only scrape the surface of the cultural iceberg. Consider the question "What can we have the gifted students research for Thanksgiving as a higher-level thinking project?" versus "How could we redesign the school's approach to Thanksgiving through an equitable lens—from lessons to whole-school activities?"

Yet, just like in the classroom, we shouldn't jump into the deeper levels of understanding without scaffolding and developing the lower levels of understanding first. PL and *courageous conversations* rely on critical debate, pushing the envelope, if you will, of comfort levels. Asking questions and prompting deep thinking result in more meaningful conversations—ultimately resulting in changing mindsets and beliefs. Facilitators should pilot the conversations, being sure to share factual and objective content about the marginalized populations, cultural beliefs, and the role culture plays on educational learning experiences. Facilitators, like teachers, should not be a sage on the stage, and frequently not even the guide on the side, but a meddler in the middle. We set up the context and the questions, but we can't afford to stay completely out of the mix either—we need to be meddling: asking questions, responding when we hear bias and inequity (remember calling out *vs.* calling in) while also supporting the participants in the conversation who are doing the same, ensuring that space is being held for all voices, and in particular that traditionally minoritized or marginalized voices in the space are being prioritized.

Connecting to the Research

Nolan and Molla's reflective professional learning model,[45] introduced earlier in this chapter in *establishing the safe zone,* supports the guiding principle of *courageous conversations* through its second interrelated process, the trigger of deliberation. For transformative PL to occur, the pedagogy of discomfort signals the disjuncture, or dissonance, which triggers deliberation, or critical reflection and critique of the values, assumptions, and beliefs that educators previously held without debate. This is not ordinary conversation. Boler and Zembylas describe how the pedagogy of discomfort engages educators in critical thinking, and to explore

> habits, relations of power, knowledge, and ethics through which the conduct of educators and students is shaped by others and by themselves. ... [A] central focus is the recognition of the multiple, heterogeneous, and messy realities of power relations as they are enacted and resisted in localities, subverting the comfort offered by the endorsement of particular norms. [46]

Educational research indicates that meaningful conversations allowing deep dives into cultural awareness promote changing perceptions and beliefs,[47] particularly when the conversations are sustained over time.[48,49] *Establishing the safe zone* in combination with the *courageous conversations* enables deeper connections, facilitating participants to share beyond surface-level assumptions and move into rigorous and divergent conversations.[50, 51]

Competencies Alignment	Standards Alignment
• NAME Multicultural Learning: Respectful engagement with diverse people • NEA Skill Areas: Institutionalizing cultural knowledge and adapting to diversity • Cultural Competencies: Recognize and redress bias in the system • Equity Literacy: Recognize; Respond; Redress; Direct Confrontation; Equity Ideology; #Fixinjusticenotkids; One Size Fits Few	• Learning Forward: Implementation (particularly in applying change research) • NAGC Programming Standards: 6.3 Equity and Inclusion; 6.4 Lifelong Learning • CEC-TAG Standards: 7.3T Collaboration; 7.1A Collaboration

Bridging the Gap Between School and Home

As teachers, we have seen the power of parental engagement in a student's success in school, as well as experienced the frustration when the parent/guardians are not actively championing for their student. The relationship between the parent, the teacher, and the student is crucial to the social and academic development of students. Parental engagement and involvement in schools unfortunately is an all-too-common struggle for teachers across K-12. Schools often focus on parental involvement—which mostly entails static activities with the teachers and/or school being the giver of information and parents the receiver. These are events like Back-to-School Night, school plays, or various forms of school newsletters and social media communications, which are all necessary pieces to maintain clear communication between the stakeholders. But, like the tip of the iceberg, these activities do not grow meaningful partnerships.

On the other hand, parental engagement recognizes the strengths parents and community members bring to the learning experience and views the parents and/or community as valuable contributors. Fostering these relationships is even more important when working with marginalized populations, where miscommunication can contribute to poor relationships between the school and parent and/or community partners. Professional learning is one avenue to strengthening these relationships. Facilitators can model for educators different strategies for engaging and communicating with parents from a strengths-based rather than deficit lens, while raising awareness about cultural differences.

Misunderstandings about definitions and conceptions of gifted education and what it means if and when a child is identified can be a factor contributing to marginalized gifted students' identification and enrollment. *Bridging the gap between school and home* acknowledges the disconnect, values the strengths of the parents and community, and seeks to actively engage all stakeholders.

Connecting to the Research

TAG's Call to Action recognizes the criticality of parent and community partnerships, including this as one of the six areas of required action.[52] The research shares a variety of ways to partner with families that are reflected in *building a bridge*. First, and similar to *taking a pulse* and *going beyond the tip of the iceberg*, knowing is critical. It is essential to learn about the children, their families and the community context in which the school is situated.[53,54] Second, embracing a strengths-based perspective is imperative; conversely, unlearning the deficit view and implicit biases that inform this view.[55,56] Finally, acknowledge the shared commitment you hold with the students, families, and community.[57]

When *building a bridge*, it is important to check yourself: part of knowing others is knowing (and checking) yourself. "A common cultural misstep is an educator assuming that a student needs to be rescued from his or her life, such as telling a Native American student, 'Don't you want to get out and make a better life for yourself, off the reservation?'"[58] What is the problem with this statement? This is a common *White savior* statement—where the young (or not so young) White teacher seeks to come in and 'save' the troubled young student of color from their 'poor' existence. Knowing others: A characteristic of gifted Native American students is a desire to return to the reservation and contribute to its success, even at a young age.[59] Know thyself: What contributed to the teachers' thoughts that the child needed to be 'saved' or that their existence was 'poor'? This is an example of deficit-thinking ideology, and it is a significant equity detour.[60]

Competencies Alignment	Standards Alignment
• NAME Multicultural Learning: Positive academic identities; Positive social identities; Respectful engagement with diverse people • NEA Skill Areas: Knowledge of students' culture; Dynamics of difference; institutionalize cultural knowledge and adapt to diversity • Cultural Competencies: Collaborate with families and the local community; Communicate in linguistically and culturally responsive ways; Recognize and redress bias in the system • Equity Literacy: Respond; Redress; Prioritization; Redistribution; One Size Fits Few; Evidence-informed equity	• NAGC Programming Standards: 6.1. Talent Development • CEC-TAG Standards: 1.1T Learner Development and Individual Learning Differences

 Identifying Grows and Glows

You may have heard the statement that teachers go into their classrooms and shut the doors until May. This misconception that teachers do not want or benefit from learning from each other appears because we tend to narrow our focus to our group of students for the year. In June 2021, Angela attended an online Abolitionist Teaching Network event and two speakers shared thoughts that resonated with her on this point—so much so that she tweeted them out to the Twittersphere. The first, Mariame Kaba, said, "We're not going to get free by ourselves. You have to organize with others. Knowledge building is a collective process. The notion of the collective, the deep belief that we are interconnected is a huge piece of abolitionist teaching." Dr. Bettina Love followed up with "'I just want to close my door and teach'—it can't be the solution. Abolition happens through community." So many times, we (yes, we can put ourselves in this box, too!) have this idea because we are protecting ourselves and our kiddos—we feel that we know what is right and we can do what is right—if the door is closed. But at the same time, this tunnel-like vision leads to professional silos of teachers. All too often, gifted teachers are already on their own in a school.

PL, however, provides an opportunity to dispel these notions by creating an environment where educators can share their glows, or what works as well as grows, or what has not. Collaboration between families and professional colleagues is the focus of Standard 7.3 of the NAGC and CEC-TAG (2013) Teacher Preparation Standards in Gifted and Talented Education. The concept of *identifying glows and grows* is not a new one—in fact, we use it all of the time in the classroom when encouraging students to share their thinking. The PL environment creates an excellent space for sharing ideas of what works or didn't work as well as brainstorming new methods of approaching the problem. Like in the classroom where a teacher guides the student talk, the facilitator is able to guide the conversation amongst colleagues to provide clarification. The guidance is key here as it redirects any misconceptions and alternative solutions. It is important to have already built a safe and brave space that encourages all ideas, where faculty feel comfortable sharing ideas that they know are growth opportunities, or even ideas that they think are glows, but after sharing, end up being grows.

Connecting to the Research

Nolan and Molla's[61] transformative professional learning model has its final callback, providing support for the glows and grows guiding principle in its third process, the transformation of professional dispositions. *Identifying glows and grows* represent the potential to show growth and change in value systems or perspectives in concrete ways through an in-depth discussion of participant-created artifacts. Remarking on the importance of benchmarks marks to measure growth in culturally responsive teaching, Geneva Gay indicates that professional learning "requires staff development of teachers that includes cultural knowledge and instructional skills, in concert with personal self-reflection and self-monitoring techniques for teaching to and about ethnic diversity."[62]

Competencies Alignment	Standards Alignment
• NAME Multicultural Learning: Pedagogy • NEA Skill Areas: Culturally self-aware (reflection component) • Equity Literacy: Recognize; Respond; Direct Confrontation	• Learning Forward: Learning Communities; Implementation • NAGC Programming Standards: 6.4 Lifelong Learning • CEC-TAG Standards: 7.3T Collaboration; 7.1A Collaboration

Cautions and Caveats: Things to Consider

As you move forward with infusing these principles into your PL, there are a few things to consider. First, you are working with adult learners, not students. Adult learners expect to be treated with mutual levels of respect and need to take ownership over their own learning. Your participants in the PL might be your colleagues, or even your boss, which could make evaluation and change a more difficult process to move through. Therefore, it is critical to maintain confidentiality when working on potentially sensitive topics and to maintain the principles throughout the PL.

Remember everyone moves through change at different rates. As the facilitator you can put all the pieces into play, but ultimately the participant must be willing to internalize and process the new understandings before lasting change. Recognizing the small changes and building on them throughout the PL is key to fostering the changing of mindsets. At the same time, you aren't there to wait for anyone to *be ready*; you are there to teach, act, move. One of Gorski's equity detours is the Pacing-for-Privilege detour,[63] when the pace of the equity matches the readiness of those that are the least invested in progress. That's not how racial equity will happen. You operate at the pace of those that are ready for the work in terms of big ideas and global changes (note: this is not the same as the *individualized learning plan*—this is big-level changes happening or decisions being made).

Finally, be ready to speak up. Conversations surrounding equity and the lack of equity often result in big emotions from all parties involved. Along with the big emotions, many misunderstandings occur because of the sharing of personal thoughts or misinformation based on personal experiences or bias. As the facilitator, you will need to be ready to monitor these conversations and step in when the lines are being crossed. You must be able to recognize when a person is asking a question with the goal of learning versus the person who is stirring the pot. Know when to call in versus call out. Be ready to meddle in the middle. And know that speaking up for equity and justice is not always easy, but it is right.

Resources

General Resources

- Video Presentation on the Equity Driven Guiding Principles, https://youtu.be/U86_3me5zts
- A Culturally Responsive Equity-Based Bill of Rights for Gifted Students of Color, https://www.nagc.org/blog/culturally-responsive-equity-based-bill-rights-gifted-students-color
- A Critical Call to Action: Supporting Equity, Diversity, and Access for Gifted Students, CEC-TAG, http://cectag.com/wp-content/uploads/2020/12/Call-to-Action-2020.pdf
- Avoiding Racial Equity Detours, http://www.edchange.org/publications/Avoiding-Racial-Equity-Detours-Gorski.pdf

Taking a Pulse

- Cultural Competence Self-Assessment, https://www.racialequitytools.org/resourcefiles/mason.pdf
- Methods for Conducting an Educational Needs Assessment, https://www.extension.uidaho.edu/publishing/pdf/BUL/BUL0870.pdf
- See additional resources in Chapter 4, Zone 1

Individualizing Professional Learning Plans 

- *Leading for Differentiation: Growing Teachers Who Grow Kids,* C.A. Tomlinson; M. Murphy, 2015. ASCD
- Moving Toward Differentiated Professional Learning for Teachers Learning to Differentiate for Gifted Students, C. Gilson in: *Best Practices in Professional Learning and Teacher Preparation: Methods and Strategies for Gifted Professional Development* (Vol. 1). Edited by A. Novak and C. Weber, 2018. Prufrock Press
- See additional resources throughout each of the chapters to individualize each Zone.

Establishing a Safe Zone 

- Guidelines for Discussing Difficult or Controversial Topics, http://www.crlt.umich.edu/publinks/generalguidelines

- Managing Difficult Classroom Discussions, https://citl.indiana.edu/teaching-resources/diversity-inclusion/managing-difficult-classroom-discussions/
- Creative Equity Toolkit, Call Out and Call In Racism, https://creativeequitytoolkit.org/topic/anti-racism/call-out-call-in-racism
- Advancing Racial Equity, Interrupting Bias—Calling Out vs. Calling In, http://www.racialequityvtnea.org/wp-content/uploads/2018/09/Interrupting-Bias_-Calling-Out-vs.-Calling-In-REVISED-Aug-2018-1.pdf
- Breakaway: Do we need safe or brave spaces? https://alternativebreaks.org/safe-or-brave-spaces/
- *Coaching for Equity*, Elena Aguilar

Going Beyond the Tip of the Iceberg 

- Identifying and Supporting Culturally, Linguistically and Economically Diverse Gifted Learners: Guiding Teachers through the Four Zones of Professional Learning, K.D. Lewis and A.M Novak, in: *Best Practices in Professional Learning and Teacher Preparation: Special Topics for Gifted Professional Development* (Vol. 2). Edited by A. Novak and C. Weber. 2019. Prufrock Press.
- Critical Multicultural Pavilion, http://www.edchange.org/multicultural/index.html
- Social Justice Books, A Teaching for Change Project, https://socialjusticebooks.org/booklists/
- *Me and White Supremacy* by Layla F. Saad
- *Everyday AntiRacism* edited by Mica Pollock

Engaging in Courageous Conversations 

- Racial Justice in Education Resource Guide (2017), National Education Association (NEA) and Human and Civil Rights (HCR), https://neaedjustice.org/wp-content/uploads/2018/11/Racial-Justice-in-Education.pdf
- *Exploring Critical Issues in Gifted Education: A Case Studies Approach* by C.L. Weber, C. Boswell, and W.A. Behrens, 2014. Prufrock Press
- *Things that Make White People Uncomfortable* by Michael Bennett
- *Courageous Conversations About Race* by Glenn Singleton
- *So You Want to Talk About Race* by Ijeoma Oluo
- *We Want to do More than Survive* by Bettina Love
- *Not Light, But Fire* by Matthew R. Kay

Bridging the Gap Between School and Home

- A Guide for Engaging ELL Families: Twenty Strategies for School by L. Breiseth, K. Robertson, and S. Lafond (note: this resource is specific to ELL), Colorín Colorado; 2011, https://www.colorincolorado.org/sites/default/files/Engaging_ELL_Families_FINAL.pdf
- Six Steps to Partner with Diverse Families by K. Buchanan and T. Buchanan, https://www.naesp.org/sites/default/files/Buchanan_JF17.pdf
- *Beyond the Bake Sale* by Anne Henderson, Karen Mapp, Vivian Johnson, Don Davies
- See additional resources in Chapter 7, Zone 4

Identifying Grows and Glows

- 5 Ways to Increase Knowledge Sharing in your Organization by D. Youngren, https://bloomfire.com/blog/522359-5-ways-to-encourage-knowledge-sharing-within-your-organization/
- Learning for Justice Classroom Resources, https://www.learningforjustice.org/classroom-resources
- Education for Liberation Network, https://www.edliberation.org/
- *Textured Teaching: A Framework* by Lorena Escoto German
- *Cultivating Genius: An Equity Framework for Culturally and Historically Responsive Literacy* by Gholdy Muhammad

Select Standards in Gifted and Talented Education that Address Equity

- The following specific standards from NAGC and CEC-TAG (2013) Teacher Preparation Standards Strands and Advanced Standards in Gifted Education Teacher Preparation address equity in the following areas: Student Learning and Program Development 1.1T and 3.2A, Assessment: 4.1T, 4.3T,4.4T, and 1.1A, Curriculum Planning and Instruction 2.3A, and Learning Environments 2.1T,2.3T, 5.2A ,6.2A and 6.3A. You can read about these standards in detail at this link: http://www.nagc.org/sites/default/files/standards/NAGC-%20CEC%20CAEP%20standards%20%282013%20final%29.pdf
- The following specific standards from NAGC (2019) Pre-K Grade 12 Programming Standards Evidence-Based Practices address equity in the following areas: Student Learning and Program Development 1.2.1, 1.2.3. and 5.8.2, Assessment 2.1.1., 2.1.2., 2.1.3, 2.2.5., 2.2.8., 2.3.1 .and 2.3.2, Curriculum Planning and Instruction, 3.3.1, 3.3.2. and 3.3.3, Learning Environments 4.4.1, 4.4.2, 4.4.3, 4.5.1, and 4.5.2. You can read about these standards in detail at this link: https://www.nagc.org/sites/default/files/standards/Intro%202019%20Programming%20Standards.pdf[64]

Notes

1 Tignor, S. (2018). 50 years, 50 heroes: Arthur Ashe, 1971. *Tennis*. https://www.tennis.com/news/articles/50-years-50-heroes-arthur-ashe-1971

2 Lewis, K. D. (2017). Culturally responsive gifted educators: Reaching every child, every day. *TEMPO, 38*(1), 14–19. https://www.txgifted.org/files/Tempo%20Issue%201%202017.pdf

3 Novak, A. M., & Lewis, K. D. (2015, November 13–15). *Equity and access in gifted programming for Hispanic youth: Targeted professional development for teachers* [Conference session]. National Association for Gifted Children Convention, Phoenix, AZ.
Novak, A. M., & Lewis, K. D. (2018, November 15–18). *Equity and access in k-12 gifted and the need for targeted professional learning for teachers* [Conference session]. National Association for Gifted Conference, Minneapolis, MN, United States.
Novak, A. M., & Lewis, K. D. (2019, July 24–28). *Guiding the gatekeepers: Using professional learning to promote equity and access in K12 gifted education* [Conference session]. World Conference on the Gifted and Talented, Nashville, TN, United States.
Novak, A. M., & Lewis, K. D. (2021, March 8–13). *Four zones of professional learning: Fostering equity in gifted programs*. [Conference session]. Council for Exceptional Children Convention. Virtual. https://exceptionalchildren.org/convention/registration/schedule-glance

4 Novak, A. M., Lewis, K. D., & Weber, C. L. (2020). Guiding principles in developing equity-driven professional learning for educators of gifted students. *Gifted Child Today, 43*(3), 169–183.

5 Novak, A. M. & Lewis, K. D. (2022). A methodological approach to designing a theory: The journey of the four zone professional learning model. *Roeper Review, 44*(1), 49–62.

6 Learning Forward. (2017). Standards for professional learning. *Learning Forward: The Professional Learning Association.* https://learningforward.org/standards-for-professional-learning
7 National Center for Education Statistics. (2018). Percentage of public school students enrolled in gifted and talented programs, by sex, race/ethnicity, and state: Selected years, 2004 through 2013–14. *Digest of Education Statistics.* https://nces.ed.gov/programs/digest/d17/tables/dt17_204.90.asp
8 National Association for Gifted Children. (2019). *Pre-K-Grade 12 gifted programming standards,* p. 17. https://www.nagc.org/sites/default/files/standards/Intro%202019%20Programming%20Standards%281%29.pdf
9 Ibid., p. 17.
10 NAGC-CEC. (2013a). *NAGC-CEC teacher preparation standards in gifted and talented education,* p. 6. https://www.nagc.org/resources-publications/resources/national-standards-gifted-and-talented-education/nagc-cec-teacher
11 NAGC-CEC. (2013b). *NAGC-CEC advanced standards in gifted education teacher preparation,* p. 5. https://www.nagc.org/resources-publications/resources/national-standards-gifted-and-talented-education/advanced-standards
12 Gorski, P. (2019). Avoiding racial equity detours. *Educational Leadership, 76*(7), 56–61.
13 National Association for Multicultural Education (NAME, 2021). *Advancing and advocating for social justice & equity.* Definitions of Multicultural Education. https://www.nameorg.org/definitions_of_multicultural_e.php
14 Ibid.
15 National Association for Multicultural Education (NAME, 2021). Social justice consciousness. *Advancing and Advocating for Social Justice & Equity. Multicultural Learning* (para 1). https://www.nameorg.org/learn/social_justice_consciousness.php
16 National Association for Multicultural Education (NAMEb, 2021). Social justice action. *Advancing and Advocating for Social Justice & Equity. Multicultural Learning* (para 2). https://www.nameorg.org/learn/social_justice_action.php.
17 National Association for Multicultural Education (NAMEb, 2021). Social justice action. *Advancing and Advocating for Social Justice & Equity. Multicultural Learning.* https://nameorg.org/learn/
18 Muñiz, J. (2019). *Culturally responsive teaching: A 50-state survey of teaching standards.* New America. www.newamerica.org/education-policy/reports/culturally-responsive-teaching/
19 NEA (n.d.), adapted from Diller & Moule (2005); Diller, V., & Moule, J. (2005). *Cultural competence: A primer for educators.* Wadsworth, Cengage Learning.
20 Muñiz, 2019; The New America Report carries a Creative Commons Attribution 4.0 International License. www.newamerica.org.
21 Gorski, P., & Swalwell, K. (2015). Equity literacy for all. *Educational Leadership, 72*(6), 34–40. https://eric.ed.gov/?id=EJ1062914
22 Nelson, S. W., & Guerra, P. L. (2014). Educator beliefs and cultural knowledge: Implications for school improvement efforts. *Educational Administration, 50*(1), 67–95. doi: 10.1177/0013161X13488595
23 Matheis, S., Kronborg, L., Schmitt, M., & Preckel, F. (2017). Threat or challenge? Teacher beliefs about gifted students and their relationship to teacher motivation, *Gifted and Talented International, 32*(2), 134–160. doi: 10.1080/15332276.2018.1537685
24 Ibid.
25 Preckel, F., Baudson, T. G., Krolak-Schwerdt, S., & Glock, S. (2015). Gifted and maladjusted? Implicit attitudes and automatic associations related to gifted children. *American Educational Research Journal, 52*(6), 1160–1184. doi: 10.3102/0002831215596413
26 Matheis et al. (2017).
27 NEA (n.d.), adapted from Diller & Moule (2005).
28 Gilson, C. (2018). Moving toward differentiated professional learning for teachers learning to differentiate for gifted students. In A. M. Novak & C. L. Weber (Eds.), *Best practices in professional learning and teacher preparation: Methods and strategies for gifted professional development* (Vol. 1, pp. 93–120). Prufrock Press.
29 Matheis et al. (2017).
30 Nelson & Guerra (2014).

31 Krisel, S. (2021, August 12). Personal communication.
32 Boler, M. 1999. *Feeling power: Emotions and education.* Taylor & Francis.
33 Gorski (2019, p. 58).
34 Scharf, A. (2018). *Critical practices in anti-bias education.* Montgomery, AL: Teaching Tolerance A Project of the Southern Poverty Law Center. https://www.tolerance.org/sites/default/files/2019-04/TT-Critical-Practices-for-Anti-bias-Education.pdf
35 Boler (1999, p. 176).
36 Nolan, A., & Molla, T. (2018) Teacher professional learning through pedagogy of discomfort. *Reflective Practice, 19*(6), 721–735. doi: 10.1080/14623943.2018.1538961
37 Jones-Roberson, J., Breedlover, L., Buchanan, M., Dailey, D., Dickson, K., Inman, T., Roberts, J. L., & Troxclair, D. (2020). *A call to action: Supporting equity, diversity, and access for gifted students.* The Association for the Gifted. Council for Exceptional Children.
38 Ford, D. Y., Moore, J. L., & Milner, R. (2005). Beyond culture blindness: A model of culture with implications for gifted education. *Roeper Review, 27*(2), 97–103. doi: 10.1080/02783190509554297
39 Briggs, C. J., Reis, S. M., & Sullivan, E. E. (2008). A national view of promising programs and practices for culturally, linguistically, and ethnically diverse gifted and talented students. *Gifted Child Quarterly, 52*(2), 131–145. doi: 10.1177/0016986208316037
40 Irby, B., & Lara-Alecio, R. (1996). Attributes of Hispanic gifted bilingual students as perceived by bilingual educators in Texas. *SABE Journal, 11,* 120–140. doi: 10.1177/0016986217752107
41 Lewis, K., Novak, A., & Coronado, J. (2015). Teachers' perceptions of characteristics of gifted Hispanic bilingual students: Perspectives from the border. *Texas Forum of Teacher Education, 5,* 71–91.
42 Ford et al. (2005).
43 Lewis, K. D., Novak A. M. & Weber, C. L. (2018). Where are gifted students of color? Case studies outline strategies to increase diversity in gifted programs. *The Learning Professional, 39*(4), 50–58. https://eric.ed.gov/?id=EJ1190300
44 Boler, M., & Zembylas, M. (2002). Discomforting truths: The emotional terrain of understanding difference. In Peter Pericles Trifonas (Ed.), *Pedagogies of difference: Rethinking education for social justice* (pp. 107–130). Taylor & Francis.
45 Nolan & Molla (2018).
46 Boler & Zembylas (2002, p. 126).
47 Clark, C. M. (2001). *Talking shop: Authentic conversation and teacher learning.* Teachers College Press.
48 Gunnlaugson, O. (2007). Shedding light on the underlying forms of transformative learning: Introducing three distinct categories of consciousness. *Journal of Transformative Education, 5*(2), 134–151. doi: 10.1177/1541344607303526
49 Moore, B. A. (2018). Developing special educator cultural awareness through critically reflective professional learning community collaboration. *Teacher Education and Special Education, 41*(3), 243–253. doi: 10.1177/0888406418770714
50 Clark (2001).
51 Moore (2018).
52 Jones-Roberson et al. (2020).
53 Buchanan, K., & Buchanan, T. (2017). Six steps to partner with diverse families. *Principal.* https://www.naesp.org/sites/default/files/Buchanan_JF17.pdf
54 Goings, R. B. & Ford, D. Y. (2018). Investigating the intersection of poverty and race in gifted education journals: A 15 year analysis. *Gifted Child Quarterly, 61*(1), 25–36. doi: 10.1177/001698621773761
55 Ibid.
56 Buchanan & Buchanan (2017).
57 Ibid.
58 Novak, A. M., Lewis, K. D., & Weber, C. L. (2020). Guiding principles in developing equity-driven professional learning for educators of gifted students. *Gifted Child Today, 43*(3), 169–183.
59 Fisher, T. (2008, January 7). *Understanding, identifying, and meeting the needs of gifted Native American students* [blog post]. http://blogs.edweek.org/teachers/unwrapping_the_gifted

/upload/2008/01/2008-01-07%20Identifying%20and%20Teaching%20Gifted%20Native %20American%20Students.pdf
60 Gorski (2019).
61 Nolan & Molla (2018).
62 Gay, G. (2000). *Culturally responsive teaching: Theory, research, and practice.* Teachers College Press, p. 214.
63 Gorski (2019).
64 NAGC/CEC-TAG (2013, pp. 1–6); NAGC (2019, pp. 1–18).

4

Zone 1

Increasing Educators' Understanding of Cultural Norms and Equity

What's the Play?

In the first zone, Increasing Educators' Understanding of Cultural Norms and Equity, teachers explore the ethnicities and cultures of their students with the intention of learning about the characteristics of their students' specific cultural backgrounds, asking questions for greater understanding and ensuring belongingness for all students. The objective of Zone 1 is to not only learn about other cultures but to understand how one's own culture, experiences, and interactions impact understanding of another culture. Additionally, this zone addresses equity and its counterpoint, inequity, in understanding how students have been marginalized in education historically, and are currently marginalized in this school, in this time. This zone is a starting point for 4ZEPL, and it is often necessary to revisit this zone at various stages of the learning process. As the learner grows in their understanding and knowledge, more questions and conversations can be held at a greater depth. As Katie's son says, the more I know, the more questions I have.

Diving into the first zone, the facilitator should narrow the focus of the cultural groups to those who are presently enrolled in the school district and building. This is important so the training can have relevancy. As an example, Native Americans and Indigenous People are represented by over 560 recognized tribal groups in the United States, but not all of these tribal groups live in all of the states. Each tribe has its own set of cultural characteristics, localized norms, and language which influences culture. For example,

DOI: 10.4324/9781003196204-5

PLC 1 Growth Group	**PLC 2** Proficient Group	**PLC 3** Extension Group
Little to no cultural & equity awareness: misconceptions related to gifted characteristics in traditionally marginalized gifted groups in the community	Average cultural & equity awareness: misconceptions related to gifted characteristics in traditionally marginalized gifted groups in the community	Culturally & equity aware: recognizes gifted characteristics in traditionally marginalized gifted groups in the community
-Facilitate Unpack culture and Whiteness, discussing the ways **the participants' culture influ**ences their teaching and their classroom. -PLC discusses how systems of oppression and bias operate in the school and community and the impact on students and families. -Facilitators provide background knowledge through multiple modalities about the traditionally marginalized students groups in **general, providing first a global** understanding and then narrowing to those groups found within the community and school.	-This group discusses culture and unpacking Whiteness, while discussing the ways the **participants' culture influences** their teaching with a deeper discussion, focusing on privilege, intersectionality, and/or upstander vs. bystander. -Facilitators situate the discussion in how racism, oppression and bias operate in this place and space. Based on the *pulse* they are given more detailed examples and may need less scaffolding. **-Facilitators provide specific** deep knowledge through multiple modalities on traditionally marginalized groups found within the district, community, and school. -Facilitators introduce the FoK Framework.	-Primary Facilitators introduce the Funds of Knowledge Framework (FoK) in a train the trainer model. -PLC shares the Zone 1 facilitation role with support from the main facilitator. -Primary Facilitator trains PLC through multiple modalities to extend knowledge on giftedness, equity, and/or traditionally marginalized gifted students groups based on *pulse*; debriefs with PLC in small groups or 1:1. -It is important to ensure that while PLC is taking on a leading role in facilitating PLCs 1 & 2 with the Lead Facilitator, that they are also engaging in new content with the Lead Facilitator.
Embedded Equity Driven Professional Learning Principles *Taking a Pulse, Individualizing Professional Learning Plans, Establishing a Safe Zone, Going Beyond the Tip of the Iceberg, Bridging the Gap between School and Home, Engaging in Courageous Conversations, Identifying Grows and Glows*		

Figure 4.1 Zone 1 in action: Sample planning chart for differentiated groups.

39 tribes live in Oklahoma. However, district tribal representation varies greatly depending on which part of the state the school district is located in. Figure 4.1 is the Zone 1 section of the Sample Planning Chart for Differentiated Groups shared in Chapter 2 (Figure 2.2), showing a general outline of what this zone might look like for three differentiated groups based on the results of *taking a pulse.*

Brief Explanation of the Research Base: Know Thyself and Know Others

Zone 1 is built upon the principle that before change can occur, one must first look inward and learn about one's self. It is not enough to just study various cultures and learn basic trivia facts; instead, we need to reflect and consider how our own understandings and misunderstandings influence our thoughts, opinions, and potential biases toward other cultural groups.[1]

Cultural self-awareness is the ability to understand the role culture and cultural experiences play in shaping one's sense of self. Those with high levels of cultural self-awareness recognize that cultural experiences influence their values, beliefs, and behaviors. These understandings may be subconscious or conscious. For example, a student who has recently immigrated to the United States from Mexico may be more aware of cultural influences as they are being immersed in new cultural experiences. These experiences often lead to a greater realization of cultural characteristics, how one's self adapts to the new cultures, and a change in mindset toward other cultures. These experiences may be positive or negative but often have a lasting impact on shaping one's understanding of culture.

Cultural self-awareness is developed through experiences, but not without engaging in self-reflection. Self-reflection is the process by which one makes sense of the cultural interaction and experiences.

> Cultural self-awareness focuses on how individuals make sense of the relationship between the culture and the self (how the culture has shaped me). Although it is highly unlikely for individuals to develop cultural self-awareness based on cultures that they have no knowledge about, accuracy and clarity of cultural knowledge are not prerequisites for cultural self-awareness.[2]

This is different from having cultural competence, which centers on knowing true and accurate information about cultural groups. Cultural self-awareness is based on understanding who you are based your own cultural experiences. Increased cultural self-awareness leads to an awareness of the influence of a cultural membership on their lives or others' lives. As teachers, developing our cultural self-awareness is crucial for serving our gifted students.

The process of developing cultural self-awareness is enhanced when one concurrently learns about cultural groups. Increasing cultural competence while developing cultural self-awareness yields the greatest positive change in understanding. We know that misconceptions often stem from misinformation. Learning about characteristics unique to various cultural groups beyond the surface level is important to the growth process and to achieving cultural competence.

The research base for equity has been discussed in depth in Chapters 2 and 3, so we will not delve into it in depth here. From a professional learning standpoint, an element to understand is the importance of not thinking of equity and inequity as a *them* issue, but an *us* or an *our students* endemic. Recognizing not just the universality of racism and inequity, but how it operates in this organization, in this school, and how it impacts our students.[3]

Put it in Play

As a general rule, we tend to suggest that professional learning starts with *taking a pulse.* You want to know where your audience is before you dive in... in many cases, you might be able to use a brief survey prior to the first meeting, so that you can plan in advance. That's the best-case scenario, but if you can't make that work, we suggest bringing differentiated ideas with you and surveying the group at the start of the session. In Zone 1, the goal is to understand cultural norms and equity, starting first with the educators' themselves, then broadening to the students and community. Thus, to *take the pulse,* you might first use a survey that gauges cultural knowledge of self and/or others. The activities in the Playbook (featured later in this chapter) offer a few suggestions. Understanding where individuals are is important so that your work can begin at a successful entry point for the cohort.

Should you divide the attendees into groups based on this pulse-taking? Is whole group the best way forward? Only you know the answer at this point! Remember, however you are *individualizing the professional learning plan,* you also need to keep in mind your limitations as the facilitator in delivering high-quality PL—just like in the classroom, don't make so many guiding reading groups that you are unable to get to all of them. Two or three groups may be a more manageable number since meeting the needs of your participants is key in this stage. A mixed-ethnicity group of participants is much more likely to have different needs than an all-White group; the lived experiences of those growing up Black in America are not equitable to those of their White peers. Assuming all teachers have the same needs when it comes to equity training is educational fallacy on par with assuming all eight-year-olds have the same educational needs just by virtue of their birthdates.

As teachers, we differentiate content, process, and product... but wait! There's one more! learning environment! Often left off the list, because what is it, anyway? When Angela taught a course called *Classroom Management for Elementary Educators,* she told her students that classroom management was really about classroom learning environment, that management is about control, and learning environment is about creating an equitable space with belongingness, love, and respect. In Zone 1, it is important to establish a sense of trust and mutual understanding. In the seven principles, we talk about *creating safe and brave zones.* Safe zones are where we feel comfortable in saying what is on our minds without fear of retribution or retaliation, while a brave zone is one in which we know we are here to learn, and we expect discomfort because it is in the disequilibrium that we know that the learning happens. Everyone has something of value to contribute to the conversation, and we can all learn from each other. Zone 1 needs to be a balance of self-reflective activities as well as group activities. This balance is important to the development of a team atmosphere and individual growth. You may only have a two-hour training, so establish this quickly! So much of facilitation is based on you—your personality as the facilitator and the tone you set from minute one.

Not only do you want to establish that trust between yourself and the attendees, but you also want to open up communication between the members of the cohort. One of the key aspects of Zone 1 is the establishment of a sense of trust and beginning the process of breaking down barriers and misconceptions. One great way to do this is using icebreakers and scenarios where the participants have an opportunity to role play and experience an uncomfortable social situation. By beginning with this type of activity, the participants are all able to experience the same situation and have a common experience with which they can relate. Another benefit of a team-building activity is that you can get teachers up and moving and out of their comfort bubble. Most of us are creatures of habit and tend to stick to the same spots (we know we have a favorite seat during faculty meetings!), but during equity work it is important that we move beyond our comfort zone and into the learning zone. In the online environment, this can be accomplished via breakout rooms or group activities in the online platform. The Playbook has several suggested activities to engage participants in Know Thyself work.

Activities are not the endgame, however. There's a phrase for when we see gifted fun, like critical thinking activities, but no content, no rigor, nothing tying it together—RAoG—Random Acts of Giftedness. Professional learning can fall into the same trap, especially where equity is concerned! We don't want to have Random Acts of Equity or Cultural Responsiveness, as those alone are no threat to racism. The content is essential. As is the *why*, the *so what*, the *debrief*. We're not saying you should be tied to a slide deck necessarily, but that the activities in isolation, without the content and the debrief, are Random Acts of Professional Learning (RAoPL). So, what is the essential content? (See Figure 4.2.)

The second part of Zone 1 is to start learning about the specific racial, ethnic, linguistic, and cultural groups of the student body demographic. Depending on the number of groups, you may want to divide up your time to focus on one or two groups, versus trying to cover all of them at once. This avoids the trap of skimming the tip of the iceberg, rather than diving deep into understanding your students.

Z1 EC: Know Thyself	Brief Explanation	Playbook Activities
We all have an identity. We all have cultures.	Everyone has a cultural identity. However some people are more aware of their cultural background and how cultural impacts their everyday experiences. Recognizing our own identities is important in being ready to serve our students.	Cultural Awareness Survey Snowball Fight_ What is Culture? Caption This! Identity Pie Chart
Whiteness is a culture.	Too often, White teachers say "but I don't have a culture, I'm just White." In reality, being White is a culture. Understanding and knowing how Whiteness has influenced and shaped your identity is essential for educators.	Snowball Fight What is Culture? Caption This!
Recognize Racism.	Being able to define, understand, and recognize racism is also important to being ready to close the equity gap. We must be able to name what we see as examples or indicators of racism in order to address them. For example: Tone Policing (focusing on the emotional delivery rather than the message itself), Privilege (advantages provided to the dominant group), White Silence (not speaking out against racism, and Microaggressions (indirect or subtle commonplace racist comments).	What is Racism? Scales Reflective Journaling Prompts
We all have biases.	We do our best to restrict them. To recognize, respond, redress, and then to cultivate and sustain a community that works without bias and discrimination. But to get to that last step, we must first *Recognize. Respond. Redress*. We can't get to *cultivate and sustain* if we think we don't have any biases and/or if we turn away when we see biased or discriminatory acts happen in front of us.	Identity Pie Chart Implicit Bias Association Test
Our identity impacts how we teach, even if we don't think it does, and even if we don't notice it.	Whether consciously or unconsciously, our experiences and identity influence our approach to instructional delivery, interactions with students, and classroom management. Therefore, knowing thyself is paramount to positively engaging with diverse learners.	Snowball Fight Caption This! Identity Pie Chart Satellite Circles

Figure 4.2 Essential content: Z1 increasing educators' understanding of cultural norms and equity: Know thyself.

As the facilitator, you will need to learn about the racial, cultural, ethnic, and linguistic groups prior to delivering the PL. A great place to begin is by pulling the demographic data for your district and looking at how the group is represented (or missing) from various programs within the district. Then, pull the school building data compared to the district, and look for variations—perhaps a neighboring school is succeeding in meeting the needs of the groups. This is a potential source of resources and expertise upon which you could draw. Next, explore the community—in what ways are each of these groups seen within and across the district? Keep in mind that the community is an essential resource in learning about the group at hand; research is very important, but it generalizes by its very nature.

As the facilitator, you will want to create activities which are respectful of your audience but are also meaningful and engaging. Remember, our end goal is to increase the number of marginalized gifted students enrolled and retained in our gifted programs. Creating a balance of group and individual activities enables learners to grow their knowledge base. Similarly, there needs to be an hourglass approach to learning. We want to start with broad understandings, narrow the focus to the student body, and then expand again to encompass gifted programming and services. Again, activities are a means to convey and/or practice content. Be sure that you are communicating all the essential content for this section of Zone 1 (Figure 4.3).

Note that this content is phrased as questions; it is not expected that you automatically know the community that you serve. It is important that you research and get to know your students, families, and community. Recall the equity literacy principles from Chapter 3: One Size Fits Few—it is important to learn about the community in which you work, as basing equity work in one cultural framework will be grounded in assumptions, not equity; and Evidence-Informed Equity—be sure to base equity work in both scholarly research and in the community and take into account student and parent voices. Zone 1 provides many opportunities for educators to identify their own areas of strengths and weaknesses. The facilitator should draw the participants' attention to not only identify their areas of weakness, but also emphasize their strengths. Equity training is not designed to blame teachers for their lack of cultural competence, but rather the purpose is to bring awareness, acceptance, and change to teacher beliefs, behaviors, and practices—with the end goal being a positive change in student outcomes.

Z1 EC: Know Others	Brief Explanation	Playbook Activities
What have you learned about the students' identity/their culture?	Focusing on the cultural groups within your school/district dive deep into understanding about each cultural group. The facilitator should reach out to experts in the cultural groups to contribute to the conversation, be purposeful in selecting factual information, and avoid myths and stereotypes.	Scaffolded Notes Learning for Justice: Social Justice Standards: Unpacking Identity
What aspects of the students' identity and culture have traditionally impacted their relationships with schooling?	Historically, have the students or their families had a positive school experience? Consider the role of culture in interactions with teachers, the structure/government aspect, administration, school to prison pipeline? Has this been a deficit view? This is a deep dive that may be done by the facilitator or as an activity during the PL. Consider how the students are represented in the curriculum & materials, as well as in the school as a whole.	Children's Literature Activities Teaching Tolerance: Magic Carpet Ride Views from a Black Man
What are the funds of knowledge and/or community and cultural wealths in your community?	Exploring the Funds of Knowledge (see Chapter 2) and cultural wealth within the community brings value to diversity and helps to reverse a school community deficit mindset.	Funds of Knowledge Activity
How does your cultural identity align with your students?	Making the connection between one's individual cultural identity and the students' within the community provides the educator with opportunities to recognize potentially discriminatory actions (intentional or not) and take meaningful steps in changing inequity within the school community	Intersection of my Cultural Identity and My Students' Cultural Identities Reflective Journaling Prompts

Figure 4.3 Essential content: Z1 increasing educators' understanding of cultural norms and equity: Know others.

Cautions and Caveats

- **Don't be afraid to use your resources.** You aren't expected to be an expert on every racial, ethnic, cultural, and linguistic group. It is okay not to know the answers, but it is *not* okay not to seek out the answers. Ask members of the varying groups for input on the PL content, research about the different groups and invite your teachers to share their expertise throughout the session.
- **Kaleidoscope view.** We all view an event or experience based on our own prior experiences, knowledge, or misunderstandings. Remember playing with a kaleidoscope as a kid, watching how the colors shifted as you turned it, or the light filtered in? Our understanding of culture, in many ways, is like a kaleidoscope; it changes based on our experiences (positive and negative) and understandings.
- **Believe in the training plan.** Changing minds can be a slow process, but if you stick to the training plan and follow the zones, you will notice changes in teachers' practices and beliefs.
- **Take 5.** Discussing race, culture, and equity—and engaging in courageous conversations—is very personal and emotional. Don't be afraid to pause the PL when things are heating up and take 5 to reflect and regroup. Keep in mind we all process emotions differently; some of your teachers may be very vocal, while others quietly chew on their thoughts. Remember that growth happens in the periods of cognitive dissonance; feelings are expected and allowing for reflection time is part of the pathway to growth. The expectation of a brave space is that discomfort, don't let it go; regroup, re-engage, and/or debrief.

Resources

Cultural Awareness Survey Options

- Cultural Diversity Awareness Questionnaire, https://edge.sagepub.com/sites/default/files/9.3_cultural_diversity_awareness_questionnaire.pdf
- Cultural Competence Self-Assessment Questionnaire (CCSAQ), https://www.pathwaysrtc.pdx.edu/pdf/CCSAQ.pdf
- Cultural Competence Self-Assessment Awareness Checklist, https://www.lacrosseconsortium.org/uploads/content_files/files/Awareness_self_assessment.pdf
- Cultural Self-Assessment Questionnaire, https://mhsfaculty.auckland.ac.nz/amh/culture.pdf
- University of Michigan Campus Climate Survey on Diversity, Equity and Inclusion, https://diversity.umich.edu/wp-content/uploads/2017/11/STAFF-SAMPLING-SURVEY.pdf
- Equity and Diversity in the U.S. A Re-Perception Quiz, http://www.edchange.org/multicultural/quiz/quizNEW.pdf
- The Multicultural Efficacy Scale: Development, Item Selection, and Reliability, https://doi.org/10.1207/s15327892mcp0704_4

White Privilege

What Is White Privilege, Really?: Recognizing White Privilege Begins with Truly Understanding the Term Itself by Cory Collins, https://www.learningforjustice.org/magazine/fall-2018/what-is-white-privilege-really

White Educator Privilege: Unpacking the Invisible Teacher Bag by Ali Hodge, https://medium.com/teachers-on-fire/white-educator-privilege-unpacking-the-invisible-teacher-bag-d6c3bcb32402

White Privilege: Unpacking the Invisible Knapsack by Peggy McIntosh, https://nationalseedproject.org/images/documents/Knapsack_plus_Notes-Peggy_McIntosh.pdf

White Privilege Checklist (abridged), based on Peggy McIntosh by Alliance of Local Service Organizations, http://also-chicago.org/also_site/wp-content/uploads/2017/03/white-privilege.pdf

Why It's Better to Talk about "Advantage" Rather than "Privilege" by Steven Aguilar, https://www.insidehighered.com/print/views/2016/11/15/why-its-better-talk-about-advantage-rather-privilege-essay

Stereotype Threat

Videos

Stereotype Threat: A Conversation with Claude Steele, https://youtu.be/failylROnrY

Facing History and Ourselves How Stereotypes Affect Us and What We Can Do by Claude Steele, https://youtu.be/KvLj3OIQHuE

Texts/Articles

Whistling Vivaldi by Claude Steele

General Resources

White Racial Identity and Anti-Racist Education: A Catalyst for Change by Sandra M. Lawrence and Beverly Daniel Tatum, https://www.teachingforchange.org/wp-content/uploads/2012/08/ec_whiteracialidentity_english.pdf

Understanding Equity Literacy Webinar, Teaching Tolerance, https://www.tolerance.org/professional-development/webinars/equity-literacy

Walk a Mile in My Redface: On Ending the Colonial in Schools, Sports Culture, Mass Media and Civic Life, TEDX Talk by Cornel Pewewardy, http://tedxtalks.ted.com/video/Walk-a-Mile-in-My-Redface-On-End

Guide for Selecting Anti-Bias Children's Books, https://www.teachingforchange.org/selecting-anti-bias-books

Weaving KidLit into Professional Learning for Gifted Educators: Shifting Perspectives and Coaching for Equitable Practices, by Katie Lewis and Angela Novak, DOI: 10.1177/02614294221078081, https://edarxiv.org/vs37w/

Professional Learning Playbook

Look for the Guiding Principle Icons by the playbook activities!

1) Taking a Pulse
2) Individualizing Professional Learning Plans 
3) Establishing a Safe Zone
4) Going Beyond the Tip of the Iceberg
5) Engaging in Courageous Conversations 
6) Bridging the Gap Between School and Home 
7) Identifying Grows and Glows

Know Thyself Activities

Activity 1: Cultural Awareness Survey

Estimated Time: 20 minutes administration; 30 minutes debrief

Materials Needed: Cultural Awareness Survey, loaded online or copies made for participants

Delivery Format: Online or In Person

Seven Guiding Principles Addressed: 

Purpose: The purpose of this activity is twofold: first, it takes the pulse of participants so that you as the facilitator can individualize learning plans as appropriate; second, it provides a reflection point for participants now and at the end of the PL, or at some point in the future.

Procedure:

- ★ Administer a cultural awareness survey. See the Resources section for several options.
- ★ Ideally this should be administered prior to the face-to-face or online interaction so that you can plan based on the results. At least a week before is ideal, as you'll want time to provide follow-up emails to non-respondents. You can also ask the administrator to have participants fill this out in person at a previous faculty meeting and collect the results and give them to you.
- ★ Confidentiality matters: however you choose to administer the survey, consider what is the best method to provide the survey so that my respondents/participants will honor their truth, not say what they think someone else wants to hear? (Consider how administration collecting paper forms will impact this). Online surveys, even if completed in person at a faculty meeting, are beneficial: all faculty complete while at the meeting, so there is less "chasing down" to do later, but the online method allows for quick transmission to you as the PL facilitator, circumventing the administrator as collector.
- ★ As Angela tells her undergrad assessment class, there are key components of a successful assessment: data collected from a quality tool, checked for bias, reliability, validity, and fairness; analysis of that data; and decisions about what to do next. Sometimes students confuse the analysis with the decisions about what to do next, but these are two very different steps. What does the data actually mean? What does it tell me about the students (participants)… about their readiness, knowledge, the context of the lesson (situation)? The second question is: What do I do with that information given the learning objective I

have today? How will I plan, or change my plans, based on the analysis, because of who is in the room?

Extensions:

★ During the activities, you can use these surveys as discussion starters.
★ Ensure at least two weeks between assessments and provide the same assessment as a post survey. Note: you should choose a survey that aligns with the content that you will be covering for the best measure of growth.
★ You may wish to use an online survey tool that provides participants an option to keep or print their results so that they can reflect on their results.

Activity 2: Snowball Fight

Estimated Time: 20 minutes

Materials Needed: Paper, pencil, space in the room

Delivery Format: In Person

Seven Guiding Principles Addressed:

Purpose: To have individuals share elements of their identity with others and engage in discussion.

Procedure:

Extension: Discuss the impact of bias and discrimination on identity. Have participants flatten the snowballs; you may even have participants express remorse to the snowballs during the flattening. When the snowballs are as close to the original piece of paper as possible, discuss whether the paper looks as neat and clean as when you started the activity, making the connection to the lasting impact of bias and discrimination on an individual's identity, sense of self-worth, self-concept, etc. There is a brief YouTube video with Tony Brent from 2012 that you can show (https://youtu.be/xleR-JUVbDA) that focuses on anti-bullying using this crumpled paper analogy.

Variations: Depending on when you do this activity (in the scope of your training—five minutes in *vs.* day two of a four-day training), the cultural and identity makeup of your participants; and what you have learned by taking a pulse, what is written on the paper/snowball can vary. For example, depending on the audience, it might be to write an example of a privilege they hold based on the color of their skin, or an example of a time when they saw or were the victim of a micro aggression.

Activity 3: What is Culture?

Estimated Time: 5–10 minutes

Materials Needed: Chart paper or digital discussion board

Delivery Format: Online or In Person

Seven Guiding Principles Addressed:

Purpose: This collaborative activity engages the participants in an open discussion sharing how they define, explain, recognize culture. This simple question, 'what is culture' is not so simple in reality to answer.

Procedure:

★ Divide participants into small groups to discuss/share/answer the question 'what is culture?'
★ Allow about five minutes for participants to share within their groups. Judge the time frame based on observation of the flow of conversation
★ Participants may elect to jot down their ideas on chart paper or share on a digital forum
★ The facilitator calls on various groups to share their responses and creates a master chart.
★ From these ideas, the facilitator guides the conversation into a deeper understanding of 'what is culture'.

Activity 4: Caption This!

Estimated Time: 15–20 minutes

Materials Needed: Online access, Google Slides, or other digital resources

Delivery Format: Digital or In Person

Seven Guiding Principles Addressed: 

Purpose: Caption This! provides an opportunity for participants to look for images of culture both seen within their neighborhoods and beyond. After selecting images that represent an aspect of culture, the participants label the image with a caption that describes the element of culture the image represents. Typically, one or two participants really get into the activity and find some awesome images!

Procedure:

★ Participants can work individually or in small groups to complete this activity. Participants will have about five minutes to go online and locate a picture that represents culture.

- ★ Participants can post their image in a shared Google Slides presentation (or another digital format) and then create a caption that describes the image.
- ★ Facilitator will invite participants to share their images and guide a discussion about the images found, highlighting any stereotypes, negative and positive connotations associated with the images.

Adaptations: Read and debrief the "Taco Night" article from EdChange. (http://www.edchange.org/publications/TacoNight.pdf) Invite participants to share ways/images of how their school recognizes or celebrates culture. Discuss the concept brought up in the article of otherness and how having a taco night can exacerbate cultural otherness rather than celebrate cultures as it may be intended. Discuss what makes cultural celebrations authentic rather than the experience in "Taco Night."

Activity 5: Identity Pie Chart

Estimated Time: 30 minutes

Materials Needed: Reproducible 4.1: Identity Pie Chart

Delivery Format: Online or In Person

Seven Guiding Principles Addressed:

Purpose: "Cultural Identity is based on membership in multiple groups that continuously interact and influence each other. Identity within these groups is affected by interaction with the dominant group and power relations among groups in society."[4] Understanding our own cultural identity is necessary before being able to understand someone else's culture. This activity helps the participants to pause and evaluate their own identities and experiences that have shaped their identity. As a springboard activity for future discussions of race and culture this is a crucial element in beginning to understand what shapes identity: who I am and who my students are.

Procedure:

- ★ Participants will create a pie chart showing how their identity is formed based on each of the following categories of identity from Gollnick and Chinn.[5] Encourage participants to reflect on how the identity categories influence who they are today. One's identity pie chart will change over time based on your experiences. For example, age is often very important when you turn 16, 18, 21, or 50! Yet, maybe the rest of the time, age may not be as important to someone.

- ★ Do not focus on actual percentages/numbers (unless you are a math person!); instead focus on dividing the pie into representative sections.
- ★ It is beneficial for the facilitator to share a sample pie chart with the participants to serve as a model.
- ★ We recommend that everyone addresses all areas, even if it is a small slice of your identity pie. This is important as some participants may elect to avoid areas that make them uncomfortable.
- ★ Depending on the audience, you may elect to keep the pie charts private between the creator and the facilitator. This sense of trust is important in establishing a safe learning environment where participants feel comfortable sharing their honest thoughts and opinions.
- ★ After participants have created their identity pie chart, it is important to follow with a conversation with each participant about their pie chart. Through these discussions the facilitator learns about the individuals' cultural identity and key influences in their lives.
- ★ As a facilitator, keep in mind that some participants will share personal information with you, that you will need to safeguard. Always ask for permission to share before sharing the personal information with the whole group.

Adaptations: If you have more time, participants can create a short video about their identity pie chart to share their narrative along with meaningful pictures for the slices.

Activity 6: Satellite Circles Activity

Estimated Time: 10–15 minutes

Materials Needed: Paper or Word document

Delivery Format: Digital or In Person

Seven Guiding Principles Addressed: 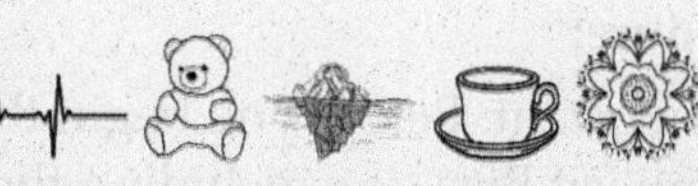

Purpose: Satellite Circles highlight the overlapping nature of culture. There are many aspects of culture that will fit your identity, but at the same time, there are many that do not necessarily apply to you. This realization is important for educators to acknowledge as they work with diverse learners who are gifted, since often, these learners do not fit the standardized mold. This activity is a companion activity to the Cultural Identity Pie Chart activity. If you haven't completed the Pie Chart, then you will first need the participants to reflect on the characteristics of identity.

Procedure:

- ★ Use your identity pie chart characteristics to fill in the satellite circles on the Reproducible.
- ★ Share a story about a time you were especially proud to identify yourself with one of the descriptors you used above.
- ★ Share a story about a time that was especially painful to be identified with one of your descriptors.
- ★ Name a stereotype associated with one of the groups with which you identify that is not consistent with who you are. Complete the sentence frame below:

  I am (a/an)_____________ but I am NOT (a/an)___________

- ★ Debrief with participants about the impact of identity, identity groups, and biases and stereotypes associated with identity groups. Share the article or video (https://youtu.be/failylROnrY) about stereotype threat with participants.

Activity 7: Implicit Bias Association Test

Estimated Time: 25–30 minutes

Materials Needed: Individual laptops for all participants for in-person delivery, link to the Race IAT, https://implicit.harvard.edu/implicit/user/agg/blindspot/indexrk.htm, TedX talk by Melanie Funchess, https://youtu.be/Fr8G7MtRNlk

Delivery Format: Digital or In Person

Seven Guiding Principles Addressed: 

Purpose: To define implicit bias and engage participants in establishing a baseline about their own implicit associations.

Procedure:

- ★ Important: Before you begin this activity, be sure to thoroughly read the Implicit Bias site, including the Ethical Considerations, https://implicit.harvard.edu/implicit/ethics.html and the FAQs, https://implicit.harvard.edu/implicit/faqs.html. You may also want to read some of the research that has been published about the IAT. Be ready to explain what the IAT *is* and what *it is not* to participants before they take it!
- ★ Watch the TedX Flour City Talk on Implicit Bias by Melanie Funchess, 16 minutes https://youtu.be/Fr8G7MtRNlk
  - ★ Discuss transformational activism and her four needed parts (starting at 14:30).
  - ★ Reflect and discuss ubuntu.

- ★ Circle back to the beginning of the TED Talk and review implicit bias. Discuss and create a universal group definition of implicit bias.
- ★ Share the link for the Race IAT, https://implicit.harvard.edu/implicit/user/agg/blindspot/indexrk.htm. Explain what the IAT is and is not—it *is* a test that measures the strengths of associations between concepts and can be used for raising awareness about implicit bias. It *is not* a diagnostic tool that identifies individuals as prejudiced or racist.
- ★ Allow time to take the Race IAT—alternatively, this can be a "takeaway" task with a follow-up debrief.
- ★ Debrief the IAT. Even with the caveat of "what this test is not" some people may not want to share their results, this is fine. Debrief general thoughts or feelings about the idea of implicit bias. Invite individuals to take other tests. Emphasize again what the test is, and what implicit bias is, with emphasis on implicit.

Activity 8: What is Racism?

Estimated Time: 20 minutes

Materials Needed: Reproducible 4.3: Definitions of Racism

Delivery Format: Digital or In Person

Seven Guiding Principles Addressed:

Purpose: To discuss definitions of racism and identify how racism is seen in the school.

Procedure:

- ★ Use Reproducible 4.3 to read through the provided definitions of racism, from DismantlingRacism.org and Dr. Ibram Kendi's definition from *How to be an Antiracist*.
- ★ Discuss the discussion questions provided on Reproducible 4.3.

Activity 9: Scales

Estimated Time: 30 minutes

Materials Needed: Balance scale and weights (online version: https://www.roomrecess.com/Tools/PanBalance/play.html); Peggy McIntosh's Invisible Knapsack article or similar list (see Resources); ripple effect story (linked) or your own

Delivery Format: Digital or In Person

Seven Guiding Principles Addressed: 

Purpose: To understand the impact of White privilege on BIPOC populations. The scale gives a visual representation of how White privilege, while it gives Whites privilege or advantage, simultaneously figuratively, and sometimes literally, pushes down on BIPOC individuals. Sometimes individuals have a picture of it as an advantage, but don't understand that it has a negative impact on others, and sometimes individuals don't recognize privilege at all. Other individuals confound monetary privilege with racial privilege. As you facilitate this activity, be ready for this discomfort and pushback (see the note below about the terms privilege *vs.* advantage).

Procedure:

★ With a virtual or physical balance scale in front of you, talk about the ripple effect, how one person's actions, whether intended or not, impact others. One such example is: http://internetstoryclub.org/fables/52_the_ripple_effect.html but there are many short stories and videos that can be used.

★ Similar to the ripple effect is a balance scale. As we put something on one side of the scale, the other side of the scale reacts. This may happen in small or large ways, depending on the weight of what we place on the scale, and of course, what is already on the other side to balance it.

★ Tell your audience that the two students are fairly similar in every way—economic status, where they live, parents and siblings, abilities in school, athletics, friends, gender, and so on. For each characteristic you mention, put a weight on each side of the scale, so that the scale is balanced. The principal difference is that one child (you can name them if you like) is White and the other is Black.

★ Using items from the McIntosh Invisible Knapsack list (or similar) that are examples of White privilege, read items aloud. For each item that you read aloud (for example, "I can choose blemish cover or bandages in 'flesh' color and have them more or less match my skin") add or take away based on the perspective from which you are reading: generally, if it is from the White perspective, remove a weight, if it is from the Black perspective, add a weight. Using that same example, since the flesh color bandage matches the White individual's skin, you'll remove a weight from the White child's side.

  ★ Unlike the previous step, do not add/remove weights evenly.

  ★ Note that when you remove a weight from one side "privilege lightens the everyday load," the other side is weighed down—the counter effect of privilege is that it creates burdens for others, or the lack of privilege is a burden or causes burdens.

  ★ The point is to recognize that privilege or advantage isn't 'cost free'—which many people assume it is; "I can't help that I get these things because of the color of my skin." The goal of this is to broaden this understanding to also recognize that there is an underbelly to privilege, that if one person is receiving it, there is a balance to the scale.

★ Using Peggy McIntosh's original list, the weight will always be removed from the White side, as the list is written as examples of White privilege. Other lists are written differently, or you may choose to reword so that you are occasionally showing examples of micro/macroaggressions or even overt racism in play. For example, items on McIntosh's original list include: "I am never asked to speak for all the people of my racial group" and "Whether I use checks, credit cards, or cash, I can count on my skin color not to work against the appearance of financial reliability." These can, in our society based on systemic and culturalized racism, be reworded to "I am [frequently/always] asked to speak for all the people of my racial group" and "Whether I use checks, credit cards, or cash, I can count on my skin color ~~not~~ to work against the appearance of financial reliability." Using these prompts, you would add a weight to the Black individual's scale.

★ After five to ten prompts, discuss the process, the examples, and the actions of the scales. Be sure to hone in on the reciprocal effect as described above. It is crucial that poverty and class are not confused with race when discussing privilege—yes, there are aspects of life that are intersectional but White privilege is not one of them.

Variations:

★ Based on readiness (based on *taking a pulse* results) rather than using an existing list from McIntosh or others in the resources section, have participants brainstorm ideas about White Privilege or White Advantage.

★ Use the term "advantage" rather than "privilege." As we've discussed (a few times!) words matter and can impact people's receptiveness to the message. Angela has been in several sessions that stress using advantage over privilege, from the Racial Equity Institute to a James Baldwin book talk with the NC Poet Laureate. This is where knowing your audience is key. The Resource section includes an essay by Stephen Aguilar that discusses the two terms.

★ This activity can also be done using microaggressions, aspects of identity (e.g., gender and sexual identity, language, exceptionalities, geography, class). The balance of power is a shift with the harm toward BIPOC and/or historically marginalized groups (the weight of the scale) and the advantage toward the historically dominant group.

★ The poem "Cause I Ain't Got No Pencil" is a powerful short poem to use when examining the ripple effect in general or rushing to judgment. For this, start with a weight on each side, and at each line read aloud, add a weight to one side for the additional step or pressure the child in the poem has. Discuss how the child has come into the school already with so much on his/her mind, only to be disciplined due to a lack of pencil. Note: this poem does not have a racial identity associated with it, and so it is an extension to use to think about ripple effect or poverty. If teachers jump to assume racial identity or culture, that is something to unpack and discuss regarding bias and stereotype. It is written by Joshua T. Dickerson, a Black author and poet, who was inspired to write the poem after witnessing a teacher in an Atlanta school require a student to remove a shoe for collateral just to borrow a pencil. https://www.protectivebehaviours.org/protective-behaviours-resources-training-room/poems/130-cause-i-aint-got-a-pencil

Know Others Activities

Activity 10: Children's Literature Connection

Estimated Time: 15–20 minutes

Materials Needed: Carefully selected read aloud book (see purpose/procedure)

Delivery Format: Digital or In Person

Seven Guiding Principles Addressed:

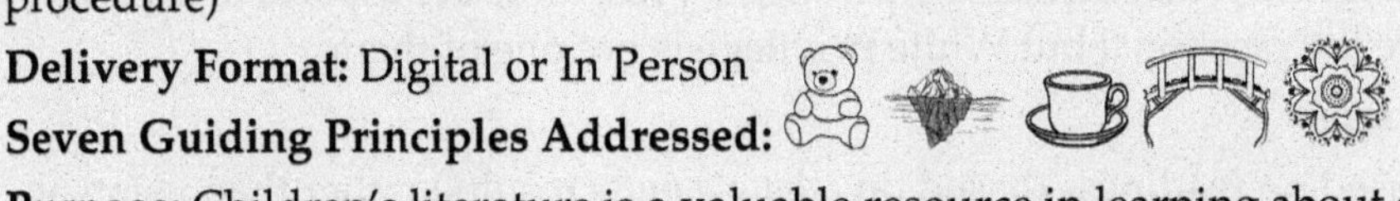

Purpose: Children's literature is a valuable resource in learning about other cultures. Experiencing cultures through stories provides a meaningful window into the world of other cultures and can act as a springboard for deeper connections and conversations amongst educators. A key in utilizing this tool is the strategic selection of books, aligning with the PL learning outcomes and goals of the session.

Procedure:

- ★ The facilitator selects the children's literature book or excerpt to be shared, being sure to follow the guidelines for selecting anti-bias children's books and review the posted KidLit article for suggestions (see Resources).
- ★ The facilitator designs activities to facilitate discussion and inquiry. Purposefully selected activities which are directly tied to the PL learning outcomes are key. Activities should be connected to the book and guide the audience to a conversation about the PL topic. Children's

literature creates a safe space for tough conversations, as the participants are discussing the characters in the book, not themselves or their own students.

- ★ The facilitator should guide the conversation from the characters in the story to text-to-self connections which allows for deeper understanding of the PL topic. Providing space for reflection is essential to the learning process.
- ★ Finally, the facilitator should make the connection between the topics covered and teaching practices.

Activity 11: Learning for Justice: Examining Identity and Assimilation

Estimated Time: 20–25 minutes

Materials Needed: Learning for Justice (formerly Teaching Tolerance): Magic Carpet Ride,

https://www.learningforjustice.org/classroom-resources/lessons/examining-identity-and-assimilation

Delivery Format: Digital or In Person

Seven Guiding Principles Addressed: 

Purpose: This activity from the Learning for Justice website is an excellent resource for examining one's own cultural identity, as well as the loss of culture. The essay Magic Carpet is a reflective piece of Mitali Perkins' own journey growing up in an American culture and the realization that she has lost part of her heritage as an adult. After reading and reflecting on this message, the audience can move through their own reflection and discussion of times when they too may have hidden a piece of their identity.

Procedure:

- ★ The facilitator will share the essay "Magic Carpet" with the audience.
- ★ Using the reflection questions guide the participants through a reflective conversation about the loss of cultural identity, the impact on their development as an adult, as well as the process of assimilation. The questions provided are meant for student use; extend the conversation using reflective prompts (discussion or journaling):
  - ★ About a third of the way through the story, Mitali Perkins writes, "Slowly, insidiously, I began to judge my heritage through colonial eyes. I asked my mother not to wear a sari, her traditional

dress, when she visited me at school." Has an incident like this happened to you and/or in your school/community to your knowledge? At your comfort level, share with the group. Discuss the implications on the classroom, from learning environment to assessment.

- ★ At the end of the first page, Mitali Perkins writes, "My decision to leave mother tongue and culture behind might have been inevitable during the adolescent passage of rebellion and self-discovery. But I wonder if things could have turned out differently." At the start of page 2, two examples are offered: picking up a book in the library, or a teacher handing the narrator a book. As an educator, what other ways could you have helped the narrator as a child?

★ What is the author's purpose in writing this piece, from an educator standpoint?

Activity 12: Learning for Justice's Social Justice Standards: Unpacking Identity

Estimated Time: 60 minutes

Materials Needed: Full PL lesson plan is provided at https://www.learningforjustice.org/professional-development/social-justice-standards-unpacking-identity; projection device connected to the Internet; pen and paper

Delivery Format: Digital or In Person

Seven Guiding Principles Addressed: 

Purpose: To define identity and understand how social justice shapes and forms our actions and the actions of our students while also understanding Learning for Justice's Social Justice Standards, specifically the five identity anchor standards.

Procedure: The online Learning for Justice professional learning lesson plan provides step-by-step directions, including when to pause for cohort discussions, when to show each of the selected videos, embedded on the website, and applications to the educators' current contexts.

Activity 13: Intersection of My Cultural Identity and My Students' Cultural Identities

Estimated Time: 15–20 minutes (depending on sharing)

Materials Needed: Reproducible 4.4: Intersection of My Cultural Identity and My Students' Cultural Identities

Delivery Format: Digital or In Person

Seven Guiding Principles Addressed: 

Purpose: This graphic organizer provides a concrete way to synthesize and analyze concepts learned in Zone 1 related to cultural identities. Being able to visualize and reflect on the similarities, differences, and commonalities between identities is an important piece of the puzzle for educators working toward changing inequities.

Procedure:

- ★ Provide participants with copies of the Reproducible 4.4 and allow for participants to fill in the graphic organizer. This step should be completed independently as the participant is able to reflect on the learning from the PL sessions.
- ★ Provide time for the participants to share out their graphic organizers and reflective prompts. This group debriefing is important in helping the faculty move forward in the change process. This should be a voluntary sharing process due to the personal nature of this exercise.

Activity 14: Stories from a Black Man

Estimated Time: 20–30 minutes

Materials Needed: TED Talk by Clint Smith, https://www.ted.com/talks/clint_smith_how_to_raise_a_black_son_in_america, blog by Clint Smith, https://ideas.ted.com/my-hopes-dreams-fears-for-my-future-black-son/ (copies for in-person delivery)

Delivery Format: Digital or In Person

Seven Guiding Principles Addressed: 

Purpose: To understand the perspective of an ethnicity/culture that may be represented in the district, that may be different from the population of the participants; likely one that will be eye-opening.

Procedure:

- ★ Optional: Begin with a discussion of free play—how participants in the room played as children, or how participants' children play.
- ★ Show the TED Talk (five minutes). Discuss the story that Clint Smith shares and invite commentary and reflection.
- ★ Share copies of Clint Smith's blog, or share the link in the online platform: https://ideas.ted.com/my-hopes-dreams-fears-for-my-future-black-son/. Ask participants to read the blog silently or in table groups aloud (the blog is fairly short; this should only take five to eight minutes).
- ★ Reflect on his second childhood story. Ask participants to engage in personal reflection first on the following questions, then have time to share and discuss. The first question might be one to have a modeling prompt available, an example of what you would share of your thought process, or an answer discussed in advance that a participant could share:
  - ★ How does Clint sharing his story of his father teaching Clint his racialized truth and awareness with Clint as a child impact your understanding of the Black experience differently than when Clint shares his childhood story of his self-taught awakening of his racialized truth and awareness?
  - ★ (Helper prompt: Did you connect to one story more, as a parent, seeing your own children through the eyes of Clint's father, or perhaps as an educator seeing your own students reflected in Clint's boyhood story?)
- ★ These are both examples of a phenomenon called 'playing while Black'—how do these examples relate to education? (You may mention at this point if you haven't called attention to the bio on the Ted Talk website that Clint Smith is a teacher, as well as a poet, writer, and activist).

Extensions:

- ★ This can be an opportunity to connect/extend to stereotypes/misconceptions and/or explore daily microaggressions that are experienced daily by Black youth specifically and/or extend to other BIPOC children. Since this is a brief activity, it can be combined with others to round out a PL experience.
- ★ Continue with a final story from Clint Smith, *The Danger of Silence*, four minutes long: https://www.ted.com/talks/clint_smith_the_danger_of_silence/transcript#t-66128

Activity 15: Funds of Knowledge Activity

Estimated Time: 30–40 minutes

Materials Needed: https://modules.nceln.fpg.unc.edu/sites/modules.nceln.fpg.unc.edu/files/foundations/handouts/Mod%204%20Funds%20of%20knowledge.pdf; online discussion group modules or meeting space; pencils/papers/printouts for in person

Delivery Format: Digital or In Person

Seven Guiding Principles Addressed: 

Purpose: To understand and record ideas of funds of knowledge in the community and households of the students served in the district, using dynamic and strengths-based language.

Procedure:

- ★ The handout has a guide; however, this can be modified, as it is created by Bank Street College for Head Start and pre-school or primary student use. https://modules.nceln.fpg.unc.edu/sites/modules.nceln.fpg.unc.edu/files/foundations/handouts/Mod%204%20Funds%20of%20knowledge.pdf
- ★ Note that the instructions are first to fill out the guide in reference to self (know thyself) and to only use the form with parents and community members once a strong relationship is formed. There is some debate around the idea of home visits, as they can be seen as performative and/or observations for the purpose of inspections/critique rather than open communication and engagement. Meeting at parks, community centers, or a student's extracurricular activity might be a more welcoming environment.

General Activities

Activity 16: Parking Lot

Estimated Time: Ongoing, throughout the PL

Materials Needed: In Person: sticky notes, markers, pens, large areas to place the sticky notes on (chart paper, but a chalk board or bulletin board works); Online: we like padlet or jamboard, but you may have a different option based on your LMS (learning management system)

Delivery Format: Digital or In Person

Seven Guiding Principles Addressed:   

Purpose: A parking lot is holding space for thoughts and questions for participants (and sometimes facilitators). The parking lot serves as a temporary holding zone until the facilitator can answer the questions or hold a group discussion to mull over the thoughts. This is an excellent strategy to help keep the PL on track during the sessions, but still enables the queries to be heard/responded to in a timely manner; it lets all participants feel their opinions/thoughts/questions are valued.

Procedure:

- ★ At the start of the session, introduce the concept of the Parking Lot:
  - ★ Throughout the session, as you come up with questions, thoughts, or ideas, if it isn't a sharing time—for example, sometimes the discussion has gone on for quite some time and we need to move on, sometimes we are working in small groups but you feel that something should be brought to the attention of the whole group, or sometimes you have a question that you might not feel comfortable voicing aloud to the whole group yet; please write it down on a sticky note provided in the center of each table and place it on the parking lot. We highly suggest that you write your name on the back of the note—this way if we don't find time to bring the question or topic to the whole group, we can make sure to get a response to you personally. Know that writing your name on the back is optional—if you prefer to remain anonymous even to us, you may choose to do so, but that limits our ability to reach out and make sure you have the answers and follow up you seek. There are parking lots located at various points throughout our meeting space (point them out—depending on the size of the group and room, you may want several parking lots at strategic points of the room).
- ★ Place several pads of sticky notes on each table/working area, along with pens or markers.
- ★ Throughout the day, several times a day, monitor the parking lot and address the questions and concerns.
- ★ Consider modeling putting a question on the parking lot during a video or read aloud by a partner facilitator.
- ★ We like to keep the notes as reflections on what is asked over the course of the session (especially in multiple-day sessions). We tape them to the side of the parking lot, in the 'garage' and occasionally reference them as growth points (the tape is because the sticky doesn't always last) or in future discussions as callbacks. Time can be tough in PL—if you don't have time to get to all the parking-lot posts, be sure to follow up with any parking-lot notes not addressed in the discussion, either through email follow-up, discussion boards after the events, or individually.

Activity 17: Scaffolded Notes

Estimated Time: 10–40 minutes

Materials Needed: Scaffolded note pages

Delivery Format: Digital or In Person

Seven Guiding Principles Addressed:

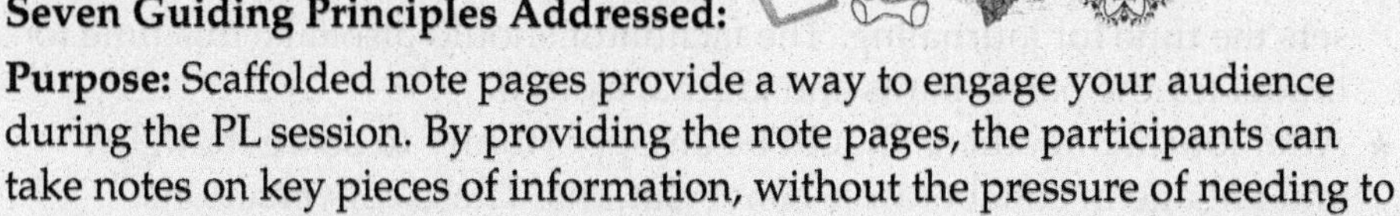

Purpose: Scaffolded note pages provide a way to engage your audience during the PL session. By providing the note pages, the participants can take notes on key pieces of information, without the pressure of needing to copy everything down, and are able to refer back to the notes at a later time. An added benefit of scaffolded notes is that they provide an active learning task for the participants, which increases focus and participation.

Procedure:

- ★ The facilitator should create the scaffolded notes to align with presentations and provide the notes to the participants prior to the PL session.
- ★ Optional: Give participants choice on whether they complete the notes. As we know some people are more auditory learners. You can also offer an emailed copy rather than a printed copy for those that are paper conscious and/or having a typing preference over writing by hand.
- ★ Modification: Many participants also prefer a copy of the slides—you can make these available in advance, with three slides on each page on the left column, and the right column available for notetaking.

Activity 18: Reflective Journaling Prompts

Estimated Time: 5–30 minutes

Materials Needed: Journal prompt, paper/Word document

Delivery Format: Digital or In Person

Seven Guiding Principles Addressed:

Purpose: Reflective journaling allows learners to process new content and knowledge. The process of reflecting provides the space for the learner to digest the new information, make connections, draw conclusions, and come to new understandings. The amount of time needed for journaling varies depending on the topic being covered, the novelty of the ideas, and depth of topic being explored. To increase the effectiveness of journaling, multiple opportunities for reflection should be embedded before, during, and after the PL. The facilitator should be purposeful in selecting the journal prompts to fit within the PL, allowing flexibility for additional reflection based on the needs of the participants. The most effective journal prompts are those which invite inquiry, are open-ended, and not self-answering.

Procedure:

- ★ The facilitator provides the journaling prompt to the participants and sets the time for journaling. The facilitator should also take this time to model for the participants and journal as well.
- ★ After journaling, there should be an opportunity to share thoughts and engage in collaborative conversations. These conversations should be voluntary as some journal prompts will invite the participant to deeply reflect sharing personal experiences. If the journal prompt is going to be shared with the whole group, the facilitator should be sure to inform the participants prior to the activity. There may be some instances where the sharing-out of responses is not necessary.
- ★ Sample journal prompts: Are we defined as people by our cultures or do shared experiences shape culture? Reflect on a time when you were the only person present with a particular trait in a room (for example, the only female, the only individual who spoke Spanish, the only newcomer to the group, etc.)—were you treated differently from the others in the room and how did it make you feel? What was something from today's PL that you were surprised to learn? What are some questions that you still have about today's topic?

Reproducibles

Reproducible 4.1: Identity Pie Chart

Directions: Create a pie chart showing how your identity is formed based on each of the following categories of culture, adapted from Gollnick and Chinn.[5] You must address all areas, even if it is a small slice of your pie. Be prepared to share with the facilitator your slices of pie that have the greatest influence on who you are today.

- **Exceptionalities:** Neurodivergent, disabilities, gifted individuals
- **Gender:** Gender identity, gender normativity, and society's expectations for your role
- **Ethnicity:** Native country of one's ancestors
- **Age:** To what extent does your age impact you (this varies at different points)?
- **Sexual Orientation:** Heterosexuality, LGBTQIA+
- **Geography:** Location where you live at a macro and micro level
- **Class:** System that differentiates groups access to economic, political, cultural, and social resources: lower, middle, upper
- **Language:** Language(s) and dialect(s) that you speak, read, or write
- **Religion:** Religions that you practice

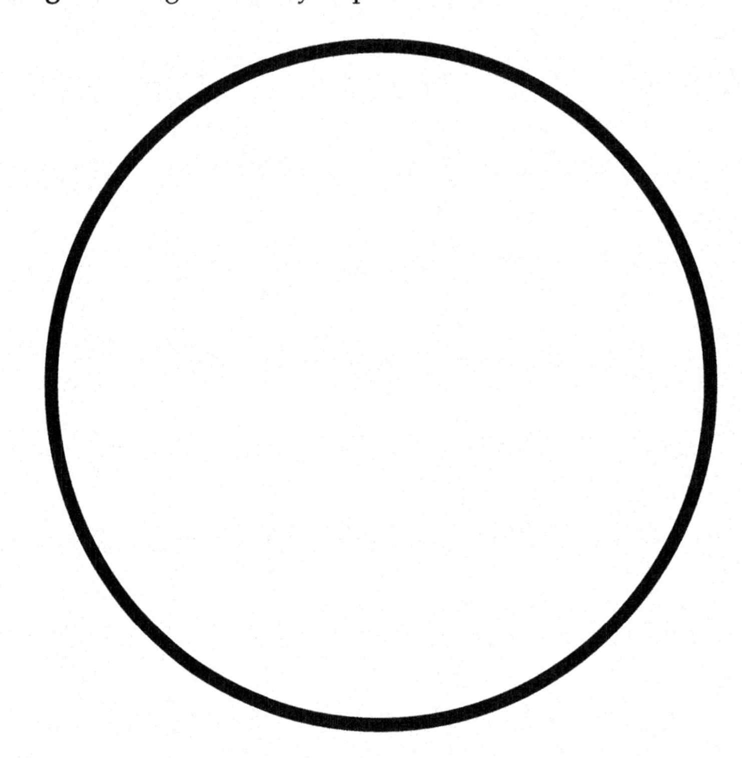

Reproducible 4.2: Satellite Circles

Directions: Using your Cultural Identity Pie Chart, fill in the Satellite Circles below with words/phrases to describe your identity.

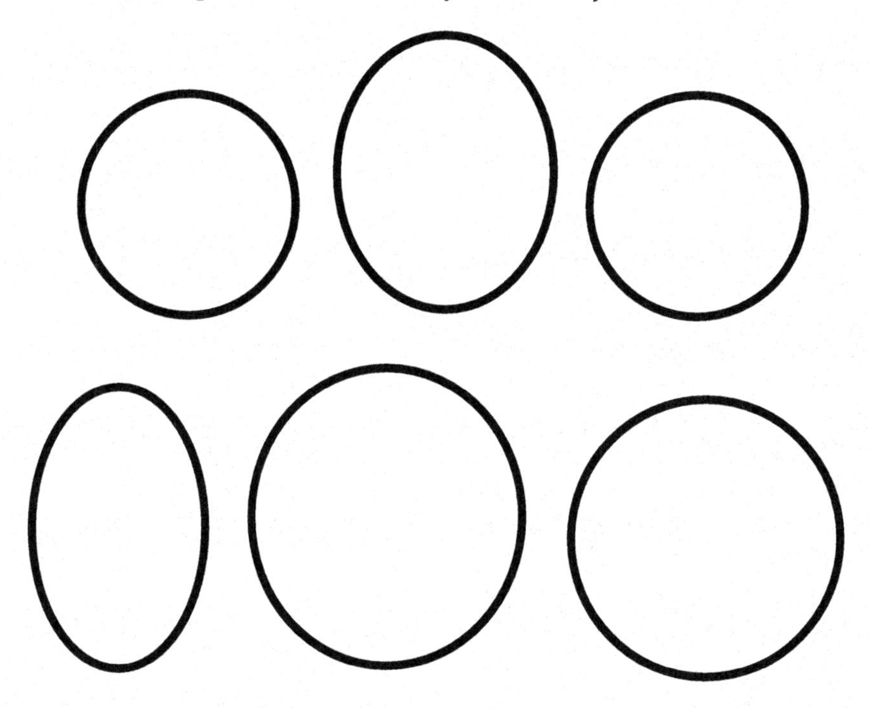

Reflect: On a time you were especially proud to identify yourself with one of the descriptors you used above.

Reflect: On a time that was especially painful to be identified with one of your descriptors.

Share a stereotype associated with one of the groups with which you identify that is not consistent with who you are. Complete the sentence frame below:

I am (a/an)______________ but I am NOT (a/an)____________

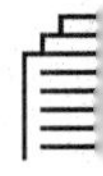

Reproducible 4.3: Definitions of Racism

Read the following definitions of racism written by DismantlingRacism.org and Dr. Ibram X. Kendi and discuss the questions below.

DismantlingRacism.org	*How to Be an AntiRacist* by Ibram X. Kendi
Racism: race prejudice + social and institutional power a system of advantage based on race a system of oppression based on race a White supremacy system Racism is different from racial prejudice, hatred, or discrimination. Racism is when the power elite of one group, the White group, has the power to carry out systematic discrimination through the institutional policies and practices of the society while shaping the cultural beliefs and values that support those racist policies and practices.	Racism is a powerful collection of racist policies that lead to racial inequity and are substantiated by racist ideas. Racist policy is any measure that produces or sustains racial inequity between racial groups. A racist idea is any idea that suggests one racial group is inferior or superior to another racial group in any way. Racist ideas argue that the inferiorities and superiorities of racial groups explain racial inequities in society.
Sources for Definitions: https://www.dismantlingracism.org/racism-defined.html https://offices.depaul.edu/diversity/education/presidents-book-club/PublishingImages/Pages/default/Kendi's%20Glossary%20of%20Terms.pdf	

Discussion Questions:

1. How are the definitions similar? How do they differ?
2. In Kendi's definition, can racism exist between racial groups, sharing an example of racism between a group of BIPOC students on a city bus (see https://www.litcharts.com/lit/how-to-be-an-antiracist/characters/smurf)? Would this meet the dismantling racism.org definition of racism? Why or why not?

We will dive into gifted education in Zone 2—but like our field, sometimes definitions in equity work can vary. It is important to clarify the definition of racism that you are using, going forward with this work. Discuss how racism is operationalized in your school. Where do you see it happening? In what ways? Be specific in your examples.

Reproducible 4.4: Intersection of My Cultural Identity and My Students' Cultural Identities

Fill in the graphic organizer; the left column consists of cultural characteristics unique to your identity, the right column consists of cultural characteristics unique to your students. The middle column contains those shared characteristics.

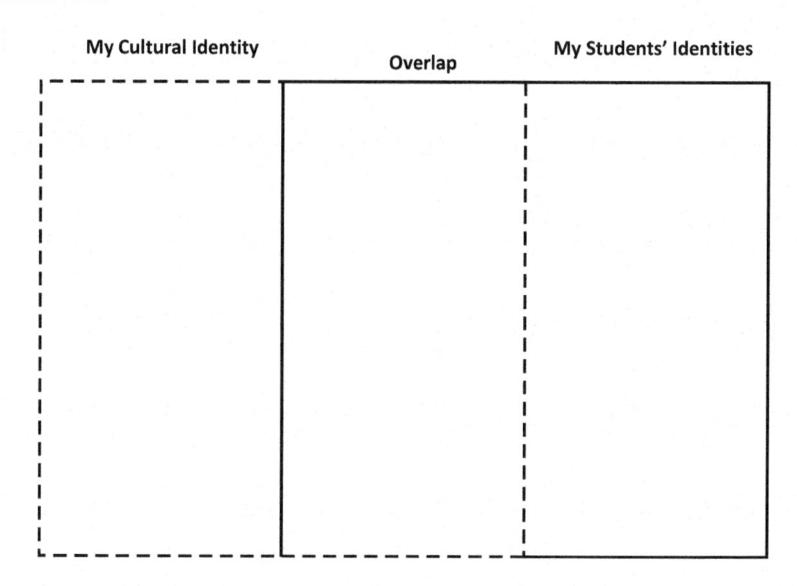

Reflect: How does understanding your cultural identity and your students' cultural identities help you become a more effective educator?

Reflect: What do you view as your strengths and areas for growth when working with students with different cultural identities from your own?

Notes

1 Boler, M. (1999). *Feeling power: Emotions and education.* Routledge.
2 Lu, C., & Wan, C. (2018). Cultural self-awareness as awareness of culture's influence on the self: Implications for cultural identification and well-being. *Personality and Social Psychology Bulletin, 44*(6), 823–837.
3 Gorski, P. C., & Swalwell, K. (2015). Equity literacy for all. *Educational Leadership, 72*(6), 34–40. http://edchange.org/publications/Equity-Literacy-for-All.pdf
4 Gollnick, D. M., & Chinn, P. C. (2013). *Multicultural education in a pluralistic society* (9th edition). Pearson, p. 13.
5 Ibid.

5

Zone 2

Increasing Educators' Understanding of Characteristics of Gifted Marginalized Students

In the 1968 Olympics, Tommie Smith broke a world record and won gold in the 200-meter race. Just as notably, he and fellow Olympian John Carlos engaged in peaceful protest on the world's athletic main stage when accepting their gold and bronze medals. Smith later remarked:

> If I win, I am American, not a black American. But if I did something bad, then they would say I am a Negro. We are black and we are proud of being black. Black America will understand what we did tonight.[1]

In schools across America, children experience the pain, pressure, fear, and anxiety of 'when will my race be a factor in the quality of my education?'

What's the Play?

Increasing Educators' Understanding of Characteristics of Gifted Marginalized Students, Zone 2, focuses on exploring how characteristics of giftedness present in various cultural groups. The zone acknowledges that the traditional characteristics of giftedness that we as teachers are often familiar with are not always accurate. Perhaps you have been given a checklist of gifted behaviors as part of the referral process; this is likely what you have ingrained as the 'gifted child.' That list of gifted traits is not the same for all students,

DOI: 10.4324/9781003196204-6

particularly for marginalized ethnic and cultural groups, as the manifestation of giftedness potential, characteristics, and behavior is influenced by culture. No two children are exactly alike, so why would we expect two gifted children to fit the same mold?

During Zone 2, the facilitator and participants explore the role that culture plays in gifted behaviors. Within this zone, the use of case studies is beneficial. You may be wondering, why Zone 2 is coming after Zone 1; why not just jump right into understanding giftedness and cultures? That's a great question! The reason is that we must first set the foundation for understanding yourself before you can understand other people. Our biases/beliefs often influence our thoughts and behaviors—unless you are aware of them and can recognize when they are directly (or more often indirectly) influencing your decisions. Then we learn about others in a broader sense before we focus on the specificity of giftedness. Zone 1's focus was Know Thyself and Know Others, through the lens of equity. It is scaffolded, which is best practice in K-12 instruction and for adult learners.

In Zone 2, we're ready to move forward into deeper understanding. For example, we may observe a student who prefers to work with peers, declines leadership roles, rarely asks questions during class though sometimes stays after class with a question, and we may initially think 'nope, not a gifted student' when comparing that student's actions with the checklist of gifted behaviors because we have been taught that gifted students are leaders who take charge in the classroom and ask all the questions. In Zone 2, we learn that within some Native American and Indigenous cultures, the emphasis is on the good of the whole, community learning, collectivism as a cultural trait over individualism, and that gifted students have the tendency to listen, learn, and wait—not asking questions during class, but waiting until after class is over. Thus, the behaviors we dismissed as *not* gifted signs are actually indicative of giftedness, influenced by cultural norms.

Just like in Zone 1, where we focused on cultural manifestations while also focusing on the broader picture of systemic and structural equity, it is important to do the same in Zone 2 within the context of giftedness. As a field, gifted education needs to strive toward equity literacy, recognizing, responding to, and redressing the historical legacy of racist power structures that built the current biased, oppressive, and inequitable system of identification. Zone 2 does not stop with recognizing cultural characteristics of racially, culturally, ethnically, and linguistically diverse (RCELD) gifted students, but continues with understanding the inequities in gifted education: recognizing how students have been minoritized and marginalized in gifted programs historically, and how they are currently underrepresented and oppressed in the time and space of the professional learning experience. Figure 5.1 is the Zone 2 section of the Sample Planning Chart for Differentiated Groups shared in Chapter 2 (Figure 2.2), which provides a general outline of what this zone might look like for differentiated groups based on the results of *taking a pulse*. Note that the pulse showed that the growth and proficient PLCs had similar levels of pre-existing knowledge for this zone and are therefore combined, leaving only two PLCs for Zone 2.

<table>
<tr><th>PLC 1
Growth Group</th><th>PLC 2
Proficient Group</th><th>PLC 3
Extension Group</th></tr>
<tr><td>Little to no cultural & equity awareness: misconceptions related to gifted characteristics in traditionally marginalized gifted groups in the community</td><td>Average cultural & equity awareness: misconceptions related to gifted characteristics in traditionally marginalized gifted groups in the community</td><td>Culturally & equity aware: recognizes gifted characteristics in traditionally marginalized gifted groups in the community</td></tr>
<tr><td colspan="2">In this example, based on the pre-assessment, neither PLC 1 or 2 has a solid understanding of giftedness in the targeted gifted population. Therefore, the activities in Zone 2 are the same:
-Discuss the impact of systemic inequities from Zone 1 on the students' educational experience. Relate that to gifted education.
-Presentation through multiple modalities and discussion of:
---What does giftedness look like in this specific culture? Who is considered gifted? What kinds of gifts are recognized or valued?
---How may giftedness present differently in the classroom from other gifted children?
-Using case studies and scenarios, facilitators should present information and have participants reflect on real-word examples, making connections to students in the classroom. Provide time for discussion and sharing opportunities.
-Facilitators should provide opportunities for job-embedded operationalization of the professional learning: have PLC 1 & 2 educators to discuss their current students' profiles, and make connections to the Zone 1 & 2 content.

Differentiation for Zone 2 is based on the level of cultural awareness and equity knowledge the PLCs demonstrated after Zone 1. For example, the facilitator differentiates the case studies, scenarios, discussion questions, and reflective prompts, mirroring the appropriate level of proximal development of the educators, allowing for their growth.</td><td>-Group members share the Zone 2 facilitation role with support from the main facilitator.
-Primary Facilitator provides supplemental knowledge through multiple modalities to extend PLC members' knowledge on giftedness, equity, and/or traditionally marginalized gifted populations based on the pre-assessment. PLC debriefs with facilitator in small groups or one-on-one depending on numbers.
-Primary facilitator provides opportunities for PLC 3 educators to discuss their current students' profiles, and make connections to the Zone 3 content to ensure they are connecting with new content and extending their knowledge.</td></tr>
<tr><td colspan="3">Throughout, provide time for self-reflective journaling prompts, discussions, and debriefs.</td></tr>
<tr><td colspan="3">Embedded Equity Driven Professional Learning Principles
Taking a Pulse, Individualizing Professional Learning Plans, Establishing a Safe Zone, Going Beyond the Tip of the Iceberg, Bridging the Gap between School and Home, Engaging in Courageous Conversations, Identifying Grows and Glows</td></tr>
</table>

Figure 5.1 Zone 2 in action: Sample planning chart for differentiated groups.

Brief Explanation of the Research Base

Culture influences all aspects of learning; therefore, it should be no surprise that giftedness does not look the same for all gifted learners. We've discussed this research in previous chapters. Giftedness presents differently based on our lived experiences as well as our ethnic and cultural backgrounds. Sustained professional learning which targets "equitable identification and assessment instruments, policies, and procedures; affective development; cultural development; curriculum and instruction; and services and programming for gifted students from all backgrounds"[2] is unequivocally essential for teachers of the gifted.

Teachers who have an education background in the field of gifted education, whether it is a certification or a degree, benefit from professional learning which has a specific focus on RCELD gifted learners,[3] as teachers may hold inaccurate beliefs about gifted characteristics,[4] particularly when asked to identify characteristics through a cultural or ethnic lens.[5] These beliefs often play a role in our recognition of RCELD gifted learners. Teachers have long been, and remain, significant gatekeepers to gifted programming through initial nominations and referrals or through secondary recommendations and checklists.[6] Zone 2 develops the foundational understanding of culturally responsive and equity-framed characteristics of gifted students. This targeted professional learning, therefore, provides potential growth points for educators to become more informed gatekeepers of gifted education, disrupting the pattern of inequities in the field.

Put it in Play

The first step in Zone 2 is to find out what your teachers already know (or think they know) about characteristics of gifted students. This is the *taking a pulse* principle—yes; again! We know, you just did that in the last zone, but cultural and equity awareness are not the same as having translated that to gifted characteristics. There are several simple ways to do this outside of using a formal instrument. The Brain Dump option involves providing a blank sheet of paper and asking participants to write characteristics of giftedness. The Choice option involves providing participants a list of 'generic' and culturally inclusive gifted characteristics, then asking them to select all the gifted characteristics. The benefit here is that it becomes a limited choice, which may highlight knowledge more effectively than a blank slate since the empty piece of paper can be frightening. These options and more are explained in further detail in the Playbook at the end of Chapter 5—but you get the point... *take a pulse!*

From our experiences, the initial review of gifted characteristics is often an eye-opening experience. If you are from a state which mandates teacher training for teachers of the gifted, then your teachers are likely to feel confident in their ability to identify gifted characteristics. As a result, you may likely face some opposition as you work to shift their mindsets while discussing gifted characteristics through an equity lens. If you are from a state where there is no required teacher training for gifted education, then you may have more legwork to put in overall, but sometimes it is a bit easier to develop teachers' foundational knowledge of giftedness while seamlessly integrating knowledge of diverse populations through an equity lens.

After establishing the starting ground, you are ready to start exploring the impact that ethnicity, culture, and equity have on the manifestation of gifted potential and characteristics. If you have multiple cultural groups to explore, we recommend diving deep into one group at a time. Like Zone 1, where we used children's literature to start the conversation, here in Zone 2, literature, case studies, or scenario-based modes of learning are fantastic ways to begin the conversation. Remember that you took a pulse for a reason! Using that data to create *individualized learning plans* (perhaps two or three groups depending on the size of the cohort) is an important step so that your entire group makes measurable growth from their starting pulse point. Accurate, meaningful, and intentional content is essential to the individualized learning plans and successful professional learning; essential content needed to increase educators' understanding of characteristics of gifted marginalized students is included in Figure 5.2.

Z2 Essential Content	Brief Explanation	Playbook Activities
What does giftedness look like?	Zone 2 starts by exploring the teachers' understanding of gifted and talented. Depending on your audience's background knowledge as determined by the *Taking the Pulse* survey, you may need to begin with an introduction to giftedness-characteristics, behaviors, what it means to be gifted, social-emotional.	Taking a Pulse Giftedness Jigsaw Think-Pair-Share Mythbusters
How do systemic inequities affect gifted students' educational experiences?	The history of segregated schooling has impacted students of color long after Brown v. Board of education, creating racialized tracking systems that perpetuate academic worlds of have and have nots, and colorized boundary lines for schools that enable funding systems that are separate and very much separate and unequal in modern day schooling. Not all marginalized student populations experience poverty, but understanding the role poverty plays in creating inequities is essential to serving gifted learners.	District Data Equity Case Study Hexagonal Thinking Activity: Equity Understanding the Culture of White Supremacy
What does giftedness look like across cultures? How does color evasiveness prohibit teachers from recognizing giftedness?	Zone 2 narrows the focus into exploring how giftedness presents in marginalized student populations. Essential content for **Z2 should zero in on the specific student population within your district.** The resources are provided for the following populations: ● Native American ● Hispanic ● African American ● Asian American?	Taking a Pulse Myth or Fact Sort **Identification Scenarios** Gallery Walk **Identification Case Study** Connecting to Current **Profiles**

Figure 5.2 Essential content: Z2 increasing educators' understanding of characteristics of gifted marginalized students.

Cautions and Caveats

- **You don't need to be the expert of all things.** Remember, as the facilitator (and participant!), it is okay not to be the expert of all things... but it is not okay not to find out the answers. The facilitator may need to invest some preparation time prior to the PL and seek out content-area experts. Remember that community members are the community experts. Don't rely solely on the peer-reviewed journals and forget the peers in front of you! Similarly, participants should be reminded that just like in the classroom, we all have our specialization areas—so just like with the curriculum, we should be willing and open to learning new things.
- **Establish a solid foundation.** Building a solid understanding of cultural groups in Zone 1 prepares the educator to be receptive to learning in Zone 2. Investing the time in Zone 1 is crucial.
- **Train your weakness.** It is okay to double back to Zone 1 if the facilitator or participant recognizes an area of cultural understanding that needs to be explored in greater depth. This is an iterative process; there is no point of no return!
- **Equity for gifted checkpoint.** Recognizing the different ways giftedness presents is only the starting point; the training journey continues into Zones 3 and 4, in which the strategies for retention and support are addressed. Remember that equity needs to be a focus, not just the cultural aspects. Make sure you are taking time to focus on the broader picture, not just the tip of the iceberg!
- **Change the talent identification process.** As the facilitator and participants explore the full spectrum of gifted characteristics, you may find that there is a disconnect between what the teachers know to be RCELD giftedness, and the identification policy measures. Hopefully, this will open a door for a conversation about changing the identification practices as well as strategies for frontloading (see Zone 3). This model itself focuses on professional learning (yeah, it's in the name!) but we don't need to stop there. Remember, the goal is overall systemic and structural change in our spheres of influence. When we identify a mismatch, how can we affect change? What steps can we take? Who do we talk to? What do we do? What processes do we enact to make this equitable? Don't stop at the PL, model the change. Be the change. Empower the participants to be change agents.

Resources

Gifted Survey Resources

- Gifted Pedagogy and Practices Scale, https://osf.io/dmy7e/
- Gifted Education Self-Efficacy Scale for Teachers, https://dergipark.org.tr/en/pub/jegys/issue/37434/432949
- Culturally Responsive Pedagogy (CRP) Self-Assessment, https://dueeast.org/wp-content/uploads/Culturally-Responsive-Pedagogy-CRP-Self-assessment.pdf *not gifted specific but very well written, includes a differentiation section, and has reflection questions

Disproportionality and Risk Ratios

- IDEA Part B Regulations Significant Disproportionality (Equity in IDEA), https://sites.ed.gov/idea/files/significant-disproportionality-qa-03-08-17-1.pdf
- Disproportionality Calculation Methodologies, https://spptap.org/wp-content/uploads/2020/03/Enc-2-Calculation-Methodologies-.docx#:~:text=Local%20Educational%20Agency%20Risk%20Ratio,the%20LEA%20(comparison%20group).
- The Other Segregation, https://www.theatlantic.com/education/archive/2019/04/gifted-and-talented-programs-separate-students-race/587614/

Resources about Giftedness Across Cultural and Ethnic Groups

- *Exploring Critical Issues in Gifted Education: A Case Studies Approach* by Christine L. Weber, Cecilia Boswell, and Wendy Behrens
- Identifying and Teaching Gifted Native American Students by Tamara Fisher, http://blogs.edweek.org/teachers/unwrapping_the_gifted/2008/01/identifying_and_teaching_gifte.html
- Understanding, Identifying, and Meeting the Needs of Gifted Native American Students by Tamara Fisher, http://blogs.edweek.org/teachers/unwrapping_the_gifted/upload/2008/01/2008-01-07%20Identifying%20and%20Teaching%20Gifted%20Native%20American%20Students.pdf
- *Case Studies on Diversity and Social Justice Education* by Paul C. Gorski and Seema G. Pothini
- Understanding, Identifying, and Meeting the Needs of Gifted Native American Students by Tamara Fisher, http://bit.ly/NAANIPTFA

- How Oklahoma's Identification of Gifted Native Students Could Serve as a National Model, article with audio interview by Robby Korth, http://n.pr/3tMDQUZ
- Black and Gifted in Rural America: Barriers and Facilitators to Accessing Gifted and Talented Education Programs, https://tpre.ecu.edu/index.php/tpre/article/view/736/68
- Why do Fewer Black Students Get Identified as Gifted? https://digitalpromise.org/2018/09/18/fewer-black-students-get-identified-gifted/
- Nurturing Gifted African American Children, https://www.nagc.org/sites/default/files/Parent%20CK/NAGC-TIP%20Sheet-Nurturing%20Gifted%20African%20American%20Children.pdf
- Ford's Female Achievement Model for Excellence, https://www.drdonnayford.com/black-females
- Whiting's Scholar Identity Model, https://www.drdonnayford.com/services3
- Bilingual Gifted Students, How can we better identify them? https://www.region10.org/r10website/assets/File/GTBilingual%20Students-Better%20Identification.pdf
- Attributes of Hispanic Gifted Bilingual Students as Perceived by Bilingual Educators in Texas, https://ncela.ed.gov/files/rcd/BE021128/Attributes_of_Hispanic_Gifted.pdf
- Hispanic Bilingual Gifted Screening Instrument, http://www.teachbilingual.com/product.cfm
- Tip Study Finds Using Local Criteria Identifies More Students as "Gifted," https://today.duke.edu/2019/08/tip-finds-local-criteria-identify-more-students-gifted
- Gifted Asian American Adolescent Males: Portraits of Cultural Dilemmas, https://files.eric.ed.gov/fulltext/EJ750763.pdf
- Asian American Gifted Students-Take a Closer Look, https://www.educationworld.com/content/asian-american-gifted-students-take-closer-look
- How The Model Minority Myth Divides Communities Of Color, https://givingcompass.org/article/how-the-model-minority-myth-divides-communities-of-color/?gclid=CjwKCAjw49qKBhAoEiwAHQVTowPoC-iW9PH_jEfgPqdgdvivf8_7wauXvlu4wBXfdmOE6N_7kWBvvRoCWhAQAvD_BwE

Professional Learning Playbook

Look for the Guiding Principle Icons by the playbook activities!

1) Taking a Pulse
2) Individualizing Professional Learning Plans 
3) Establishing a Safe Zone
4) Going Beyond the Tip of the Iceberg 
5) Engaging in Courageous Conversations 
6) Bridging the Gap between School and Home 
7) Identifying Grows and Glows 

Activity 1: Take a Pulse!

Estimated Time: 20–30 minutes administration; 20–30 minutes analysis and 'what's next decision-making'

Materials Needed: Instrument of choice (see Resources section)

Delivery Format: Digital or In Person

Seven Guiding Principles Addressed:

Purpose: To gauge participants' current levels of understanding of the professional learning objectives to plan effectively and with the participants in mind; use of pre-PL measures have the benefit of potentially measuring growth when also used as post-PL measures at least two weeks apart.

Procedure:

★ Administer a pre-assessment to gather information about the participants' current understandings of giftedness, including culturally and equity-related manifestations of giftedness. We recommend this take place prior to the planned PL (a week or two ahead of time) to give you time to disaggregate the data and plan.

★ Break down the results of the assessment (disaggregate the data) and look for trends. Be sure to note if participants need background knowledge in gifted characteristics in general; if they would benefit from more specific targeted knowledge in racially, culturally, ethnically, and linguistically diverse gifted students, and inequities in gifted education; or if they need the whole slate.

★ Your entire participant group may not have the same knowledge base—you may find that two or three groups naturally emerge from your data. Or perhaps only one significant group and two or three individual outliers. This is where we go back to our 'just like the kiddos' line… every participant has the right to be challenged, to learn something new, every day. That's true for PL, too! That's where differentiated PL and the individualized learning plans come in. So now you have taken that data and adjusted your plans, what are you going to do during the PL, how will you adjust the content based on what the participants know and want to know, but also, how will you adjust groupings?

Variations:

★ The Resources section has a few survey options.

★ Earlier in the chapter, we suggested activity options—the Brain Dump *vs.* Choice. These are written as individual activities. If you do not have the opportunity to *take the pulse* prior to the PL experience, these can be opening individual or group activities. We recommend having an overstacked set of slides or two or three decks to choose from so that you have several different options already planned and ready to go, based on how the participants respond to the opening activity.

Extension:

Repeat the opening assessment after the PL experience, ideally allowing at least two weeks to pass between assessments. To ensure confidentiality, ask participants to provide a random ID used to match their pre-test with their post-test. This can be something simple like the two-digit birth month and the last four digits of their cellphone number; something that is simple, not likely to be duplicated among the sample, and that will stay the same between the two data collection points. Analyze the data and compare the pre- to the post-test for growth.

Activity 2: Giftedness Jigsaw

Estimated Time: 30 minutes

Materials Needed: NAGC Definition of Giftedness https://www.nagc.org/sites/default/files/Position%20Statement/Definition%20of%20Giftedness%20%282019%29.pdf printouts or links, group space, breakout rooms (online)

Delivery Format: Digital or In Person

Seven Guiding Principles Addressed: 

Purpose: The purpose of this activity is to provide a foundational understanding of the nature and needs of gifted learners. While this 30-minute activity is only the starting point of learning about gifted learners, it does provide a good overview of 'what is giftedness?' The facilitator should plan on providing further PL to expand on these key ideas, whether it is embedded throughout the 4ZEPL sessions or provided as a supplemental PL.

Procedure:

- ★ Begin with a jigsaw activity of the NAGC Position Statement: A Definition of Giftedness that Guides Best Practice. A jigsaw involves starting participants with a home group, then moving to expert groups to learn content, and then moving back to home groups for a final discussion. In the home group, they have a problem or task to solve.
- ★ For this jigsaw, participants will focus on answering the question: In what ways does the NAGC position statement reflect the current gifted education policy and programming in the district? Jigsaws begin with a few minutes in the home groups for an initial discussion of the problem.

★ Assign one (or more) members of each home group to an expert group, making sure that every home group has one member going to each expert group. Assign each expert group one of the five key points from the NAGC Position Statement: A Definition of Giftedness that Guides Best Practice (e.g., gifted students come from all racial, ethnic, and cultural populations, as well as all economic strata).

★ Within the expert groups, participants should unpack the statement and be prepared to share out with their home groups. They should share text-to-text or text-to-self connections and relate the NAGC position statement with the current policy and programs in the district. Provide ten minutes in the expert groups.

★ Return to the home groups. Instruct the participants that they are not simply reporting out their content, but sharing the content in a way that applies it to the original question at hand: In what ways does the NAGC position statement reflect the current gifted education policy and programming in the district? If participants are unfamiliar with the gifted education policy and program, then access to these documents should be provided for review. Provide 15 minutes for the final home group.

Modifications: If the participants have no background knowledge of gifted education, the facilitator will need to consider addressing all the core areas of GT, e.g., identification, assessment, instruction, social-emotional. Most of this content is embedded throughout the 4ZEPL; however, the facilitator should be prepared to spend additional time to fill in any knowledge gaps. In some ways, it will be easier to focus on equity with a group of gifted educators without prior knowledge as we can sometimes get stuck in the 'but this is how I have also done it' mentality.

Activity 3: Myth or Fact Sorting Activity

Estimated Time: 10–15 minutes

Materials Needed: Reproducible 5.1: Myth or Fact Gifted Characteristics Sort

Delivery Format: Digital or In Person

Seven Guiding Principles Addressed: 

Purpose: The purpose of this activity is to identify the misconceptions about gifted characteristics and marginalized student populations. The activity can be utilized as a pre/post assessment tool, or anticipatory activity.

Procedure:

- ★ The facilitator will share the myth or fact sort activity with the participants.
- ★ Participants will identify the myths/facts.
- ★ Facilitator will guide a discussion where myths are dispelled. This sort of activity should be the beginning of a longer PL session related to the particular diverse student population in your district.
- ★ The activity could also serve as a post-assessment of the PL session.

Activity 4: Identification Case Study

Estimated Time: 20–25 minutes

Materials Needed: Reproducible 5.2: Identification Case Study

Delivery Format: Digital or In Person

Seven Guiding Principles Addressed: 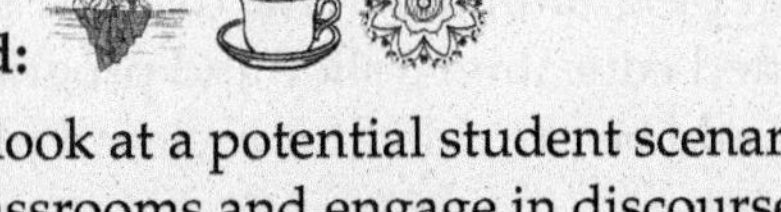

Purpose: This activity helps teachers look at a potential student scenario which they may encounter in their classrooms and engage in discourse about whether to refer the student for further evaluation for identification. After participants decide to refer or not to refer, they are presented with two potential outcomes based on the result of their decision. These conversations will help participants apply their new understandings of the impact of culture, color-evasiveness, and systemic racism on the presentation of giftedness in a realistic situation.

Procedure:

- ★ Provide the participants a copy of the student scenario and have them work in groups to decide whether they would refer the student for further evaluation. In their groups, they should discuss reasons for or against the referral.
- ★ Based on the decision of the group, the facilitator should share Doorway #1 or Doorway #2 and lead a discussion on the results of the decision to refer/not to refer.
- ★ Then, the facilitator should share the second doorway option and discuss how the student outcome may be altered with a different approach.
- ★ Guide the conversation back to the teachers' current students and possible scenarios. Discuss what other outcomes may have occurred based on input from the parents, teachers, or students.

Activity 5: District Data

Estimated Time: 30–45 minutes

Materials Needed: Access to district data, Access Denied report \h https://www.education.purdue.edu/geri/new-publications/gifted-education-in-the-united-states/) with data pulled from the individual state, copies for each group; optional: pencils, pens, highlighters

Delivery Format: Digital or In Person

Seven Guiding Principles Addressed: 

Purpose: To examine data for individual districts and compare to state-level missingness data from the *Access Denied* report.

Procedure:

- ★ Facilitator should pull report for the state from https://www.education.purdue.edu/geri/new-publications/gifted-education-in-the-united-states/
- ★ Facilitator should become familiar with the terms used in *Access Denied* (see the Executive Summary https://www.dropbox.com/s/d6u13umiv7a8i6y/Access%20Denied%20Executive%20Summary.pdf
- ★ Prior to the PL experience, determine how the groups will access the data: Will they be pulling data? Will it be provided? Will they be collating or disaggregating data or will everything be provided?
- ★ The essence of this activity is to compare the district-level data to the state-level data provided in *Access Denied*, which was completed using data from the Office of Civil Rights (OCR), which is federal data. Teachers may think "but we don't have that issue here" or "that's a 'them' problem." The goal is to dig into the data and see what the numbers are in this space and place.
- ★ One statistic that is fairly easy to calculate with a calculator is a Risk Ratio (RR). This is found by dividing the 'risk' of one outcome for children in one ethnicity by the 'risk' of that same outcome for children in all other ethnicities (the comparison group). A risk ratio of 1.0 is proportional, while RR of 2.0 means that a child is twice as likely to be identified than those of other ethnic groups and a RR of 0.5 means that this is an area of underrepresentation, and this ethnic group is half as likely to be represented in gifted programs. The formula is: ((Gifted Black Students ÷ All Black Students) × 100) ÷ ((All Gifted Students ÷ All Students) × 100) = Risk Ratio

Activity 6: Equity Case Study: (Racist) Terms of Endearment

Estimated Time: 30–45 minutes (depending on role play)

Materials Needed: Overhead or shareable copy of the Gorski and Pothini case study, http://www.edchange.org/cases/Terms-of-Endearment.pdf

Delivery Format: Digital or In Person

Seven Guiding Principles Addressed: 

Purpose: To discuss and role play a real-life situation in which racism occurs in gifted classrooms.

Procedure:

- ★ Facilitator should thoroughly review Gorski and Pothini's equity case study and present it to the PLC as a case study for discussion. The case study is not written for a gifted classroom, but a simple gifted twist is that it is an honors or gifted Math classroom.
- ★ After a discussion of the provided case study questions, extend Question 4 (how would you approach the situation) into role playing. Note that there are several key factors: (a) stopping the racist action and the excuses for the racist action, (b) checking in on Reggie, who is increasingly uncomfortable in the situation, and (c) checking in on Keisha, who was pointing out racist behavior and chastised for her reaction to the racist behavior. You may choose to role play the strategies in isolation, but if so, emphasize that addressing these factors are not 'either/or' but 'both/and.'

Activity 7: Connecting to Current Profiles

Estimated Time: 20 minutes

Materials Needed: Follow-up activity, use this in tandem with another activity of choice

Delivery Format: Digital or In Person

Seven Guiding Principles Addressed: 

Purpose: To provide opportunities for job-embedded operationalization of the professional learning through discussions of current students' profiles.

Procedure:

An important aspect of effective PL is authentic transfer of learning—the chance for educators to put their learning into practice in an environment that is useful and practical. We both loved 'Make it Take it' PD sign-ups as early career teachers in the Virginia Public School district where we both taught. Why? Because we went for an hour, and instead of sitting and listening to someone talk, we got to do something *crafty* that we could use the next day or week! And of course, it checked off one of our many required hours. *Score!* There are no crafts in this activity, much to our 22-year-old selves' chagrin, but the job-embeddedness is there.

- ★ This activity builds off several of the other activities, with the key being to connect the work to students in the gifted program, identification profiles, or students in class. Of note, Giftedness Jigsaw, Myth or Fact Sort, Identification Case Study, Myth Busters, and the Identification Scenarios Gallery Walk all lend themselves to Connecting to Current Profiles as an add-on activity.
- ★ Using specific profiles or data—ideally student portfolios if those are available—use examples from the student body to foster connections and deepen understandings with the material. When needed, based on confidentiality, names can be redacted, but generally PLCs are within schools, so this method is a powerful tool to use to transfer the hypothetical learning to real students at hand. Facilitators should stay close at hand to listen for *safe and brave spaces*, ensure that dynamic rather than deficit thinking is expressed, and that the application of the content is accurate.

Activity 8: Myth Busters

Estimated Time: 30 minutes

Materials Needed: Myth Busters video https://www.youtube.com/watch?v=MDJst-y_ptI (8 minutes), copies of Myths article from NAGC https://www.nagc.org/myths-about-gifted-students for groups; chart paper, markers or computers with internet access and jamboard/padlet

Delivery Format: Digital or In Person

Seven Guiding Principles Addressed: 

Purpose: To recognize the popularized myths and stereotypes about gifted education and gifted learners and understand the literature behind the truth.

Procedure:

- ★ Start by showing the eight-minute Myth Busters clip. Explain that this clip was created by students in a Maryland school.
- ★ Provide copies of the NAGC myths article to the groups. Explain that marketing research tells us that if we write the myths, that's what people will remember—so instead of writing about the "myths," the

goal of the PL experience today is to reformulate the article into a list of "truths" about gifted education and gifted learners.

- ★ Provide participants 10–15 minutes to create a Top Ten list—these can be from reworking items from the video or article, or knowledge from a previous PL session (suggestion: provide ten minutes, check in at seven minutes, and decide at that point if you need to give them extended time beyond the three minutes). Most of these involve rewriting, so typically this activity doesn't take long; it depends on how much debate/discussion the groups put into the activity.
- ★ Have the Top Ten lists posted around the room (or on padlet/jamboards—the online posting can be done even with an in-person facilitation—save some trees!) Have the groups review others' work and reflect a bit on similarities/differences. Allow a few minutes for discussion based on what they see/notice/wonder about the posted lists.
- ★ Ask: Why do these myths and stereotypes exist? Why are they pervasive? How can they be broken?
- ★ Follow Up: What role does the media/television/movies/books have in perpetuating myths and stereotypes?

Activity 9: Understanding the Culture of White Supremacy

Estimated Time: 45 minutes

Materials Needed: Copies of White Supremacy Culture for each group https://www.dismantlingracism.org/uploads/4/3/5/7/43579015/okun_-_white_sup_culture.pdf, Reproducible 5.5: Personal Commitment, copies for each participant (note: there are two per page)

Delivery Format: Digital or In Person

Seven Guiding Principles Addressed: 

Purpose: The purpose of this activity is to unpack the meaning of White supremacy culture—what it is and what it is not—as well as to make connections to the field of education. Participants will explore possible impacts of this culture on gifted education, programming, and policy.

Procedure:

- ★ This is another jigsaw activity, like the NAGC Position Statement: A Definition of Giftedness that Guides Best Practice but using the characteristics of the White Supremacy Culture article. Start the jigsaw with home groups, then moving to expert groups to learn content, and then moving back to home groups for a final discussion. In the home group, participants have a problem or task to solve.

★ Jigsaws begin with a few minutes in the home groups for an initial discussion of the focus question: In what ways do the characteristics of White supremacy culture impact equity and access in gifted education?
★ Assign one (or more) members of each home group to an expert group, making sure that every home group has one member going to each expert group. Depending on numbers, assign each expert group two or three of the characteristics of White supremacy culture: perfectionism, sense of urgency, defensiveness, quantity over quality, worship of the written word, only one right way, paternalism, either/or thinking, power hoarding, fear of open conflict, individualism, I'm the only one, progress is bigger/more, objectivity, and right to comfort.
★ Within the expert groups, participants should unpack the statement and be prepared to share out with their home groups. They should share text-to-text or text-to-self connections and relate the characteristics of White supremacy culture with the current policy and programs in the district. Provide 15 minutes in the expert groups.
★ Return to the home groups. Instruct the participants that they are not simply reporting out their content, but sharing the content in a way that applies it to the original question at hand: In what ways do the characteristics of White supremacy culture impact equity and access in gifted education? If participants are unfamiliar with the gifted education policy and program, then access to these documents should be provided for review. In the final home groups, participants should also discuss: In what ways can the antidotes support equity and access to gifted education? Provide 20 minutes for the final home group.
★ After the final home group, allow time for sharing out.
★ Provide a copy of Reproducible 5.5 (one half-sheet per person) to participants, asking participants to fill out their name and school/workplace in the first two blanks. In the third blank "As a ____," participants write their racial/ethnic identity, followed by a characteristic of White supremacy that the participant commits to addressing. In the next set of blanks, participants use the antidotes that they have learned about, and choose which antidotes that they will use to address the characteristic of White supremacy they have chosen to address (participants can use the information provided in the article to complete these blanks). There are sentence starters for the final two lines: "I believe this is important because," and "I believe I can make an impact in my sphere of influence through." Have participants take their personal commitments with them but encourage them to share/post in a public place—ideally these are not secretive but points of honor that your school is working toward together.

Activity 10: Think-Pair-Share

Estimated Time: 5–10 minutes

Materials Needed: None

Delivery Format: Digital or In Person

Seven Guiding Principles Addressed: 

Purpose: This flexible strategy is a great way to allow participants to reflect on a question, prompt, or new concept prior to engaging in discourse with their peers, while at the same time allowing an opportunity for conversation during the pair moment so that everyone gets an opportunity to bounce ideas off and receive feedback on their current thoughts. The strategy allows everyone an opportunity to share out without having to go person to person. The last step is the sharing step, which is adaptable to either one representative per group or jotting the thoughts down on a shared thought board.

Procedure:

- ★ The facilitator poses the question/prompt to the participants and allows a few minutes for everyone to reflect on the question and write down their thoughts.
- ★ After a few minutes, the facilitator directs the participants to turn and talk to their neighbor or group members sharing out their thoughts and engaging in a meaningful discussion. The facilitator should circulate during this time.

Modification:

Jot/Sketch-Pair-Share—Have you ever gotten to the sharing part, and you couldn't remember the original thought you had? Angela likes to use Jot-Pair-Share when working with students and teachers alike. It's the same except the thinking step is a jotting or sketching step, in which thoughts are written down, or sketched, in a formal sketch notes style, or just generally "sketched" using a combination of words, pictures, and phrases.

Activity 11: Identification Scenarios Gallery Walk

Estimated Time: 10–30 minutes

Materials Needed: Case studies on Reproducible 5.2: Identification Case Study

Delivery Format: Digital or In Person

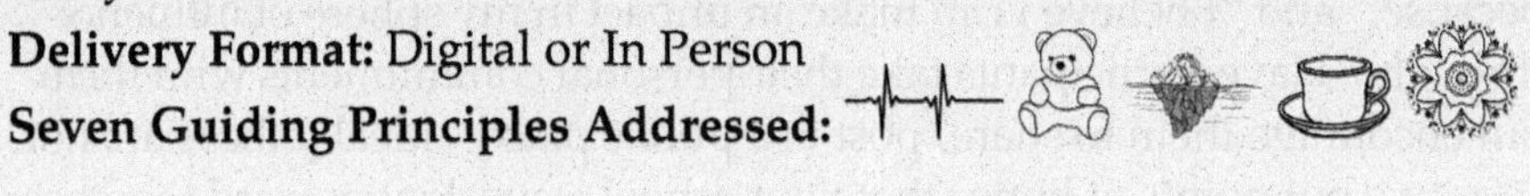
Seven Guiding Principles Addressed:

Purpose: The use of scenarios provides an opportunity to explore realistic student situations where gifted characteristics and behaviors may be overlooked due to misunderstandings—created either by the lack of teacher knowledge or potential bias. Scenarios can be used as an anticipatory activity, post activity, or even the main activity when accompanied by scaffolded questions.

Procedure:

★ Determine the purpose of using the scenario prior to designing the activity and align your PL content to the scenario. Scenarios can be implemented in a variety of ways: pre-assessment, post-assessment, breakout group activities, and more! In general, select high quality scenarios. When you are just getting started using full case studies, it is often easier to use those that are ready made.

★ For this activity, put the scenarios around the room, as a gallery walk. Note that the scenarios reflect characteristics of bilingual and BIPOC gifted students, but do not share with the participants that these students are gifted/should be referred at the outset- the purpose of the activity is for them to discuss and discover this throughout their conversations and receiving the information in Step 3.

★ Step 1: For the first walk through, have participants walk through with an initial reaction. Ask them to write their thoughts on a sticky note (it's up to you—have these private or collect them—if you collect them, we recommend having a folder or envelope at that gallery station to collect the initial thoughts). The question on the table is: Should this child be referred for gifted services? Note, this is not the same as: Is this child exhibiting gifted behaviors? Something that individuals may ask to unpack, depending on where you are in the training. Encourage the participants to make their own decisions as to what this means based on their best judgement.

★ After the initial gallery walk, discuss the definition of giftedness in the district manual or policy and go over the identification criteria. If your individual district doesn't have a definition and/or criteria, refer to state level policy, and then to national policy (for a definition). This is a good time to clarify the gifted behaviors vs. identified for gifted services conundrum that may be on many educators' minds. There are many conceptions of giftedness, but to achieve internal consistency of a program, we need to identify for the program that we are providing for our students (see Zone 3 for additional support).

★ Step 2: Provide time for a second gallery walk. Once again, the question on the table is: Should this child be referred for gifted services? Participants may alter their opinion if they choose. On this round, again using sticky notes, teachers can write questions that they have about the student scenarios. What is the unknown information, based on the identification protocol in the district? What assumptions can they make, based on the district protocol and known information about the student regarding gifted referral/identification?

★ Step 3: The facilitator should now provide information regarding characteristics of bilingual and BIPOC gifted children, making sure that this information is inclusive, culturally responsive, and equity informed. Ensure that the information provided reflects these characteristics.
★ Step 4: Allow time for one final gallery walk, again, offering an opportunity for posting questions, responding to earlier questions that the participants asked (themselves or they might respond to a peer's question). Ask them, one more time, if they would refer the student for gifted services. If these thoughts were collected earlier, collect them again (for a pre-post measure) or if they were kept private, ask participants to write their current thoughts near their previous answer in their journals to reflect on their earlier response. Was it different? The same? If it was the same, were the reasons the same?
★ Guide the participants through a conversation reflecting on the information shared and the process of the scenarios. Encourage participants to make text-to-text, and text-to-self connections by drawing their new understandings to their current classrooms. Ask participants to share their thoughts on the referrals of the students.
★ Modification: If you are training a group of gifted teachers or facilitators that likely already know the district's gifted definition and identification policies, Step 1 should be omitted.

Activity 12: Hexagonal Thinking Activity: Equity

Estimated Time: 25–30 minutes

Materials Needed: Hexagonal Thinking Cards (copies of Reproducible 5.4: Hexagonal Thinking: Equity, scissors, envelopes, or paper clips to keep materials together for groups)

Delivery Format: In Person (to modify for digital, you can use google slides to recreate the activity, following these directions: https://youtu.be/6BSxQepDY7k)

Seven Guiding Principles Addressed:

Purpose: The Hexagonal Thinking activity comes from a strategy of Stern et al.[7] in their book *Learning that Transfers*. This activity helps the learner manipulate concept cards as a visual way to see how different concepts are related. A hexagon has six sides, which means the concept could have multiple connections, while at the same time limiting the repetition of the connections.

Procedure:

- ★ This activity works well in a group as the participants can share their thought process. However, it could also be completed independently, if necessary.
- ★ Share the hexagon cards with your participants and ask them to sort the cards according to the relationships between the concepts. The arrows are used to point out 5 meaningful connections across the 12 cards. These five connections will be shared out at the end of the group work (or individual reflection) time. An overarching question to guide the discussion should be posted in the room: How do structural inequities in society contribute to inequities in gifted education?
- ★ Note that none of the cards are specific to gifted education—that is intentional. The goal is to make the connections. None of the cards reference teacher recommendations, testing, bias—all the typical reasons we list for underrepresentation. In this activity, we are looking at the broader picture, that is, that these are symptoms of the problem: systemic and structural racism.

Reproducibles

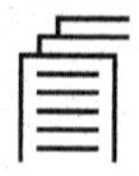

Reproducible 5.1: Myth or Fact Gifted Characteristics Sort

Directions: Share the left column with the participants and have them sort the cards into either myth or fact columns.

Myth or Fact? Gifted children are always asking questions in the classroom.	**Myth:** Some gifted children are observers first and ask questions at a later time. It is a sign of respect in some cultures to observe, watch, and listen—rather than immediately asking questions.
Myth or Fact? Gifted children are the leaders in the classroom.	**Myth:** In collective societies, it is more about teamwork and working together, than being the leader. Gifted children may choose to work together as a team, sharing their ideas as part of the group, rather than taking charge. Similarly, in some cultures, females defer to males. Gifted girls may defer to the males in the group as part of their cultural characteristics.
Myth or Fact? Gifted children are naturally curious.	**Fact:** Gifted minds tend to be quite curious! How they showcase that curiosity may vary greatly. Their expressions and manifestations of curiosity may not be what you'd expect.
Myth or Fact? Gifted children are always early readers with an advanced vocabulary.	**Myth:** While this is true of many gifted children, students who are English language learners may struggle with their reading and vocabulary. These students should be assessed in their native language. Alternatively, a child may be gifted in ways other than verbally/linguistically.

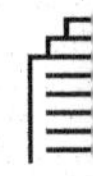

Reproducible 5.2: Identification Case Study

Sylvia, a six-year-old, was born in Nuevo Laredo and had been taken care of by her maternal grandparents for most of her life. Her grandparents volunteered to raise Sylvia so that the parents were able to come to the United States to finish graduate school. During this time, Sylvia only spoke in Spanish and did not attend a formal school. Shortly after her parents' graduation from school, they decided to have Sylvia come and live with them in the United States. Her parents registered her for school shortly after her arrival in mid-October of her first-grade year. Sylvia's language proficiency was evaluated, and she was placed into an English Language Development program as an emergent English language learner.

During the first month of school, Sylvia rarely interacted with her peers and when she did, it was usually to ask a question. Her first-grade teacher, Ms. Smith frequently observed Sylvia being unable to perform most of the tasks that were assigned, unless it was a group assignment. A month after starting school, the ESL teacher remarked to Ms. Smith that she was shocked at how quickly Sylvia was picking up the English language. Ms. Smith and the ESL teacher engaged in conversation and wondered if Sylvia was potentially a gifted child. Ms. Smith was not sure as she didn't feel Sylva showed any initiative and was very dependent on her peers during assignments. Ms. Smith felt that it was puzzling how quickly the girl was learning English. Ms. Smith pulled her math benchmark tests, which as a whole, were not impressive, yet the straight computation section was perfect. At the end of Sylvia's first month in school, Ms. Smith held a parent conference, during which time she expressed the concerns that she had about Sylvia's poor academic progress. At the meeting, Sylvia's parents told the teacher that she was very talkative now in English and enjoyed the Saturday trips to the local science museum. They said that Sylvia had recently developed an interest in monarch butterflies, so much so, she had checked all the books in the library and was reading them nightly and had even colored a map of the monarch migration path going past her grandparents' home in Nuevo Laredo. During the parent conference, Ms. Smith makes a recommendation for the next steps for Sylvia. As a teacher present during this conference, what would you recommend?

Doorway #1

During the parent conference, Ms. Smith focuses on the lack of social interaction and poor academic scores on benchmark exams. Ms. Smith explains to the parents that while Sylvia was picking up the English language quickly, it would be in Sylvia's best interest to continue in the ESL program for an extended period. Additionally, Ms. Smith expresses high levels of concern

over Sylvia's lack of social interaction and dependency on her peers. Her parents agree that she is a quiet child at home and preferred to work in the same room as them. At the suggestion of Ms. Smith, the parents agree to pursue a referral by the school psychologist, speech and language therapist, and special educator to determine if she had a disability. By the end of the first semester, Sylvia was diagnosed with a language disability, and began working with the special educator, ESL teacher, and the school counselor. Sylvia was frequently pulled out of the first-grade classroom for a variety of supports which the specialists believed were addressing her social, emotional, and academic needs. At the end of the school year, when the teachers meet, they recommend that Sylvia repeat first grade. Her parents agreed with this plan.

Doorway #2

Thinking a referral for gifted services might benefit Sylvia, Ms. Smith requests the ESL teacher and the gifted resource teacher join the meeting. As a team, the classroom teacher, ESL teacher, GT teacher, and parents discuss options for fostering Sylvia's growth. It is agreed upon that further evaluation should be completed to determine if Sylvia would be eligible for gifted services. By the end of her first term in first grade, Sylvia did not qualify for gifted services but was placed into a bridge program where the teachers could foster her critical thinking and problem-solving skills. Sylvia enjoyed working with the bridge program where she was able to explore more about Monarch butterflies. The ESL teacher continued to work with her to develop her English language proficiency skills. Over time, Mrs. Smith noticed an increase in Sylvia's confidence in the classroom as well as increased scores on her benchmark tests. At the end of the year, Mrs. Smith, the ESL teacher, the gifted resource teacher, and the parents met again to discuss Sylvia's progress. Everyone agreed that Sylvia should be reevaluated for gifted services in the fall.

Reproducible 5.3: Identification Scenarios

Directions: Read the student scenario and decide to refer or not to refer.

Shiloh

Shiloh lives with his grandmother on the reservation. He does not plan to pursue college, as he prefers to stay close and work with the elders. His standardized test scores are in the top 5% but between his attendance record and his performance in the classroom the teachers are considering retaining him. Shiloh seems to enjoy math class where he easily makes connections between mathematical concepts and calculates complex problems in his head. He stays after class to ask questions and learn more about concepts.

Elijah

Elijah's record indicates he ranges from high to average academic performance. He never turns in homework or the annual science fair project. Elijah is a happy child who enjoys humor. In the classroom, he likes to showcase his talents to his peers, which often results in disciplinary actions. He is curious about science, mathematics, and has asked his teacher if he could be part of the gifted program.

Maria

Recently, Maria emigrated with her family from Mexico. She is very quiet in class and does not volunteer to answer questions. She always turns in her assignments on time although she is frequently late to school. Typically, her work reflects a strong understanding of the content knowledge and creative ideas. Maria has repeatedly declined a position on the chess team because she takes care of her two younger siblings after school.

Alejandra

Alejandra is a bilingual student who is scoring well on standardized tests and average in the classroom assessments. She prefers to work in groups and will defer to a male student any leadership roles. She had perfect attendance for the first nine weeks but lately has missed several days. She apologized for absences but says that she is needed to help with her family.

Lorenzo

Lorenzo is a Spanish-speaking student with a solid school attendance record. He is interested in science and hopes to study biomechanics in college. He scores in the top 10% on his standardized tests, has As and Bs on his report

card but is currently failing English. He translates for his parents when they come to the school for conferences. Lorenzo works part time after school to help his parents pay the bills. He was recently offered a full-time job, but it would require him to drop out of school.

Oscar

Oscar is bilingual but still struggles with written English Language Arts skills and tasks. He often turns in incomplete writing assignments, with the explanation that he didn't have anything to say. Oscar enjoys oral storytelling and has created many of his own characters. He prefers to work in groups and talk ideas over with his peers. He often volunteers to be the group leader or the presenter.

Zuhey

Zuhey is interested in learning about animals. She speaks Spanish and is learning English. Her reading is below grade level, but her math is on level. She mostly struggles with word problems in math. She has already memorized sight words and is quickly developing her vocabulary. She enjoys coming to school to be with her peers especially on days when pizza is offered at lunch.

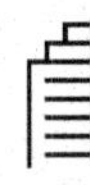

Reproducible 5.4: Hexagonal Thinking: Equity

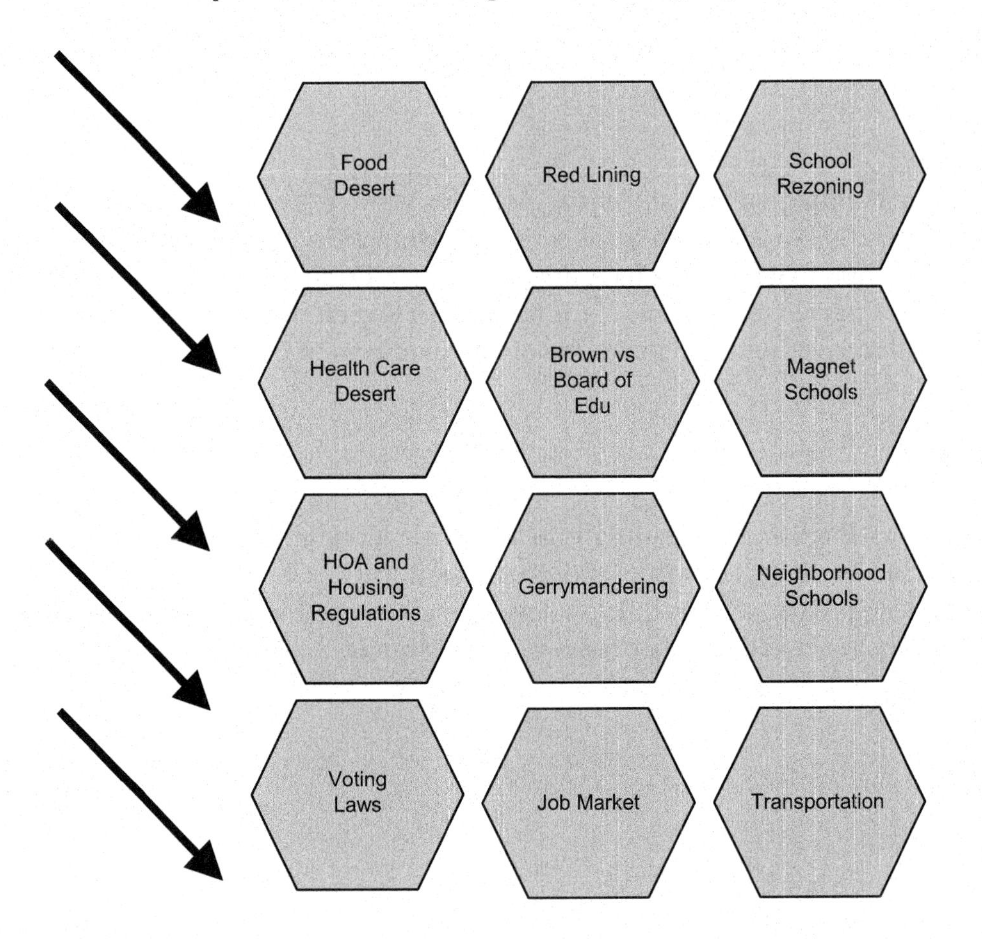

Reproducible 5.5: Personal Commitment

I, ____________________________, am committed to dismantling White supremacy in our community of ____.

As a _____________________, I commit to address the _____________________

____

characteristic of White supremacy culture by focusing on the antidote of ____

____.

I believe this is important because ____

____.

I believe I can make an impact in my sphere of influence through __________

____.

I, ____________________________, am committed to dismantling White supremacy in our community of ____.

As a ___________________________, I commit to address the ________________

____

characteristic of White supremacy culture by focusing on the antidote of ____

____.

I believe this is important because ____

____.

I believe I can make an impact in my sphere of influence through __________

____.

Notes

1 BBC News. (2008). 1968: Black athletes make silent protest. *BBC News. On this day.* http://news.bbc.co.uk/onthisday/hi/dates/stories/october/17/newsid_3535000/3535348.stm
2 Ford, D. Y. (2014). Segregation and the underrepresentation of Blacks and Hispanics in gifted education: Social inequality and deficit paradigms. *Roeper Review, 36*(3), 143–154. doi: 10.1080/02783193.2014.919563
3 Plunkett, M., & Kronborg, L. (2011). Learning to be a teacher of the gifted: The importance of examining opinions and challenging misconceptions. *Gifted and Talented International, 26*(1–2), 31–46. doi: 10.1080/15332276.2011.11673587
4 Baudson, T. G., & Preckel, F. (2013). Teachers' implicit personality theories about the gifted: An experimental approach. *School Psychology Quarterly, 28,* 37–46. doi: 10.1037/spq0000011
5 Lewis, K. D., Novak, A. M., & Coronado, J. (2015). Teachers' perceptions of characteristics of gifted Hispanic Bilingual students: Perspectives from the border. *Texas Forum of Teacher Education, 5,* 71–91.
6 Novak, A. M., & Jones, K. D. (2020). Gatekeepers in gifted: A case study of the disproportionality of gifted black youth in elementary program. *Journal of Cases in Educational Leadership,* 1–17. doi: 10.1177/1555458920976736
7 Stern, J., Lauriault, N., & Ferraro, K. (2017). *Tools for teaching conceptual understanding, elementary: Harnessing natural curiosity for learning that transfers.* Corwin.

6

Zone 3

Increasing Classroom Support for Educators and Gifted Marginalized Students

Michael Jordan is well known not just for his enigmatic smile and his talents on the basketball court, but for his inspirational words about persistence in the face of failure. He openly discusses his emotional tears when he didn't make his high school varsity team as a sophomore, and the 26 times he was trusted to take the game-winning shot and missed. Jordan states, "Obstacles don't have to stop you. If you run into a wall, don't turn around and give up. Figure out how to climb it, go through it, or work around it."[1] As educators, we need to take a critical view of the systems and structures in which we work. After Zone 2, we understand that they are perpetuating the oppression of students of color and creating barriers to their identification and participation in gifted programs. We need to take a note from MJ's playbook: as we're working for transformative change, meet our students' needs by climbing, going through, or working around the obstacles.

What's the Play?

Within Zone 3: Increasing Classroom Support for Educators and Gifted Marginalized Students, we turn our focus to the *now what* question. In Zone 1, we learned about equity and focused on cultural awareness and responsivity using a two-prong approach: Know Thyself and Know Others. Zone 2 followed with putting the knowledge of equity and culturally responsive teaching into play within the gifted context. *Now what?* Often districts focus on changing their identification practices with the end-goal of increasing

DOI: 10.4324/9781003196204-7

diversity amongst identified gifted students, and then when districts achieve more equity, they pat themselves on the back and perhaps move on. But that is just a starting point. They must also disrupt the inequities that exist: reform how gifted programming, curriculum and support systems are created and implemented so that the newly identified students are set up for success. The end goal is not identification; it is retention and student success. Zone 3's goal is to strategically train faculty to support students and fellow faculty members before, during, and after the identification process. Gifted learners need systemic sustenance as they move through K-12 education; this involves multiple layers of support from various stakeholders on the educational team.

First, we need to provide social support systems. Marginalized gifted students need peer and professional mentors with whom they can identify. Identity groups, peer support programs, and community mentor programs have been successful in gifted programs. For example, a bilingual Hispanic gifted learner can connect with other peers within the gifted program, research high profile, successful Hispanic professionals such as Sonya Sotomayor, and be matched with opportunities to work with local mentors on special interest projects. Goals and topics in professional learning include the facilitation of identity groups, developing community and mentor relationships, setting up mentor programs, and facilitating successful peer-support programs.

A second goal for gifted programs that can be achieved through professional learning is revamping the gifted curriculum to be more inclusive. For example, if your district identifies a high population of bilingual students, but the gifted curriculum is only offered in English, the program doesn't adequately represent or serve your student population. Zone 3 works to help districts and teachers find ways to support English language learners by modifying the curriculum. PL topics might include integrating the Ford-Harris/Bloom-Banks Matrix,[2] Black English as a language, and other strategies to ensure your curriculum is both equitable and equity-infused. It is key that this curricular support is seen as talent development and provided before, during, and after the identification process.

Finally, Zone 3 is professional learning support for educators of gifted students as they grow and develop as professionals. This support for teachers expands beyond just curriculum changes to include mentoring and advocacy-focused professional learning sessions. As a gifted teacher, often a sole practitioner in the building, how can you be a mentor to others? How can you model your teaching for others to learn? How can you advocate beyond your role? As a classroom teacher, how can you advocate for gifted learners?

Figure 6.1 is the Zone 3 section of the Sample Planning Chart for Differentiated Groups shared in Chapter 2, Figure 2.2. This section offers the third zone's outline of the differentiated PLCs based on the initial pulse-taking. The three PLCs are back in their three original groups in this zone.

PLC 1 Growth Group	**PLC 2** Proficient Group	**PLC 3** Extension Group
Little to no cultural & equity awareness: misconceptions related to gifted characteristics in traditionally marginalized gifted groups in the community	Average cultural & equity awareness: misconceptions related to gifted characteristics in traditionally marginalized gifted groups in the community	Culturally & equity aware: recognizes gifted characteristics in traditionally marginalized gifted groups in the community
-Facilitators present through multiple modalities and engage PLC in discussion of the teacher supports that exist in the district to help provide equity in the gifted classroom and/or for gifted learners. -Educators will engage in guided exploration of practical and actionable resources that can support traditionally marginalized gifted learners and have an opportunity to put resources to use in their lesson planning with the guidance of the facilitator and in collaboration with their PLC members. -Educators will be asked to try lessons using the supports, then reflect and report back at the next PLC meeting. -Educators learn information about and engage in discussion regarding non-instructional supports (e.g., mentorships, affiliate groups) for minoritized gifted learners. -Educators identify human resources available within their district who can support gifted programming- for example the ESL teacher may have strategies to support second language acquisition.	-Facilitators present through multiple modalities and engage PLC in discussion of the teacher supports that exist in the district that help to provide equity in the classroom and/or for gifted learners. -Facilitators present through multiple modalities different tools that support equity in gifted curriculum. -Facilitators provide an example of inequitable curriculum from the district. Educators discuss ways to modify it for equity and identify practical, actional ways to provide resources in the classroom to support minoritized gifted students. -Educators discuss instructional (frontloading and talent development) and non instructional supports available for gifted learners and identify practices in their districts that are commensurate practices. -Educators identify human resources available within their district who can support gifted programming- for example the ESL teacher may have strategies to support second language acquisition.	-Facilitators present through multiple modalities a variety of tools that support equity in gifted curriculum. -PLC conducts a review of school and district gifted curriculum for equity/inequity; discuss ways to modify the curriculum for equity and identify practical, actional ways to provide resources in the classroom to support minoritized gifted learners. -PLC discusses the concept of reparations and what/how this looks like in gifted education. -PLC identifies human resources available within the districts who can support gifted programming- for example the ESL teacher may have strategies to support second language acquisition. -Facilitators provide opportunities for educators to plan together, share ideas, and for demonstration teaching.
Throughout, provide time for self-reflective journaling prompts, discussions, and debriefs.		
Embedded Equity Driven Professional Learning Principles *Taking a Pulse, Individualizing Professional Learning Plans, Establishing a Safe Zone, Going Beyond the Tip of the Iceberg, Bridging the Gap between School and Home, Engaging in Courageous Conversations, Identifying Grows and Glows*		

Figure 6.1 Zone 3 in action: Sample planning chart for differentiated groups.

Brief Explanation of the Research Base

We know that professional learning and requirements for teacher training regarding gifted education vary significantly from state to state. Beyond the basic crash course in gifted education that some educators receive, there are very few ongoing specialized PL opportunities, unless, of course, the individual is personally motivated to pursue a master's degree or learn more about the field of gifted education. This lack of teacher knowledge is shown to have a detrimental effect on the identification of and instruction for gifted learners.[3] Zone 3 seeks to disrupt inequities by developing teachers' knowledge base through intentional PL focused on classroom support for both students and teachers. We know the powerful impact high-quality, sustained PL has on changing teacher beliefs and instructional practices (see Chapter 1). Teachers who feel more confident in their instructional abilities are more likely to change their practices after experiencing a change in student outcomes.[4]

Experiencing positive change is necessary for internalizing change because of self-efficacy. Self-efficacy, as defined by psychologist Albert Bandura, is one's belief in their capability to achieve, do, or perform a task. Self-efficacy is developed when one experiences success or failure, which is why support throughout professional learning is essential to long-term success. We know that often a lesson doesn't go as planned, and support structures are helpful for exchanging ideas when trying out a new lesson or strategy.

We can develop self-efficacy in four different ways.[5] First, mastery experiences: if we experience success, then we feel more confident that we can complete the same or a similar task again. Tasks which are too easy to accomplish provide a false sense of efficacy which can be jolted when one experiences failure. Therefore, experiencing a small amount of challenge before overcoming the obstacle results in greater strides in building self-efficacy. The second way to develop self-efficacy is through vicarious experiences. We develop self-efficacy when we see someone who we identify with experiencing success. This results in the mentality: well, if he can do it, then surely, I can, too! During PL, the coach models lessons, shares revised curriculum and a multitude of other successful experiences to enable the potential development of vicarious self-efficacy.

Social persuasion is the third way to increase self-efficacy, though this is the most unreliable method, as one relies solely on verbal praise to improve self-efficacy. However, there is some value in utilizing social persuasion to increase perceived self-efficacy, as the temporary boost in confidence can be enough motivation to try a new task. Then, the new attempt is often enough to experience success, which parlays into the development of self-efficacy through one of the other methods. Finally, self-efficacy can be manifested through the purposeful planning of experiences in a low-stress environment.[6] The sense of safety fostered is conducive to the development of efficacy. Consider scaffolding instructional support for gifted teachers in a low-stress environment, encouraging them and assisting them with modifying, adapting, and/or changing their standardized gifted curriculum to meet the needs of a diverse gifted student population with support *vs.* assigning this daunting task for them to complete on their own. Which scenario is more likely to build self-efficacy? Similarly, identifying the readily available resources within the school building and district, complete with looking up emails and perhaps even making the first contact, while sitting around a table as a team, makes change seem not only possible, but achievable. Remember that gifted teachers often operate as silos in a building full of grade-level teams, and collaboration and support is refreshing, since changing on their own can seem a formidable task. We want to work smarter, not harder.

Simply being identified for gifted services does not automatically result in a successful experience in programs for marginalized gifted students, hence the focus on both recruitment and retention. Marginalized gifted students are more likely to decline services than White gifted students.[7] There may be negative perceptions of what it means to be gifted, based on the expectations of the program, or based on the traditional racial composition of the program.

Perhaps you have heard a parent or student say that the gifted program just means more work. Before you dismiss children as *lazy*, consider: does the program remove the child from their class for an hour, a half-day, a full day? And are the children then required to make up the work that they missed from their regular school day? Are the children given any choice in their curriculum in the gifted program? Does it reflect them and their interests? One of Angela's kids, Jay, didn't want to be gifted in Language Arts, just in Math. Why? Only the Math gifted program was fun. Jay didn't like going to the ELA gifted class because they didn't like the work they were doing, and it wasn't worth having to miss class, be miserable there, and then having to make up all the work they missed while out of the room. It was a *punishment to be gifted*. Now the funny thing—Jay was the only ELA kiddo being pulled for gifted third grade, but the teacher wasn't allowed to be adjust the material to meet Jay's interests because of a requirement to follow the district curriculum.

The second part of "what it means to be gifted" is based on the traditional racial composition of the program. Many of the marginalized gifted learners' characteristics studied in Zone 2 included collaboration and collectivism cultures,[8] where value is placed on the cohesiveness of the group, in belongingness. Children may experience trepidation when faced with the choice of exiting their class, a blended group of students with some that look like them, to go to a gifted class amidst a sea of mostly (or in some cases, all) White faces. Another negative perception of the gifted program may come from within the student's peer group. It may not be socially acceptable to stand out academically or to be the only one from the peer group who participates in the gifted program.[9]

Zone 3 is essential to helping build a support system for the students by preparing the teachers to create a learning environment that is responsive to the affective needs of the gifted learners, as well as actively looking for ways to meaningfully engage all ethnic and cultural groups academically in the gifted program. A mentor who can provide guidance and encouragement significantly contributes to the long-term success of a marginalized gifted student. Research shows the benefit of support systems for developing and retaining marginalized gifted students.

Put it in Play

In Zone 3, professional learning is divided into two major focus areas: training that transforms student programming and PL that provides educator support (Figure 6.2).

Z2 Essential Content	Brief Explanation	Playbook Activities
Support Systems for Identified Marginalized Gifted Students	Marginalized gifted students may struggle in traditional gifted education programs for a multitude of reasons. Zone 3's focus is transforming gifted programming so that the students are able to flourish in their learning environment. A key focus is an equitable learning environment and curriculum before, during, and after identification. Attention must be focused on both essential academic and affective, or social-emotional, supports.	Hexagonal Thinking: Giftedness & Identity This is Who I Am: A Photo Essay for Gifted Learners Making Your Presence Known Fostering Growth through Mentorships
Support Systems for Educators of the Gifted	Gifted teachers need support as they transform gifted curriculum which includes content and strategies in equity, cultural responsiveness, and advocacy. Gifted teachers benefit from continued PL support as they continue to grow in their understanding of the impact of culture and systemic racism on giftedness and gifted and talented programming.	Equity Detectives: Identifying Inequities in K-12 Current Events Infusing Cultural Responsiveness Connecting Funds of Knowledge to Gifted Instructional Strategies It takes a Village: Engaging with Instructional Specialists Writing Culturally Responsive Enrichment Lessons and Curriculum Units Demonstration Teaching

Figure 6.2 Essential content: Z3 increasing classroom support for educators and gifted marginalized students.

Starting with scaffolding but leading to an eventual transformation of the gifted curriculum and learning environment for students, not only before but during the identification process and throughout the program, is essential to the long-term retention and success of marginalized gifted learners. PL in Z3 focuses first on the social-emotional well-being of the marginalized gifted learners followed by the development of an equitable and equity-driven curriculum for academic success.

The second half of Z3 PL focuses on the support structures for the educators. Gifted educators need continual coaching as they modify and differentiate the gifted curriculum to best fit the needs of the diverse learners and grow as advocates and leaders themselves. It is beneficial to invite instructional support specialists to these PL sessions, as they can provide insight into accommodations, modifications, and share contact details for other individuals who can offer further assistance. For example, the ESL teachers can share strategies and instructional tools.

Cautions and Caveats

- **Be prepared with a game plan.** Zone 3 covers a lot of information, and the facilitator needs to have a game plan for approaching it. Identify the most critical areas to address first, as well as those areas which are easily achieved. Remember the benefits of short-term success often lay the groundwork for future wins.
- **Develop a sense of team unity.** Educators often find themselves working in silos, but in equity work we need to rely on each other and foster a sense of team unity to provide multiple levels of support for our students and teachers.
- **Identify position coaches.** Instructional support requires multiple human resources. The facilitator, along with the participants, should identify different people to serve as the position coach taking the lead to develop areas. For example: an educator with a background in special education may spearhead the revision of gifted curriculum to meet the needs of twice-exceptional learners. Seek experts from within!
- **Create organization charts**. Throughout the Zones, you will most likely encounter at least one small problem area that grows larger as you begin to address it. Flexibility is key; education is a living organism which grows and adapts to its environment. Create a chart to organize areas to be addressed now or in the future and identify who

needs to address the concerns. Remember the Parking Lot activity from Chapter 4? You can make one just for you!

Resources

Articles

- Tiered Lessons: One way to Differentiate Mathematics Instruction, https://www.davidsongifted.org/gifted-blog/tiered-lessons-one-way-to-differentiate-mathematics-instruction/
- Leveled Questions for ELLs, http://fspsscience.pbworks.com/w/file/fetch/80214878/Leveled_20Questions_20for_20ELLs
- A Culturally Responsive Equity-Based Bill of Rights for Gifted Students of Color, https://www.nagc.org/blog/culturally-responsive-equity-based-bill-rights-gifted-students-color
- Approaches to Multicultural Curriculum Reform by James Banks, https://www.teachingforchange.org/wp-content/uploads/2015/11/Banks_James.pdf
- Finding a Mentor for Your Gifted Child, https://www.davidsongifted.org/gifted-blog/finding-a-mentor-for-your-gifted-child/
- Mentor Relationships and Gifted Learners, https://www.davidsongifted.org/gifted-blog/mentor-relationships-and-gifted-learners/

Literature Tools

- "Taco Night" by Paul Gorski, http://edchange.org/publications/TacoNight.pdf
- "Becoming Joey" by Paul Gorski, http://edchange.org/publications/becoming-joey.pdf
- Teacher Spotlight Case Studies, National Association for Multicultural Education, https://www.nameorg.org/learn/case_studies_in_enactments_of.php

Webinar

- Prejudice Reduction and Collective Action: Integrating the Anti-Bias Framework into All Disciplines Webinar, Teaching Tolerance, https://www.tolerance.org/professional-development/webinars/prejudice-reduction-and-collective-action-integrating-the
- Meeting the Needs of Gifted Learners at a Distance—A Focus on Grades 4–8, https://www.youtube.com/watch?v=lcOPaz0tJhI

- A Framework for Teaching Critical Thinking, https://vimeo.com/403459157

Books

- *Recruiting and Retaining Culturally Different Students in Gifted Education* by Donna Ford
- *Textured Teaching: A Framework* by Lorena Escoto Germán
- *Start Here, Start Now: A Guide to Antibias and Antiracist Work in Your School Community* by Liz Kleinrock
- *Empowering Underrepresented Gifted Students* edited by Joy Lawson Davis and Deb Douglas
- *Coaching for Equity* by Elena Aguilar
- *Cultivating Genius* by Goldy Muhammad

Professional Learning Playbook

Look for the Guiding Principle Icons by the playbook activities!

1) Taking a Pulse
2) Individualizing Professional Learning Plans 
3) Establishing a Safe Zone
4) Going Beyond the Tip of the Iceberg 
5) Engaging in Courageous Conversations 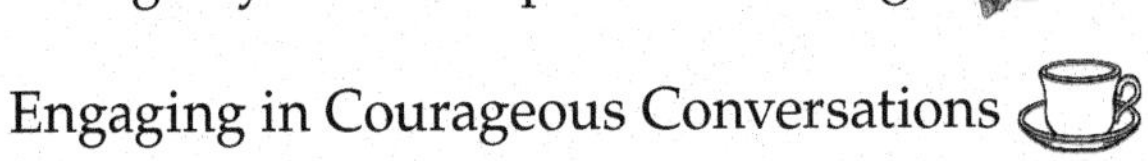
6) Bridging the Gap between School and Home 
7) Identifying Grows and Glows 

Activity 1: Hexagonal Thinking: Giftedness and Identity

Estimated Time: 25–30 minutes

Materials Needed: Hexagonal Thinking Cards (copies of Reproducible 6.1: Hexagonal Thinking: Giftedness and Identity, scissors, envelopes or paper clips to keep materials together for groups)

Delivery Format: In Person (to modify for digital, you can use google slides to recreate the activity following these directions: https://youtu.be/6BSxQepDY7k)

Seven Guiding Principles Addressed:

Purpose: The Hexagonal Thinking activity comes from a strategy of Stern et al.[10] in their book *Learning that Transfers*. This activity helps the learner manipulate concept cards as a visual way to see how different concepts are related. A hexagon has six sides, which means the concept could have multiple connections, while at the same time limiting the repetition of the connections. The purpose of this activity is to discuss the intersections of giftedness and identity.

Procedure:

- ★ This activity works well in a group as the participants can share their thought process. However, it could also be completed independently, if necessary.
- ★ Share the hexagon cards with your participants and ask them to sort the cards according to the relationships between the concepts. The arrows are used to point out 5 meaningful connections across the 12 cards. These five connections will be shared out at the end of the group work (or individual reflection) time. An overarching question to guide the discussion should be posted in the room: How do giftedness and identity intersect for a gifted child? How does a society's picture of a gifted child potentially inhibit their understanding of who they are?
- ★ Recommended Extension: The Hexagonal Thinking: Giftedness and Identity Activity would be a great activity for K-12 students to complete as part of their processing.

Activity 2: This is Who I Am: A Photo Essay for Gifted Learners

Estimated Time: 20–30 minutes

Materials Needed: NAGC Campaign Posters for Giftedness Knows No Boundaries: http://www.giftednessknowsnoboundaries.org/posters-page, tablet or device to take pictures, photo editing software, access to a printer

Delivery Format: In Person

Seven Guiding Principles Addressed: 

Purpose: This activity raises awareness about cultural diversity of gifted learners. The activity helps educators raise awareness of the role culture plays on giftedness, first by completing the activity and then taking it back to the classroom as a practical activity to help gifted learners analyze and evaluate their own giftedness.

Procedure:

★ This PL activity provides a tangible strategy which gifted educators can take back to their classrooms. Taking a turn-key approach, the facilitator should present the strategy to the team and ask the participants to complete the This is Who I am Photo Essay.

★ Begin by sharing the NAGC Campaign Posters for Giftedness Knows No Boundaries (http://www.giftednessknowsnoboundaries.org/posters-page) followed by a discussion centered around the concepts learned in Zones 1 and 2, where the focus was on recognizing giftedness across cultures. Pose the question: If we were to create one more poster for the campaign which highlights our gifted student body, what would it look like? What would be the slogan?

★ Following the brainstorm, the teachers working in groups will create additional campaign posters, which could be hung around the school, or shared out through social media.

★ Next, the facilitator challenges the gifted teachers to take this activity back to their classrooms and ask their gifted students to create their own This is Who I Am Photo Essay. The gifted learners should be encouraged to reflect their own cultural identities in their photo essay along with a slogan.

★ At the following PL session, gifted teachers will share out the student work and reflect on what they have learned about their gifted students through this process.

★ Recommended Extension: Share these posters with the Family and Community Partners to raise awareness about what it means to be gifted (see Zone 4 for more ideas of how to involve the families and community members).

Activity 3: Making Your Presence Known

Estimated Time: 20–30 minutes

Materials Needed: A Culturally Responsive Equity-Based Bill of Rights for Gifted Students of Color, https://www.nagc.org/blog/culturally-responsive-equity-based-bill-rights-gifted-students-color

Delivery Format: Digital or In Person

Seven Guiding Principles Addressed: 

Purpose: This activity is designed to empower marginalized gifted learners to learn how to advocate for themselves.

Procedure:

- ★ This PL activity begins with the teachers reviewing the Culturally Responsive Equity-Based Bill of Rights for Gifted Students of Color, focusing on Rights VI. Curriculum and Instruction and VII. Social and Emotional, appraising strengths and weaknesses of the current gifted curriculum and instruction at their school. This assessment will be utilized as a starting point for revamping instructional content and practices, in a future PL session.
- ★ The facilitator guides the discussion through the following prompts:
    - ★ In what ways are we meeting the expectations of the Bill of Rights for Gifted Students of Color?
    - ★ What are possible impacts for students if we fail to meet these rights?
    - ★ How do these rights connect to Zones 1 and 2?
    - ★ How can we do better? Where do we begin?
- ★ Note: Making the Bill of Rights for Gifted Students of Color visible in the school building is a low-hanging fruit for increasing equity. Facilitators and gifted teachers should hang copies of this document within the building as well as sharing them on social media.
- ★ Recommended Extension: Gifted educators should take this exercise back to their classroom and work through the following discussion prompts with their gifted students:
    - ★ What is a Bill of Rights? What is the purpose of a Bill of Rights?
    - ★ What surprises you about the Bill of Rights for Gifted Students of Color?
    - ★ How does it make you feel after reading the Bill of Rights for Gifted Students of Color?
    - ★ How can we do better? Where do we begin?

Following the classroom discussion, gifted educators can bring the big ideas back to the next scheduled PL session to continue the conversation and take action on some of the student and teacher recommendations for where to begin with increasing equity in gifted programs.

Activity 4: Fostering Growth through Mentorships

Estimated Time: 15–20 minutes initial planning, plus additional time for mentoring

Materials Needed: Board and dry erase markers or chart paper and markers, two articles on mentors for gifted learners (see Resources)

Delivery Format: Digital or In Person

Seven Guiding Principles Addressed: 

Purpose: One of the contributing factors to poor retention of marginalized gifted students is the lack of support within gifted programs. By providing PL on identifying and supporting mentors for gifted students, educators are better equipped to facilitate mentorships.

Procedure:

- ★ During this PL, the facilitator will work with the gifted teachers to identify potential mentors available to support marginalized gifted students, beginning with unpacking the purpose of the mentoring program. The following questions should be explored:
  - ★ Who are the mentees? What are their student profiles? What do we know about their Funds of Knowledge and cultural backgrounds?
  - ★ What is the purpose of the mentor–mentee relationship? Is it teacher-driven or student-driven? What are the desired outcomes?
  - ★ Who is available to mentor? Other gifted peers? Community partners? Or is the mentor a famous person whom the student can look up to as a role model? (Note: it is likely that you will want to establish all three types of mentor–mentee relationships. The process of selecting a qualified mentor is the same, whether it is a gifted peer, community partner, or famous person.)
  - ★ What do we know about the possible mentors? What are their profiles/qualifications? What do we know about their commitment to equity?
- ★ The next step in the PL is for the facilitator to a review of the expectations of what a good mentor–mentee relationship looks like:
  - ★ Establish the goals and expectations for the mentoring relationship. How involved is the commitment? What kinds of support is the mentee looking for? What times during the day/week will the mentor and mentee be available to meet? Where/how will they meet? How long is the relationship expected to last?

- ★ Communication is essential. A strong relationship requires willingness to give and receive. As with any relationship, there will be some misunderstandings, but a willingness to work through the conflicts is essential to the health of the mentor–mentee relationship. Both parties must be equally invested in the desire for the relationship to be beneficial.
- ★ Recognition of efforts. Receiving positive feedback and accolades builds self-efficacy for both parties. This is especially important for the student who may have lower confidence and needs validation. However, the mentor who is volunteering his time also needs reassurance that his efforts are worth his time and valued.
- ★ Create opportunities for growth. The establishment of opportunities for growing as a learner is essential to the long-term success of the marginalized gifted learner. These opportunities will look different based on the circumstances, but just like in the classroom, we are scaffolding the learning process and the mentor will need to scaffold the authentic learning process.

★ Pass out and/or share the links to the two brief articles about gifted children and mentor relationships (see Resources section). Lead a brief discussion about the role of the mentor and potential challenge in finding a mentor for gifted youth. Finally, have participants create a t-chart pairing the gifted students with potential mentors. Prior to sharing any of the potential mentor–mentee pairings, the gifted teachers should reach out to the mentors to confirm their willingness to participate as well as the expectations for the relationship. Remember, that as a general rule, people do not like to be voluntold! The same considerations should be kept in mind when approaching the gifted learner about the mentorship, especially when pairing students. You will want to be sure that the gifted learner is willing to be paired with the peer mentor.

★ Note: Don't hesitate to also ask the gifted learner if they have someone in mind who would be a good mentor. Some gifted learners may already have a relationship with someone who would be an excellent mentor or have someone in mind who they would like to work with.

★ Modification: Depending on participant readiness, be ready to provide support with Funds of Knowledge or cultural background information. Refer to Zone 2 activities for resources.

Activity 5: Equity Detectives: Identifying Inequities in K-12 Current Events

Estimated Time: 15–20 minutes

Materials Needed: Access to the internet to find examples, computer, projector

Delivery Format: Digital or In Person

Seven Guiding Principles Addressed: 

Purpose: The purpose of this PL activity is to draw attention to curriculum, instructional activities, and current events which highlight the inequities still present in K-12 classrooms due to the actions of teachers, school administrators, and textbook publishers. Moving beyond raising awareness of current events, this activity challenges the gifted teacher to reflect on their own instructional activities and curriculum to be equity-minded and take action to disrupt inequities.

Procedure:

- ★ The facilitator prepares a slide deck of images and current event articles which highlight inequities in education. The activity works best when the examples are from the last five to ten years as this creates relevancy and illustrates the point that equity is a problem *today*, not just in the past. Here are few examples to get you started
  - ★ In September 2021 in an Oregon school district, a staff member appeared at work wearing blackface to protest the COVID vaccine mandate.
  - ★ In March 2021, a Texas teacher assigned students a chivalry assignment in which girls were instructed to act in manners that would be pleasing to the male students, for example: outside the classroom, ladies cannot show intellectual superiority if it would offend the men around them.
- ★ While participants view the images in the slide deck, encourage them to reflect on their initial reactions by journaling or sharing through a digital discussion board. The facilitator should monitor an open discussion in which participants not just share their responses to the inequities but they begin to question and critique these examples, sharing ideas of how to disrupt these inequities. The facilitator may need to scaffold this part of the conversation with intentional prompts or provide examples, as needed.
  - ★ Potential Prompts:
    - ★ In what ways does the (current event) present an equity issue?
    - ★ How does this (current event) disrupt power dynamics or marginalize one group over another?

- ★ How can we, (as faculty/as administrators), engage in providing anti-oppressive curriculum?
- ★ Is there a different narrative that we can share to tell this story?

★ Next, the facilitator challenges the participants to pause and reflect on their own school building and curriculum to identify areas where inequities exist. In groups, participants should identify find real-world examples of similar inequities that exist in their spheres of influence, as well as possible ways to counteract or change these curriculum, policies, or practices. As the facilitator, explain that this is not a Gotcha exercise, but a group think to identify and disrupt inequities and embrace change together. As teams share images of the content which perpetuates inequity, allow each group several minutes to facilitate a short whole group discussion for all participants to contribute additional ideas for change.

★ Recommended Extension: Challenge the gifted teachers to take this activity back to their classrooms and ask the students to identify areas where they see inequities in their school. The gifted teachers lead the students through the process of evaluating and creating alternate assignments/materials. Finally, the gifted teachers return to the follow-up sessions to debrief and share out.

Activity 6: Infusing Cultural Responsiveness

Estimated Time: 15–20 minutes

Materials Needed: Reproducible 6.2: Infusing Cultural Responsiveness in Academic Vocabulary and Language Instruction, sample lessons from gifted teachers

Delivery Format: Digital or In Person

Seven Guiding Principles Addressed: 

Purpose: As many gifted children possess an advanced vocabulary, it can come as a surprise to gifted teachers when there may be gaps in vocabulary. This PL activity helps the educator consider ways to infuse cultural responsiveness throughout their instruction by targeting academic vocabulary and language.

Procedure:

★ Beginning with responsive academic vocabulary, the facilitator walks the PL group through the process of scaffolding activities to be more inclusive. As needed, the facilitator may review tiered vocabulary words or move straight into a discussion around gifted learners and language acquisition.

- ★ Leveling vocabulary is the process of differentiating the use of academic language to provide the necessary scaffolding to support the learner. For example, if students are asked to consider the relationship of cup–saucer, some gifted learners may struggle to answer the question as they may be unfamiliar with the word saucer, never having used a formal tea set in their home. Saucer in this context is a Tier II vocabulary word. By leveling the vocabulary, the teacher can provide visual images to provide the context for understanding the term, use synonyms which are more familiar (Tier I), or remove vocabulary terms that are biased.
- ★ Reinforcement and practice activities provide the opportunity for students to apply new vocabulary terms in context—such as in conversations or writing prompts. This does not mean the student is completing repetitive worksheets or other meaningless tasks! Remember Gifted 101: more of the same is not enrichment!
- ★ Vocabulary acquisition refers to the process of learning new words. There are many vocabulary strategies, from using your context clues to synonym replacement. It is important for the gifted learner to be exposed to multiple strategies so that they can select the one that works best for them. Keep in mind these strategies work only if the student has the background knowledge for the other words in the sentence. Nothing is more frustrating than to be told to use your context clues, and not know any of the other words in the sentence.
- ★ Code-switching occurs when the speaker switches between two or more languages in conversation. Code-switching occurs naturally when learning a second language; however gifted learners who enjoy word play will intentionally code-switch for emphasis in their conversations.
- ★ Sentence lifting/retelling/role-playing are avenues for the gifted learner to apply newly acquired vocabulary words. Sentence lifting is a teaching strategy where the teacher selects an exemplary student sentence from a writing. Using this sentence as an example, the teacher has the class analyze it, breaking down the components of writing (grammar, mechanics, or spelling) being exemplified. Retelling and role-playing are culturally responsive literacy strategies where the learner demonstrates their ability to recall and visualize a story.
- ★ Revising is a key element of the writing process. To be effective, the revising process needs to allow the writer multiple opportunities to critically think about their writing and utilize the same writing structure (e.g., personal narrative writing, realistic fiction, or short answer).

- ★ Teachable moments are gold moments in the classroom. Capitalize on these moments to draw gifted learners' attention to new vocabulary or language structures. Often the teachable moments are more impactful because of the personalized connection—which makes the learning process more authentic.

★ Working in teams, teachers workshop ways to apply these culturally responsive understandings to their own lesson plans. It is helpful to have gifted teachers bring sample lessons with them to this PL, so that this PL session can be a working session. Guiding the teams to critically access their existing lesson plans, the facilitator helps the team to make connections between culturally responsive language acquisition and gifted learners. For example: We know gifted learners crave depth and complexity. We also know marginalized gifted learners may not have as many Tier II and Tier III words. Therefore, a scaffolded lesson plan where students explore relationships between words to unlock the meaning of unfamiliar words. Cognates are a great way to challenge gifted learners! For example: the math activity may ask students to identify which of the following shapes are a *composite* shape. If the gifted learner is unfamiliar with the word composite, the teacher can provide a cognate word: composition. The word composition may be more familiar to the student as they frequently write compositions in English class. The gifted educator asks the student to explore the two words—composite and composition—to identify the Latin root word. Upon further exploration, the gifted learners would identify that the root word is *componere*, which means to put together. From here, the gifted learner (guided by the teacher) applies these new understandings to derive meaning from the unfamiliar word, composite, thus understanding that a composite shape is a shape that is made up of other shapes.

Activity 7: Connecting Funds of Knowledge to Gifted Instructional Strategies

Estimated Time: 20–30 minutes

Materials Needed: Reproducible 6.3: Connecting Funds of Knowledge to Gifted Instructional Strategies

Delivery Format: Digital or In Person

Seven Guiding Principles Addressed: 

Purpose: This activity provides a graphic organizer for educators to use as they consider ways to modify their instructional practices to be more equitable. The participants connect the Funds of Knowledge with gifted expressions and instructional strategies to modify their instruction.

Procedure:

- ★ The facilitator shares the Reproducible 6.2: Connecting Funds of Knowledge to Gifted Instructional Strategies with the participants. Working in small groups, participants consider ways to modify their instruction utilizing knowledge of the Funds of Knowledge, and gifted expression. This list of modifications can be referred to in a future PL when participants work to revamp their current gifted curriculum.
- ★ Note: There are more Funds of Knowledge beyond the three listed on Reproducible 6.3, therefore it would be worthwhile to consider, as a team, additional ways in which to address these understandings in the classroom. See Resources from Chapter 4 for more information regarding the Funds of Knowledge.

Activity 8: It Takes a Village: Engaging with Instructional Specialists

Estimated Time: 10–15 minutes

Materials Needed: Reproducible 6.4: It Takes a Village: Engaging with Instructional Specialists

Delivery Format: Digital or In Person

Seven Guiding Principles Addressed: 

Purpose: Gifted teachers often feel like they are lone wolves, especially when they are the sole gifted teacher for several buildings or the entire district. This PL activity focuses on identifying and leaning on readily available human resources within the district. The purpose of this activity is to help gifted teachers' network and reach out to colleagues who may have an area of expertise which will support the marginalized gifted students' long-term success in the gifted program.

Procedure:

- ★ The initial step is to identify which resources are already being accessed by the gifted teachers. The facilitator creates a t-chart showing the three types of resources found in schools: human resources (subject matter experts), capital resources (textbooks, software, education programs and materials), financial resources (school district funding, PTA funds, grant money).
  - ★ In teams, educators complete the t-chart with examples of the various types of resources being used in their programs.

 - ★ The facilitator guides the discussion using the following prompt: In what ways are we effectively utilizing available resources? Are there resources that we are not accessing? Who can share a creative way utilizing limited resources?
- ★ Next, the conversation focuses on identifying ways to access human resources to support gifted programming, which may not already be utilized. The facilitator shares Reproducible 6.4: It Takes a Village: Engaging with Instructional Specialists. Working in groups the PL team first completes the instructional need column based on the individual needs of their marginalized gifted students. Next, the group identifies subject matter experts in the school who may be able to meet this instructional need. Finally, the PL team considers the level of involvement which they are asking from their subject matter experts. People are often willing to help but may be wary of taking on a large time commitment. By identifying specific needs and length of time commitment the gifted educator will be more successful in gathering support from other teachers.
- ★ The facilitator tasks each PL member to reach out to one human resource between now and the next PL session. If time allows, the initial contact can be made that day via email. By providing a concrete timeline and a check-in point, the facilitator is adding in a layer of accountability for the gifted teachers. This is important to ensure that we are actively taking steps forward to strengthen the gifted education program, and empowering participants to become change agents and advocates.

Activity 9: Writing Culturally Responsive Enrichment Lessons and Curriculum Units

Estimated Time: 30–60 minutes, ongoing

Materials Needed: Current lesson plans, gifted and talented scope and sequence, if applicable

Delivery Format: Digital or In Person

Seven Guiding Principles Addressed: 

Purpose: The purpose of this activity is to provide a structured time for gifted educators to revise, modify, or create culturally responsive enrichment lessons and curriculum units. The ultimate goal is to revise the entire curriculum; however, this task may be too big to tackle in one time. Rather, it would be beneficial to plan several PL sessions throughout the school year dedicated to lesson planning and curriculum unit development. Because lesson planning may be automatic to veteran teachers, it is especially important to slow down the lesson planning process to critically assess each lesson for equity and the principles of cultural responsiveness.

Procedure:

★ Gifted teachers should bring their lesson plans and enrichment curriculum materials to the PL, to make this a working PL session. If this is your first time working through lesson plans with an equity lens, it is best to begin with revising one lesson plan. Once the team is comfortable and agile with the process then you can move at a quicker pace.

★ Keeping in mind that there are a variety of lesson plan templates and demographic data varies by district, this activity is flexible and adaptable.

★ This activity begins with the teachers participating in a turn-and-talk where they walk through the lesson plan in its current form. This process helps the teacher think through all the parts of the lesson (Anticipatory Set, I Do, We Do, You Do, Closure).

★ Next, the facilitator will ask the teachers to highlight/markup the lesson plan for key elements:

  ★ Does the lesson plan consider students' Funds of Knowledge (FoK)?

  ★ Does the lesson plan incorporate the cultural capital and assets the marginalized gifted learners are bringing with them?

  ★ Does the lesson plan differentiate to accommodate multiple cultural backgrounds readiness, affect, and learning profiles?

  ★ Are the activities engaging and meaningful for the learner?

  ★ Do the activities align with the student learning outcomes?

★ Following the lesson plan markup, educators will work together to modify the lesson to increase its effectiveness. With the goal of being able to affirm:

  ★ All gifted learners will be challenged and engaged in the lesson.

  ★ All gifted learners have access to necessary scaffolding to excel.

  ★ All gifted learners will have an opportunity to synthesize and reflect on the learning process and make connections to their own cultural identity.

★ Once the teachers have a quality lesson plan, the next step is to implement the lesson. The facilitator should make themselves available to co-teach or observe the lesson as requested to provide feedback. The gifted teachers should reflect on their lesson delivery and make notes of *glows and grows*, as well as collect student samples to bring back to share at the next PL session. This is an essential step in the process as it allows for the teacher to grow in their understanding of culturally responsive teaching, opportunities to talk through any potential problem areas, as well as to share 'aha' moments with their colleagues.

Activity 10: Demonstration Teaching

Estimated Time: 30–45 minutes

Materials Needed: Reproducible 6.5: Equity-Driven Classroom Observation Form

Delivery Format: Digital or In Person

Seven Guiding Principles Addressed: 

Purpose: Demonstration teaching is an opportunity for the gifted facilitator to model effective equity-driven teaching practices. Demonstration teaching is a tool which is underutilized during PL; however, the benefits can be exponential. Being able to observe a master teacher implement a new strategy, interact with students, and reflect on the instructional delivery are powerful teaching tools. Demonstration teaching can continue the experience with PLC members recording or livestreaming lessons, using the feedback form for feedback and discussion.

Procedure:

★ The facilitator works with the gifted teachers to arrange a day and time for a lesson demonstration. During the demonstration, the facilitator can model equity-driven instructional practices while the gifted teacher observes the lesson. To increase the effectiveness of the lesson observation, the facilitator should provide the teacher with Reproducible 6.5 Equity-Driven Classroom Observation Form. This form is intended to be used as a growth measure, not as an evaluation tool. The form provides purpose to the observer by providing concrete items to focus on observing.

★ Following the demonstration lesson, the gifted teacher should complete the observation form and arrange a time to meet with the facilitator to debrief about the observation.

Extensions:

★ The gifted teacher arranges a time with the facilitator to observe a similar gifted lesson. With the roles being reversed, the facilitator is now able to provide feedback to the gifted teacher as they implement their equity-driven lesson. Again, the purpose of the observation is to develop our teaching skills; it is not to evaluate the teacher for contract renewal. It is very important to make this clear to both the gifted teachers and administrators so that trust is established, and the teacher can profit from constructive feedback.

★ PLC members record lessons and post to an LMS or Google Drive and/or arrange a time to livestream the lesson. The same feedback form can be used as in the first extension activity as an opportunity for feedback.

Reproducibles

Reproducible 6.1: Hexagonal Thinking: Giftedness and Identity

You're different. You're special. You're not like the rest of them.	You are a proud example for your community!	Why don't you understand this? I thought you were gifted!	Now you fit in! You are with others just like you!
You are so articulate for a Black girl!	You should constantly achieve. That's what gifted kids do. Failure is not an option.	I'm the teacher, here! What are you trying to prove?	Is it harder to achieve now that everyone is at your level?
Being around those white gifted kids has changed you. You don't even talk like us!	We are proud of you!	But you're Korean, aren't you good at Math?	Represent our school well! When you are on that stage, you are HMS!
You should not stand out. Don't speak up or raise your hand. Blend in. It's better if they don't know you.	You belong in this community.	No homework again today? That gifted program should teach you some organizational skills..	We've run out of classes. Would you like to help teach or do an independent study?

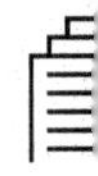

Reproducible 6.2: Infusing Cultural Responsiveness in Academic Vocabulary and Language Instruction

Tiered Vocabulary Words	What do we know about culturally responsive academic vocabulary and language instruction?	What do we know about gifted learners and language acquisition?	How can I apply this to my classroom?
Tier I: Words which are commonly used in everyday conversations (e.g., triangle, angle, corner)	Evidence of leveling vocabulary words (Tier 2 and Tier 3) Evidence of reinforcement and practice activities Use of vocabulary acquisition strategies (word structure, apposition, context clues, synonym replacement) Provide code-switching opportunities Sentence lifting/ Retelling/ Role-playing Revising (phonetics, markers, syntax, and vocabulary) Teachable moments	Gifted kids need less repetition to learn vocabulary. Gifted learners enjoy playing with language. Gifted brains crave depth and complexity. Gifted learners learn a second language at an accelerated rate. Gifted students interact with language in different (storytelling, visual, and artistic) ways. Gifted kids may utilize improvisation, humor, imagery, music, and/or movement in language acquisition.	

Reproducible 6.3: Connecting Funds of Knowledge to Gifted Instructional Strategies

Connecting Funds of Knowledge to Gifted Instructional Strategies			
Funds of Knowledge	**Gifted Expression**[11]	**Gifted Instructional Strategies**	**In what ways can you apply these understandings in your classroom?**
Home Language	Code switching	Word games (idioms, puns, riddles, etc.), improv, creative writing extensions, scenario and simulation-based activities, role-plays	
	Expressiveness of gestures, body language, and the ability to interpret these	Creative movement, dance, drama, kinesthetic activities, creating melodies, role-plays, improv	
	Humor and sense of humor	Word games (idioms, puns, riddles, etc.), role-play and storytelling activities, vocabulary activities, research, improv	
	Richness of imagery in informal language	Oral presentations, storytelling, creative writing, simulations, role-playing, poetry slams, song creation, improv	

Family Values and Traditions	Enjoyment of and ability in music and rhythm, creative movement, dance, and/or dramatics	Creative movement, dance, drama, kinesthetic activities, creating melodies, critical- and creative-thinking scenarios, storytelling	
	Articulateness in role-playing and storytelling	Oral presentations, storytelling, creative writing, simulations, role-playing, critical- and creative-thinking scenarios	
	Enjoyment of and skills in group activities and problem-solving	Debates, discussions, speeches, critical- and creative-thinking scenarios, research	
Scientific Knowledge	Originality of ideas in problem-solving	Riddles, puzzles, scenarios, ethical debates, creative problem solving, future problem-solving, critical- and creative-thinking scenarios	
	Problem centeredness or persistence in problem-solving	Debates, seminars, maker space, invention convention, future problem solving, creative problem-solving, critical- and creative-thinking scenarios	
	Ability to improvise with commonplace materials	Kinesthetic activities, science experiments, inventions, loose parts play, maker space, critical- and creative-thinking scenarios	

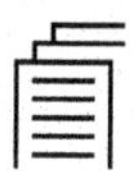

Reproducible 6.4: It Takes a Village: Engaging with Instructional Specialists

Instructional Need	**Who within the school has experience or an area of expertise?**	**What level of involvement are you requesting from the subject matter expert?**
Example: I have a gifted student who is Spanish-speaking. I need help modifying my enrichment activities.	Example: The ESL teacher has resources for modifying curriculum.	Example: I would like some ESL strategies to apply to my lesson plans. I would like someone to come to my classroom and support the student during the lesson. I will ask for 90 minutes of support, 30-minute observation, and 60 minutes of follow-up.

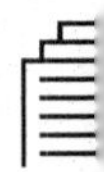

Reproducible 6.5: Equity-Driven Classroom Observation Form

During the observation, you can take notes, but your focus should be on the instructional delivery that you are observing rather than completing this form. Reflect on the form and complete it following the observation. Remember your goal is to make observations not judgments.

Classroom Environment
What does the classroom *feel* like during the lesson?
Describe the student engagement (make observations, use examples).
How does the teacher engage with different learners in the room (make observations, not judgments)?
In what ways is it evident that the teacher knows every child beyond the surface level?
Share any evidence you see of "warm demander" in action.
What is one takeaway about the **classroom environment**?

Instruction and Materials
How is the lesson culturally responsive, or how does the teacher modify the lesson to be culturally responsive?
What materials used in the lesson are culturally responsive? How do you know?
How does the teacher engage all gifted learners in a challenging learning environment?
What scaffolded supports do you observe? To whom are they provided?
What aspects of cultivating genius, historically responsive equity literacy do you observe in the curriculum? (Identity meaning-making, Skills, Intellect, Intellect, Criticality, Joy)
What is one takeaway from this observation about **instructional delivery or materials**?
Assessment
Do the students understand the material? How do you know?

What examples of lean-in assessment are evident?
What examples of equitable assessment are evident? (Mathematically sound, Value knowledge over environment or behavior, Support hope and growth, Grades are simple and transparent, Build up soft skills, but don't grade them)
What is one takeaway from this observation about **instructional delivery or assessment**?

Reflections and Connections
What aspects of the lesson are equitable or equity-driven?
In what ways does this lesson, the lesson delivery, and/or the learning environment connect to the "Talent Scout" *vs.* "Deficit Detective"? Provide examples.
What questions do you have for the debrief/discussion?
What growth opportunities or ideas would you like to share during the debrief/discussion?

Key Terms
warm demander: Lisa Delpit's phrase for when teachers "expect a great deal of their students, convince them of their own brilliance, and help them to reach their potential in a disciplined and structured environment."[12]
lean-in assessment: aligning assessment to the student's personal learning story[13]
cultivating genius aspects:[14]
• **identity meaning making:** instruction that enables students to learn about themselves or others
• **skills:** instruction increases learners' abilities in a specific content area
• **intellect:** instruction refines students' mental acuity and builds knowledge
• **criticality:** instruction grounded in learners' critical thinking about equity, power, and disrupting systems of oppression
• **joy:** instruction that encourages students to see joy in themselves and others
equitable assessment examples:[15]
• **mathematically sound:** standards-based grading, use a 0–4 scale instead of 0–100; ditch the 0, weigh recent growth over initial scores
• **value knowledge over environment or behavior:** assessment measures knowledge, it is not a reward or a punishment, points aren't taken off for tardies, sloppiness, or missing names (behaviors), grade the students' knowledge of the content only
• **support hope and growth:** mistakes are a part of the learning process, value the process of learning and growth; provide opportunities for revision and resubmission and test retakes, replacing current scores (current level of mastery) not half-points or partial points. It's not teaching a "bad lesson"—unless humanity and grace are "bad lessons."
• **grades are simple and transparent:** students should know how they're going to be evaluated before they turn in assignments. Use clear, concise, rubrics that are aligned with the content to be assessed (valuing knowledge over behavior/ environment).
• **build up soft skills, but don't grade them:** motivation is important, but it's not worth a grade; not everything done in class should be worth points. We complete work to learn and grow, not because it goes in the gradebook; support the development of intrinsic motivation.
deficit detective and talent scouts:[16] a paradigm shift required of teachers to be talent scouts rather than deficit detectives. Rather than focusing on deficits and eliminating students because they are not performing high in all, or not exhibiting talents in the dominant cultural characteristics, teachers provide children opportunities for talent to manifest itself by exposing them to advanced content and enriching experiences and observing students demonstrating creativity and critical thinking skills. Thus, instead of looking for ways that students shouldn't be in gifted programs (deficit detectives), teachers are talent scouts, searching for students exhibiting points of promise.

Notes

1 Allan, T. J. (2015, November, 24). How Michael Jordan's mindset made him a great competitor. *USA Basketball.* Youth News. https://www.usab.com/youth/news/2012/08/how-michael-jordans-mindset-made-him-great.aspx
2 Ford, D.Y. (2013). Ford-Harris/Bloom-Banks Matrices. *Samples.* https://www.drdonnayford.com/sample-ford-harris-matrices
3 Ford, D.Y., Moore, J. L., & Milner, R. (2005). Beyond culture blindness: A model of culture with implications for gifted education. *Roeper Review, 27*(2), 97–103. doi: 10.1080/02783190509554297
4 Guskey, T. R. (2016). Gauge impact with 5 levels of data. *Learning Forward, 37*(1), 32–37.
5 Bandura, A. (n.d.). *Self-efficacy.* https://www.uky.edu/~eushe2/Bandura/BanEncy.html#sources
6 Ibid.
7 Winsler, A., Gupta Karkhanis, D., Kim, Y. K., & Levitt, J. (2013). Being Black, male, and gifted in Miami: Prevalence and predictors of placement in elementary school gifted education programs. *The Urban Review, 45,* 416–447. doi: 10.1007/s11256-013-0259-0
8 Torrance's Creative Positives (1998), as adapted by Smutny, J. F., Bolaños, O., Haydon, K. P., & Estrada Danley, G. (2012). *Discovering and developing talents in Spanish-speaking students.* Corwin.
9 Grantham, T. C., & Biddle, W. H. (2014). From bystander to upstander teacher for gifted black students accused of acting White. *Gifted Child Today, 37*(3), 178–187. doi: 10.1177/1076217514530117
10 Stern, J., Lauriault, N., & Ferraro, K. (2017). *Tools for teaching conceptual understanding, elementary: Harnessing natural curiosity for learning that transfers.* Corwin.
11 Torrance's Creative Positives (1998), as adapted by Smutny et al. (2012).
12 Safir, S. (2016). Equity vs. equality: 6 steps toward equity. *Edutopia.* Education equity. https://www.edutopia.org/blog/equity-vs-equality-shane-safir
13 Ibid.
14 Muhammad, G. (2020). *Cultivating genius: An equity framework for culturally and historically responsive literacy.* Scholastic.
15 Feldman, J. (2020). *Accurate and equitable grading: Your district's grading system could be perpetuating inequities.* National School Boards Association. https://www.nsba.org/ASBJ/2020/February/Accurate-Equitable-Grading
16 Siegle, D. (n.d.). Be a talent scout not a deficit detective. *National Center for Research on Gifted Education.* Recommendations for Improving Gifted Education. https://vimeo.com/596617943

7

Zone 4

Increasing and Developing Partnerships with Parents and the Community

"I am America. I am the part you won't recognize. But get used to me. Black, confident, cocky; my name, not yours; my religion, not yours; my goals, my own; get used to me."[1] These words by boxer Muhammad Ali reflect what our students think and feel, but perhaps may not say. *See me. Know me. Value me.* For who I am, not for who I could be, if only I changed into what your picture of giftedness is. Do not tell me that my intellect is valued, and my participation is integral on the team, but only if I leave my Black English and hoodie at the door. Part of the equity work we are embarking on in the 4ZEPL is the reformation of gifted education. Developing genuine relationships with the parents and communities built on understanding and trust is part of the groundwork in establishing new, equitable programs that are reflective of the children being served.

What's the Play

Zone 4: Increasing and Developing Partnerships with Parents and the Community zeros in on utilizing the families and communities to support gifted learners. There is a triangle of relational learning in education; relationships exist between the teacher and student, student and parent/community, and parent/community and teacher. We know that when all three legs of the triangle are connected, the student achieves the greatest academic and social

DOI: 10.4324/9781003196204-8

PLC 1 Growth Group	**PLC 2** Proficient Group	**PLC 3** Extension Group
Little to no cultural & equity awareness: misconceptions related to gifted characteristics in traditionally marginalized gifted groups in the community	Average cultural & equity awareness: misconceptions related to gifted characteristics in traditionally marginalized gifted groups in the community	Culturally & equity aware: recognizes gifted characteristics in traditionally marginalized gifted groups in the community
-Facilitators present in multiple modalities the basic tenets of FoK, primarily focusing on strengths/assets based viewpoints and cultural capital. -As part of ongoing and sustained work, PLC 3 received training to continue to support PLC 1 in this role (see Zone 1). -PLC members attend events within the school community. -Facilitators support PLC as they review current parent and community engagement opportunities focused on gifted programming assessing for level of impact and quality of engagement. -Facilitators and PLC members explore avenues to involve the local members of the historically minoritized communities in gifted programming. -PLC creates a plan to welcome parents and community to the school and/or a community space for information sessions about the program; PLC works with the planning committee to ensure that there is a panel of speakers that can address any concerns that arise about the gifted programming.	-Facilitators train PLC to conduct home visits and build asset-based relationships with families and the community, per the FoK framework. -PLC works with facilitators to review current parent and community engagement opportunities focused on gifted programming assessing for level of impact and quality of engagement. -PLC works with facilitators to explore avenues to involve local members of the historically minoritized communities in gifted programming. -PLC plans information sessions for parents and community; researches expert speakers to invite that will provide culturally relevant input on the gifted programming.	-PLC members conduct home visits and build asset-based relationships with families and the community, per the FoK framework; mentor PLC 2 with this work. -PLC begins to work with administration to revise current parent and community engagement opportunities focused on gifted programming assessing for level of impact and quality of engagement. -PLC creates an action plan with at least two local community members input to involve local members of the historically minoritized communities in gifted programming. -PLC plans and conducts information sessions for parents and the community, serving as the expert speakers.
Throughout, provide time for self-reflective journaling prompts, discussions, and debriefs.		
Embedded Equity Driven Professional Learning Principles *Taking a Pulse, Individualizing Professional Learning Plans, Establishing a Safe Zone, Going Beyond the Tip of the Iceberg, Bridging the Gap between School and Home, Engaging in Courageous Conversations, Identifying Grows and Glows*		

Figure 7.1 Zone 4 in action: Sample planning chart for differentiated groups.

success. Too often, however, one or more of the links of the triangle is broken. This could be due to deficit thinking on the part of the educator, a lack of trust of governmental entities on the part of the parents and community, or an unwillingness (or forgetfulness) on the part of the student to share. While there are many and varied causes of the disconnect, educators who are effective at fostering authentic relationships with the family and school partnership find greater yields in their students' outcomes. Zone 4 seeks to develop all the triangle links to foster the greatest potential for student success. Figure 7.1 is the Zone 4 section of the Sample Planning Chart for Differentiated Groups, initially shared in Chapter 2, Figure 2.2 which shows a general outline of what Zone 4 might look like for three differentiated groups based on the results of taking a pulse.

Brief Explanation of the Research Base

The importance of family, school, and community partnerships is widely recognized within the field of education. Through a compilation of the research from the past 20 years, Katie and her colleagues identified benefits of strong family–school partnerships; these include

> (a) higher academic achievement and grades; (b) increased student sense of well-being; (c) better school attendance; (d) positive student and parent perceptions of both classroom and school climate; (e) positive student attitudes and behaviors; (f) increased student readiness to do homework; (g) increased student time spent with parents; (h) higher educational aspirations; and (i) increased parental satisfaction with teachers.[2]

When there are positive relationships between parents and teachers, there are direct positive effects on student outcomes beyond academics; overall, these students develop a stronger skill set of social-emotional aptitudes as well as healthier relationships with their peers. The PTA (Parent Teacher Association) National Standards for Family-School Partnerships[3] identify six research-based standards for how families and schools can work together to student academic success.

- **Standard 1: Welcoming All Families into the School Community**—focusing on inviting families to become involved in the school community, recognizing the value in their contributions to the learning environment as well as building relationships between families.

- **Standard 2: Communicating Effectively**—going beyond the one-way street of communication to developing two-way lines of meaningful communication about student learning and growth.
- **Standard 3: Supporting Student Success**—fostering the development of the whole child by working with families and educators to guide both social-emotional and academic development.
- **Standard 4: Speaking Up for Every Child**—empowering families with the tools to be advocates for their children.
- **Standard 5: Sharing Power**—uplifting the importance of shared decision-making, that families and educators should be equal partners in advocating for appropriate policies, practices, and programs.
- **Standard 6: Collaborating with Community**—knowing and utilizing the resources available within the school and community to enrich and expand learning experiences for the students.

Developing strong family-community partnerships requires sustained commitment from all stakeholders. While this may seem like a daunting task, it is a worthwhile endeavor. Successful partnerships recognize all stakeholders as equal partners at the table; therefore, it is important to raise the question: how will each group benefit and contribute to this relationship? How can I, in my (school-based or district, teacher or administrator) role make sure that all voices are not just brought to the table (inclusion) but that all parties know that their contributions are welcomed, needed, and valued (belongingness)? PL facilitators should spend significant time on this content in professional learning experiences.

Gifted coordinators who are initiating this conversation must first determine which stakeholders will be the points of contact, brainstorm the stakeholders that should be at the table, and take a critical look from a counter point of view: which voices are missing from the conversation? Sometimes it helps to view the question from the view of *whose voice is or has traditionally been missing* versus *who do we need to invite*? Engage the community leaders in this brainstorming session. Mariame Kaba quotes her father, Moussa Kaba, in *We Do This 'Til We Free Us*, saying "Collectivity: because everything worthwhile is done with others."[4] One of the points of Zone 4 is to remove gifted teachers and administrators from their historical silos—we are part of a community of stakeholders that are invested in creating equitable gifted services for all gifted children.

When working with marginalized groups of students, it becomes essential to nurture authentically healthier relationships with the family and school partners. Historically, these relationships have been fraught with tension and mistrust (from both ends!); therefore, the impetus is on the educators to take the initiative to open the doors to healthier relationships. PL plays an important role in preparing educators to provide meaningful opportunities to invite the stakeholders to participate in the gifted school community. Specifically, healthy sustainable partnerships rely heavily on the establishment of open lines of communication, cooperation, respect, trust, and equity. Knowledge and understanding of these qualities can be developed through PL, with content focused on enhancing understanding of cultural differences in addition to situational and organizational factors that have posed traditional barriers to school community partnerships such as schedules, time availability, and language differences.[5] PL can also focus on the soft skills necessary for effective communication. Most importantly, PL must focus on the underlying cause: an understanding of the systemic racism and disparate inequities that have caused these barriers.[6] Hopefully you're not tired of sports analogies yet! Why is it that after a losing season, the coaches are frequently under review? Players are responsible for their knowledge of the game, their ability to carry out plays, their teamwork, and yes, of course, their skills! But it is the coach's job to provide that knowledge, the plays, foster teamwork, and provide coaching to hone their players' skills. As facilitators of high-quality professional learning experiences, we must provide not just the skills, but the knowledge and understandings that support the skills. In working authentically with the parents and community, our goal is to work together to disrupt these inequities.

Zone 4 is heavily grounded in the Funds of Knowledge approach, discussed in detail in Chapter 2, so we won't be overly repetitive in describing the research base here. The essence of FoK is that individuals, households, familial groups, and sometimes communities, have developed, over time, skills and knowledge that enable them to thrive within their cultures. By welcoming the families and communities into the classroom, by celebrating and valuing these funds of knowledge, we create connections for the students, value their homeplace, and meaningfully engage with their families through their ways of knowing. One of the FoK founders states, "you can know the academic standards inside and out, and write the most creative lesson plans, but if positive, affirming, and mutually respectful relationships are not the norm in our classrooms, no learning will take place."[7] As we get to know our communities, two of the equity literacy principles come to mind: *one size fits few* (know who is at the table, e.g., a Puerto Rican family, rather than generalizing to a broader group, i.e., Hispanic) and *evidence-informed equity* (textbooks and research are principal resources, but so too are the community stories).[8]

Put it in Play

Increasing family and community partnerships is essential. The first step should be to *take the pulse* by surveying your teachers to find out how they are currently engaging with family and community partners. Educators have varying degrees of experience and levels of comfort related to community engagement. Understanding their prior experiences, interactions, and expectations are important moving forward in Zone 4. It is equally important for the facilitator to understand the perspectives of the parents and community members. It is recommended to also reach out to your partners to gather input from them regarding their experiences and expectations of involvement with the gifted, as well as to be aware of the district's policies regarding family and community partnerships.

Zone 4 centers on *bridging the gap between school and home,* and bringing community partners to the table as equal partners. Creating an authentic process for communication is a key focus of Zone 4, as participants who have experienced failed partnerships are more likely to resist involvement in schools. The onus is on educators to reach out to families and partners to repair broken lines of communication. This is a process that can move very quickly in some ways, but may move significantly more slowly in others. For example, opening the lines of communication by increasing the number of emails, flyers, or social media posts is a relatively quick process. However, diving deeper into more integrated partnerships takes more time as there are more steps in the process.

In Zone 4, we foster discussions about what works when we engage with partners, and how to create mutually beneficial and authentic relationships. This requires some self-reflection for both the individual and the institution. Encourage candid conversations about what has worked well in the past for engaging communities, as well as things that fell flat. This is another great opportunity to reach out beyond the gifted world and see where/how other organizations have experienced success. There's no need to reinvent the wheel; however, if the wheel is broken, don't be afraid to replace it with a better one!

Inviting community members to the table to engage in an open discussion on how to strengthen the family community partnership starts the listening conversation. Listening and learning about community partners is essential to nurturing a successful relationship (see Zone 1). Just like in our personal relationships, we need to remember to hear the other side of the conversation if we are to maintain a healthy relationship. Consider the venue for these conversations, is it best to invite the community members to join you at the school, or perhaps it would be better to join them at the local community center.Finally, consider how many people to invite to the meeting—is this a small group conversation or a town hall meeting?Each serves a purpose—but sometimes deeper conversations are more likely to develop during smaller groups where participants feel more comfortable sharing versus the larger audiences where few voices can be heard.

Change takes time, and building trusting authentic relationships does as well. After inviting community members in for initial conversations, follow up on those conversations and continue the conversation. Just as you send a follow up note to a parent after a conference, the community members should receive a follow up communication. Remember, this is not the school running a meeting with parents and community invited, it is everyone's meeting. Treat it as such.

Be sure that leadership roles are spread throughout the various stakeholders, and that all members of all groups are part of even what may seem like the smallest decisions (e.g., meeting time, place, menus, speakers, agendas, print or email invitations, childcare options, whether the meeting is recorded, what kind of sign-in is required). During the meetings, it is important to remember the Funds of Knowledge, all that was learned in Zones 1 and 2 (keep in mind, the zones are iterative—jump back as needed) and remain judgment free and open to listening to all stakeholders—all partners. Engage your best listening skills and focus on affirming and validating any concerns or ideas the partners bring to the table.

Courageous conversations in Zone 4 will not only need to occur between the educators, but also with the family and community members. These conversations should take place in smaller settings, as opposed to larger gatherings, so that a sense of trust can be established along with an opportunity for all participants to feel comfortable sharing their thoughts. The PL should focus on training the teachers to conduct these conversations with the families of their gifted learners instead of relying solely on the administration to coordinate the conservations. Content should also include the history of systemic racism and inequities, and a review of Funds of Knowledge and/or deficit vs. dynamic thinking as needed, based on the results of *taking a pulse*. Figure 7.2 shows the essential content for this zone, assuming your participants are ready to move forward. Dip back into Zones 1 or 2 as needed for a review of FoK, deficit thinking, and/or community or cultural assets of your local population.

Z4 EC	Brief Explanation	Playbook Activities
Self and Community Study Study	Just like in Zone 1, this content area starts off with knowing thyself and knowing others. Begin with gathering and identifying the types of family and community engagement activities for gifted programs already in existence. Critically evaluate the activities for their effectiveness, purposefulness, equity, and cultural relevance. While getting to know 'thyself' and what has been offered and attempted in the past, begin to establish relationships- honest, genuine, and meaningful relationships- with families and community members. Work together to establish a plan moving forward.	Get to Know Your Families Putting Yourself in Their Shoes Keep it, Revise it, or Trash it Activity Connecting Funds of Knowledge to Family & Community Partnerships
Developing a Family and Community Gifted Engagement Plan	Develop an engagement plan that is respectful, purposeful, equitable, and creates belongingness with the students, family, community, staff, and faculty of the school. This may include plans for workshops and seminars, but is not limited to Informational sessions. Participants will develop culturally responsive and equitable community programming which is inclusive of the unique cultural characteristics of the student population. A communication plan should be embedded within the engagement plan or an additional plan.	Creating a GT Plan for Developing Community Partnerships Multilayer Communication with Gifted Families Families & Friends of the Gifted Booster Club Planning Organizer PMI Organizer for Families & Friends of the Gifted Booster Club Equal Partnership Scale Checks & Balances Building a Gifted Education Family, Community, and School Collaborative Council

Figure 7.2 Essential content Z4 increasing and developing partnerships with parents and the community.

Cautions and Caveats

- **Following the rules and regulations.** School districts have policies and procedures in place for community and parental engagement, some of which are non-negotiables such as clearances. As the facilitator, you will need to be aware of these policies and appoint people responsible for enforcing them. You will need to know which rules can or cannot be changed or adjusted to increase family and community involvement before creating a new community partnership plan.
- **Valuable volunteers.** Acknowledging and thanking your family and community partnerships is important in growing your Team Gifted support. Community members who invest their time and resources in your gifted program should be recognized for their contributions. It can be as simple as sharing thank-you notes from the students or a shout-out on social media.
- **Reciprocal rewards.** When fostering partnerships, it is important that both parties have an equal stake in the project. This requires some give and take from both parties. For example, if you invite a community leader to come speak at the gifted education seminar, then in return the school may offer that leader the use of the multipurpose room for their next community event.
- **Voluntold doesn't work.** Don't forget everyone is juggling multiple responsibilities—whether it is family, job, or community-service–related. Be sure to provide many options for contributing to the gifted program. Mandating X number of hours can backfire since some families simply do not have any more time in the day. Instead, share several options for the families and community to actively contribute to the gifted program.
- **Home field advantage.** Keep in mind the advantage the home team has during competitions. When you invite someone into your community, you already have the advantage of a comfortable environment. Instead of always inviting the partners to your school building, consider reaching out and meeting the partners on their home fields (e.g., the community hall or neighborhood park).
- **Just do it!** Nike's slogan says it all. Sometimes we are hesitant to reach out again to a family or community group based on our own past experiences. However, we need to commit ourselves to giving it another full-hearted attempt, because this could be the time that the partnership is successful.

Resources

Websites

- Funds of Knowledge Toolkit, https://www.k12.wa.us/student-success/access-opportunity-education/migrant-and-bilingual-education/bilingual-education-program/funds-knowledge-toolkit
- How to Use Funds of Knowledge in your Classroom and Create Better Connections, https://www.notimeforflashcards.com/2018/02/funds-of-knowledge.html#:~:text=Funds%20of%20Knowledge%20are%20collections,families%2C%20communities%2C%20and%20culture.
- NAGC Resources for Parents, https://www.nagc.org/resources-publications/resources-parents and Recursos Para los Padres de Familia, https://www.nagc.org/resources-publications/resources-parents/recursos-para-los-padres-de-familia
- Parent TIP Sheets, https://www.nagc.org/resources-publications/resources-parents/parent-tip-sheets

Articles

- "Taco Night" by Paul Gorski, http://edchange.org/publications/TacoNight.pdf
- "Becoming Joey" by Paul Gorski, http://edchange.org/publications/becoming-joey.pdf
- Theorizing Social Justice: Funds of Knowledge as Praxis, https://digitalcommons.unomaha.edu/cgi/viewcontent.cgi?article=1054&context=ctlle
- Using Families' Funds of Knowledge Literacy to Enhance Family-School Relationships, https://rdw.rowan.edu/cgi/viewcontent.cgi?article=3764&context=etd

Books

- *Bright, Talented, and Black* by Joy Lawson Davis
- *Culturally Responsive Teaching in Gifted Education* edited by C. Matthew Fugate, Wendy Behrens, Cecelia Boswell, and Joy Lawson Davis
- *Beyond the Bake Sale* by Anne Henderson, Karen Mapp, Vivian Johnson, and Don Davies
- *Families and Educators Together: Building Great Relationships that Support Young Children* by Derry Koralek Karen Nemeth Kelly Ramsey
- *Powerful Partnerships: A Teacher's Guide to Engaging Families for Student Success* by Karen Mapp, Ilene Carver, and Jessica Lander

Professional Learning Playbook

Look for the Guiding Principle Icons by the playbook activities!

1) Taking a Pulse
2) Individualizing Professional Learning Plans 
3) Establishing a Safe Zone
4) Going Beyond the Tip of the Iceberg
5) Engaging in Courageous Conversations
6) Bridging the Gap between School and Home
7) Identifying Grows and Glows 

Activity 1: Get to Know Your Families

Estimated Time: 15–20 minutes

Materials Needed: Paper, or online software

Delivery Format: Digital or In Person

Seven Guiding Principles Addressed: 

Purpose: This activity provides a needs-assessment for the teachers to reflect on the current level of interactions with the families and community. These questions are designed to provide a reflective opportunity for educators to share what is already known, working, and what they perceive to be potential barriers. Similarly, there are reflective prompts which should be shared with the families and community members to gain insight into their levels of communication with the teachers in the gifted program.

Procedure:

★ Educators use the discussion prompts and the facilitator should guide a conversation to learn how gifted teachers are interacting with the marginalized gifted students' families and communities. This is an important first step in identifying areas where communication is working or not working.

★ At the same time, the reflective questions for families and community members should be shared with the stakeholders. These questions may be shared in an open response formed through an online survey tool, like survey monkey, or paper copy. If possible, the reflective questions should be shared with individual families as well as asked in a more open forum. This is important, as some families may not feel comfortable sharing their thoughts in a whole-group discussion.

★ The facilitator should take notes on the key takeaways from the discussion and address any questions during the future PL sessions.

Activity 2: Putting Yourself in Their Shoes

Estimated Time: 10–15 minutes

Materials Needed: "Becoming Joey" and "Taco Night" by Paul Gorski

Delivery Format: Digital or In Person

Seven Guiding Principles Addressed:

Purpose: The purpose of this activity is to help the PLC team develop empathy toward families and community members. By putting themselves in the shoes of their students' families, gifted educators gain new insights into the impact of culture and everyday life. In turn, gifted teachers are better positioned to create meaningful partnerships.

Procedure:

- ★ The facilitator shares "Becoming Joey" by Paul Gorski with the PLC team. Following a think-pair-share format, the facilitator invites the participants to first read the poem and reflect on the following prompts:
  - ★ What are your initial reactions to reading the poem?
  - ★ How do you relate to Joey?
  - ★ If you were Joey's parent, what would your advice be to him?
  - ★ Do any of your students remind you of Joey?
  - ★ If you were Joey's teacher, what would your advice be to him?
- ★ After engaging in a discussion on the reflection prompts, the facilitator guides the conversation to the parent perspective. Again, engaging in a think-pair-share format, invite the PLC team to reflect on the following discussion prompts
  - ★ If you were Joey's parent, what would your advice be to him?
  - ★ Write a poem, letter, or email from the parents' perspective to the gifted teachers.
- ★ Invite the PLC teams to share their perspective writings and transition the conversation to parental involvement in schools. Share "Taco Night" with the teachers and ask them to engage with the text, thinking about the following prompts:
  - ★ What are your initial takeaways from this story?
  - ★ What events does our school district have that are similar in nature to taco night?
  - ★ Where did the school district misstep in their intentions of creating a taco night?
- ★ Diving into conversation with the PLC team, discuss "Taco Night," making connections between the text and Z1 and Z2 concepts.
- ★ This activity prepares the PLC team to move into Playbook Activity 3: Keep It, Revise It, or Trash It.

Activity 3: Keep It, Revise It, or Trash It

Estimated Time: 20–30 minutes

Materials Needed: Chart paper, or digital organizer; Reproducible 7.2: Keep It, Revise It, or Trash It

Delivery Format: Digital or In Person

Seven Guiding Principles Addressed: 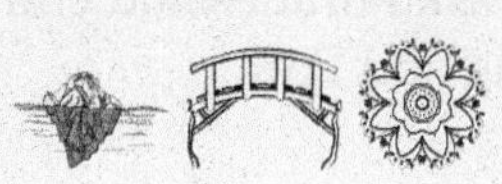

Purpose: This activity is designed to help gifted educators objectively assess their current events for parents of gifted children and community. By obtaining a clear picture of the current partnership plans, the team is better prepared to revise, modify, and create new more inclusive gifted families and community partnerships.

Procedure:

- ★ Working in groups, teachers generate a list of all the current events and activities for parents of the gifted which are scheduled to occur throughout the school year.
- ★ From the list, each event should be carefully assessed for the value of the activity using Reproducible 7.2: Keep It, Revise It, or Trash It. With an ultimate decision of whether to keep the event, revise it to be more effective, or trash it altogether.

Activity 4: Connecting Funds of Knowledge to Families and Community Partnerships

Estimated Time: 15–20 minutes

Materials Needed: Reproducible 7.3: Connecting Funds of Knowledge to Families and Community Partnerships

Delivery Format: Digital or In Person

Seven Guiding Principles Addressed:

Purpose: The purpose of this activity is to help gifted teachers make direct connections with the Funds of Knowledge, the families of their gifted students and ways to incorporate this understanding into meaningful school-based partnerships. While this activity seems similar to a Z3 playbook activity, the focus here is not instructional strategies or pedagogy, rather it is on the development of genuine, meaningful connections and open communication.

Procedure:

- ★ Working in PLC teams, gifted teachers should reflect on the Funds of Knowledge activities from Zones 1–3. If needed, the facilitator may need to provide additional training on FoK. The facilitator should share the Reproducible 7.3: Connecting Funds of Knowledge to Families and Community Partnerships; working in teams the PLC groups can create questions to ask families and community members related to gifted programming and FoK.

★ To ensure quality questions, the facilitator should have the PLC teams share out their questions and provide feedback to help wordsmith any questions which need revision, as well as to review for any possible missing questions.
★ As an extension of the activity, the participants can take the questions back to the classroom and reach out to their families to initiate the conversation. Before this, the facilitator should review the expectations for establishing a sense of trust with families as well as any district specific community engagement policies and procedures.
★ At the following PLC session, the facilitator should lead a debriefing activity, in which participants share their findings from the family sessions with the group, taking care to maintain the confidentiality of the families.

Activity 5: Building a Gifted Education Family, Community, and School Collaborative Council

Estimated Time: 30–60 minutes, repeated over several days

Materials Needed: Chart paper, or digital organizer; phone, email, computers

Delivery Format: Digital or In Person

Seven Guiding Principles Addressed: 

Purpose: This activity begins the process of building your Gifted Education Family, Community, and School Collaborative Council (feel free to personalize the name) and is designed to help your gifted team (teachers, administrators, district support) authentically engage parents and community members. This activity centers Standard 5 and 6 from the PTA: Sharing Power, and the importance of uplifting shared decision-making with families and educators as equal partners and advocates for their children, and Collaborating with Community, which is knowing and making use of school and community resources in order to enrich the learning experiences of our children.

Procedure:

★ Facilitators should lead a discussion with participants to recognize the importance of having all stakeholders as equal partners at the table. Prompts include:
  ★ How will each stakeholder group benefit and contribute to this collaborative committee?
  ★ How can I, in my (school-based or district, teacher or administrator) role make sure that all voices are not just brought to the table

(inclusion) but that all parties know that their contributions are welcomed, needed, and valued (belongingness)?

★ Facilitators then lead a discussion (whole group or small group depending on the pulse of the room) to help participants identify potential stakeholders: family of gifted students and community members. Ask participants to view their lists with the question in mind: *whose voice is or has traditionally been missing* versus *who do we need to invite*?
★ Review district policies on volunteer participation, as needed, and adjust meeting times and locations to ensure successful participation.
★ Have participants invite members and for the next meeting, repeat this process, including the invited members. This will ensure that all stakeholders are included.
★ Begin to identify the roles, expectations, time commitments, and purposes of the collaborative council.
★ Be sure that leadership roles are spread throughout the various stakeholders, and that all members of all groups are part of even what may seem like the smallest decisions (e.g., meeting time, place, menus, speakers, agendas, print or email invitations, childcare options, whether the meeting is recorded, what kind of sign-in is required).
★ Parent involvement can vary from district to district; just as your gifted program should mirror your student population of the school, your collaborative council should also be representative of your school and community. Be intentional in your invitations so that you are including voices that represented your students. You may not be overwhelmed with enthusiastic "yes, I am happy to join" from the start! Respect those that are guarding their space and time due to work, family, and/or physical and mental health. But don't give up! Go to the next person on the list. It's okay to start with a smaller group and build when you gain momentum; this is likely a better play than a disproportionate representation of voices on your collaborative council.
★ Activities 6–9 include the participation of this collaborative council.

Activity 6: Creating a Plan for Developing Community Partnerships for the Gifted and Talented Program

Estimated Time: 40 minutes (first day), repeated activity or continued

Materials Needed: Reproducible 7.4: Goal Planning Worksheet; Reproducible 7.5: Multilayer Communication with Gifted Families; computers or chart; paper/markers; previous community engagement plans

Delivery Format: Digital or In Person

Seven Guiding Principles Addressed: 

Purpose: This activity provides a structured meeting place for the gifted teachers and/or administrators along with the collaborative council to create an engagement plan that is respectful, purposeful, equitable, and creates belongingness with the students, family, community, staff, and faculty of the school.

Procedure:

The length of time will vary depending on existing (or lack of) community engagement plans. It begins with sketching a base outline, reaching out to administrators, and reworking the outline prior to a final product. It is key to remain flexible during the development process, keeping in mind that this plan should be a living document. Minor revisions and adjustments are to be expected as relationships are developed. The collaborative council will be involved in this activity.

- ★ The facilitator will be guiding the participants in creating a GT plan for community engagement. This conversation should occur after completing Activity 1 Get to Know Your Families and Activity 2, Keep It, Revise It, or Trash It.
- ★ Beginning with the end in mind, the facilitator guides the conversation from identifying both short-term and long-term goals for community engagement using Reproducible 7.4. Goals should be forward thinking—Where do we want to be in the next 5 years?—as well as considering shorter goals—Where do we want to be by the end of the academic year?
- ★ This may include:
    - ★ Plans for workshops and seminars but not limited to informational sessions
    - ★ Culturally responsive and equitable community programming which is inclusive of the unique cultural characteristics of the student population
- ★ After goals are established, the facilitator will guide the teachers through considering a realistic number and type of events/activities/etc. to accomplish the goal for the first year.
- ★ Finally, the group should identify how they will measure the effectiveness of these events/activities.

Activity 7: Families and Friends of the Gifted Workshops Planning Organizer

Estimated Time: 20 minutes or more

Materials Needed: Reproducible 7.6: Families and Friends of the Gifted Booster Club Workshops Planning Organizer; Reproducible 7.7: PMI Organizer for Families and Friends of the Gifted Booster Club

Delivery Format: Digital or In Person

Seven Guiding Principles Addressed: 

Purpose: The purpose of this activity is to get educators, administrators, and the collaborative council thinking creatively about ways to actively engage families in the gifted program, beginning with providing professional learning experiences for families and community members. When designing workshops, it is important to keep in mind that the events/activities must be mutually beneficial. One way to evaluate the workshop is the use of the Plus Minus Interesting (PMI) Strategy. This strategy enables the learner to broaden their thinking, consider different perspectives, as well as weighing the pros and cons of a decision.

Procedure:

★ The collaborative council will be involved in this activity.
★ Working in teams, brainstorm ideas for the family and friends of the Gifted workshop/events. Using the graphic organizer (Reproducible 7.6) consider ways to actively involve the partners and then the sustainability of the activity.
★ Next, participants complete the Family and Friends of the Gifted Booster Club PMI (Reproducible 7.7) to further refine the workshop potential and anticipate any possible problem areas.
★ Decide the details for each specific workshop, obtain administrative approval to move forward and advertise the event.

Activity 8: Equal Partnership Scale

Estimated Time: time will vary

Materials Needed: List of community partnerships events/activities related to gifted programming; notepaper; Reproducible 7.8: Equal Partnership Scale

Delivery Format: Digital or In Person

Seven Guiding Principles Addressed: 

Purpose: The purpose of this activity is to review each outreach activity/event to ensure that they are mutually beneficial. There does not need to be a 1:1 ratio; however, there needs to be an overall balance; equity literacy principles favor prioritizing the benefits for the marginalized students, families, and communities. This is an activity that is used directly after Activity 6, and again after Activity 7; it could also be used after both 6 and 7 are finished, considering both lists of events/workshops/activities at the same time.

Procedure:

★ The collaborative council will be involved in this activity.
★ After brainstorming ideas for events, participants will use a balance scale to determine if the event is mutually beneficial to all invited stakeholders. Working in small groups, participants will consider each event/activity/workshop suggested in Activity 6 and/or Activity 7 and the potential benefits for both the GT program and the families and community.
★ Sort the results of Activities 6 and/or 7 into two categories: Benefits for the Gifted Education Program and School Community and Benefits for the Marginalized Gifted Families and Community
★ Adjustments to the number of events or types of activities should be made to equitably balance the scale, keeping in mind that equitable does not necessarily mean equal.

Activity 9: Checks and Balances

Estimated Time: 15–20 minutes

Materials Needed: Reproducible 7.9: Checks and Balances; list of planned community engagement activities

Delivery Format: Digital or In Person

Seven Guiding Principles Addressed: 

Purpose: The purpose of this activity is to ensure that the learning outcomes and goals of the gifted program will be met through the planning of family and community engagement activities. Validity measures whether the equity goals of the gifted and talented program will be met through the planned event. It is possible to plan a fun event that is not valid. Reliability is a measurement of consistency. Will this event meet the intended outcomes in the same way every time or are there too many variables? Critically assessing the planning GT activities is an important step in ensuring the sustainability of the community engagement.

Procedure:

- ★ The collaborative council will be involved in this activity.
- ★ The facilitator guides the participants in a critical review of the planned family and community engagement activities. Using the Reproducible 7.8: Checks and Balances, the participants will review each activity for validity and reliability.
- ★ If an activity does not meet, or is low on, either criteria, then the facilitator guides the participants to, improve, revamp, or remove the activity.

Activity 10: Multilayer Communication

Estimated Time: 15–20 minutes

Materials Needed: Reproducible 7.5: Multilayer Communication with Gifted Families; chart paper and markers or computers

Delivery Format: Digital or In Person

Seven Guiding Principles Addressed:

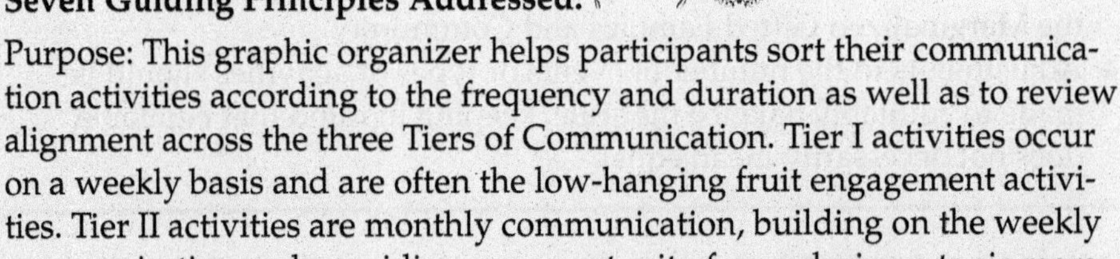

Purpose: This graphic organizer helps participants sort their communication activities according to the frequency and duration as well as to review alignment across the three Tiers of Communication. Tier I activities occur on a weekly basis and are often the low-hanging fruit engagement activities. Tier II activities are monthly communication, building on the weekly communication and providing an opportunity for exploring a topic more in-depth. Tier II is yearly communication which would include activities that are ongoing throughout the year or are a once-a-year occurrence. It is important to have alignment between the three tiers so that each activity, event, and communication is purposeful.

Procedure:

- ★ A communication plan should be embedded within the engagement plan or as an additional plan. Reproducible 7.5: Multilayer Communication with Gifted Families walks through questions about communication to facilitate creating goals and processes for communicating with families.
- ★ Working with the previously created GT plan and workshop organizers, this PL allows for teachers to review their communication activities for depth and complexity. The goal here is to ensure that the various forms of communication are relevant, meaningful, and interconnected.
- ★ When gaps are identified, the facilitator guides the participants through the process of organizing and revising the activities to create a more balanced and holistic communication plan.

Reproducibles

Reproducible 7.1: Get to Know Your Families

Get to Know Your Families Reflection Prompts for the Teachers	
What do you know about your marginalized gifted students and families?	
What do you want to learn about the families and/or communities?	
What barriers are preventing you from getting to know these families? What support do you need to overcome these barriers?	
Who on the staff works closest with these families?	
What would be valuable for the faculty to know?	
How could you facilitate more individualized interactions with the families and community?	

Get to Know Your Families Reflection Prompts for the Families and Community Members	
What do you know about the gifted and talented program?	
What do you want to know about the gifted and talented program?	
What are barriers preventing you from getting to know the gifted teachers?	
Which teachers do you rely on for information about gifted programming?	
What would be valuable for the faculty to know about your child?	
What would be valuable for the faculty to know about your family?	
What can you share that would help faculty to better understand your culture?	
How could the school facilitate more individualized interactions with the families and community?	

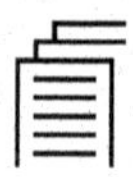

Reproducible 7.2: Keep It, Revise It, or Trash It

Name of Event/Activity	
What is the purpose of the event/activity?	
How much time and resources (human/capital/material) are invested in the event?	
In what ways are the community partners involved as absorbers (passive) or doers (active)?	Absorbers:
	Doers:
In what ways is it culturally responsive?	
In what ways is it equitable?	
In what ways is it meaningful?	
Keep it, Revise it, or Trash it?	

Reproducible 7.3: Connecting Funds of Knowledge to Families and Community Partnerships

Connecting Funds of Knowledge to Families and Community Partnerships			
Fund of Knowledge	Gifted Expression[9]	Create some questions that you could ask families to learn about their funds of knowledge. Remember you must first establish trust and good rapport with the families and community before asking these questions.	In what ways can you apply these understandings in the development of an equitable and culturally relevant partnership between the families, community, and the gifted program?
Home Language	Code Switching		
	Expressiveness of gestures, body language, and the ability to interpret these		
	Humor and sense of humor		
	Richness of imagery in informal language		
Family Values and Traditions	Enjoyment of and ability in music and rhythm, creative movement, dance, and/or dramatics		
	Articulateness in role playing and storytelling		
	Enjoyment of and skills in group activities and problem-solving		
Scientific Knowledge	Originality of ideas in problem-solving		
	Problem centeredness or persistence in problem-solving		
	Ability to improvise with commonplace materials		

Reproducible 7.4: Goal Planning Worksheet

Working together, the gifted education leadership team should create both long-term and short-term goals for increasing meaningful family and community partnerships. As you are crafting your goals, keep in mind the SMART goal planning process (S-specific, M-measurable, A-achievable, R-relevant, T-timely).

GT Plan for Developing Community Partnerships		
Goal Term	Things to Consider	Goals for Family and Community Engagement of the Marginalized Gifted and Talented Student Population
Long-term (5 Year)	• Alignment with the local educational plan for gifted education • Focus on equity • Aligned with areas in need of improvement based on the Get to Know Your Families Surveys • Respectful and purposeful • Creates belongingness with the students, family, community, staff, and faculty of the school	Goal 1: Goal 2:
Short-term goals (current academic year)	• Alignment with 5 year goals • Focus on equity • Culturally responsive and equitable community programming which is inclusive of the unique cultural characteristics of the student population • A communication plan	Goal 1: Goal 2:

Next, take each of the short-term goals and match them to the current activities, events, and/or workshops available to determine any gaps.

Short-Term Goal	Activities/Events/Workshops	What is missing?
Goal 1		
Goal 2		

Reproducible 7.5: Multilayer Communication with Gifted Families

Multilayer Communication with Gifted Families

Tier I: Weekly Communication

List the ongoing communication between GT teachers and families.
In what ways is there a balance of consuming and doing?
In what ways it inclusive of all cultures?
In what ways it meaningful?

____
____
____
____
____
____
______

Tier II: Monthly Communication

List the ongoing communication between GT teachers and families.
In what ways is there a balance of consuming and doing?
In what ways is it inclusive of all cultures?
In what ways is it meaningful?
How does this build on or support the Tier I communications?

____
____
____
____
____
____
______

Tier III: Yearly Communication

List the ongoing communication between GT teachers and families.
In what ways is there a balance of consuming and doing?
In what ways is it inclusive of all cultures?
In what ways is it meaningful?
How does this build on or support Tier I & II communications?

____
____
____
____
____
____
______

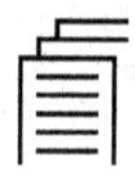

Reproducible 7.6: Families and Friends of the Gifted Booster Club Workshops Planning Organizer

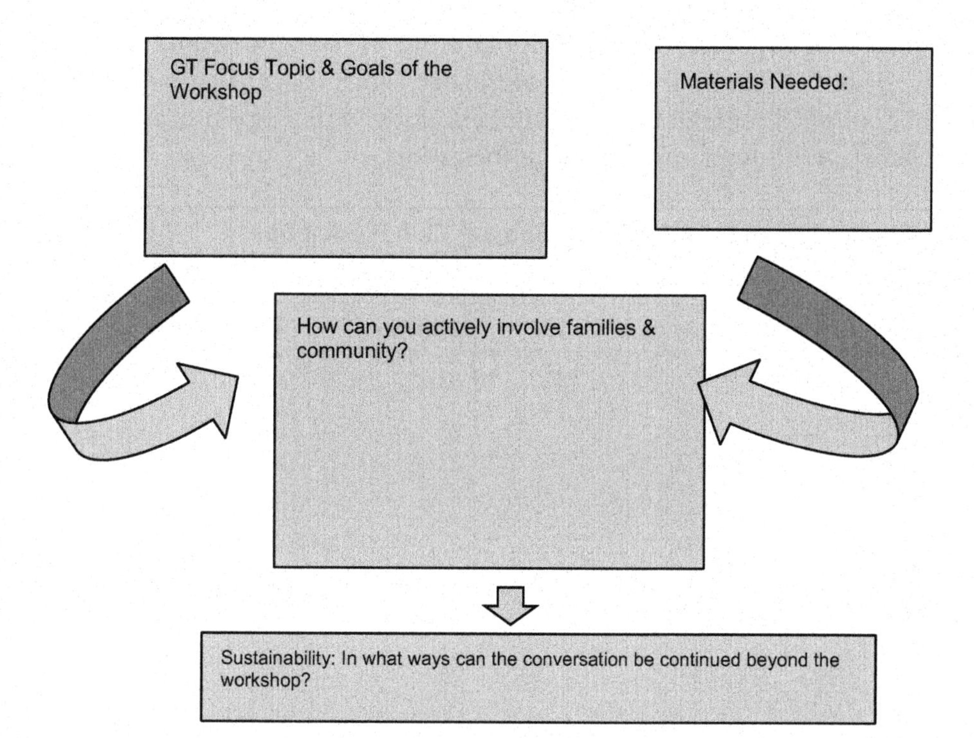

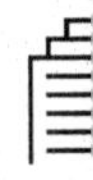

Reproducible 7.7: PMI Organizer for Families and Friends of the Gifted Booster Club

The following organizer is useful in planning the specific details of individual workshops. Thinking about the workshop's purpose and goals, the faculty members would pull out the plus (benefits of the workshop), minus (potential problems), and interesting aspects of the event.

Families and Friends of the Gifted Booster Club Workshops		
Name of the Specific Workshop:		
Plus	**Minus**	**Interesting**

Reproducible 7.8: Equal Partnership Scale

Directions: Working in small groups, educators consider each event/activity/workshop and the potential benefits for both parties. The goal is to keep the scale balanced with both parties mutually benefiting. Adjustments to the number of events or types of activities should be made to equitably balance the scale, keeping in mind that equitable does not necessarily mean equal. The scale does not necessarily need to be a 1:1 ratio, depending on the weight of individual items; equity literacy principles favor prioritizing the benefits for the marginalized students, families, and communities.

For example: a gifted characteristics workshop would benefit the school community by raising awareness of giftedness and the gifted program, while for the community a benefit could be childcare during the event for parents attending the school meeting, while also learning about giftedness and the programmatic options available to their children.

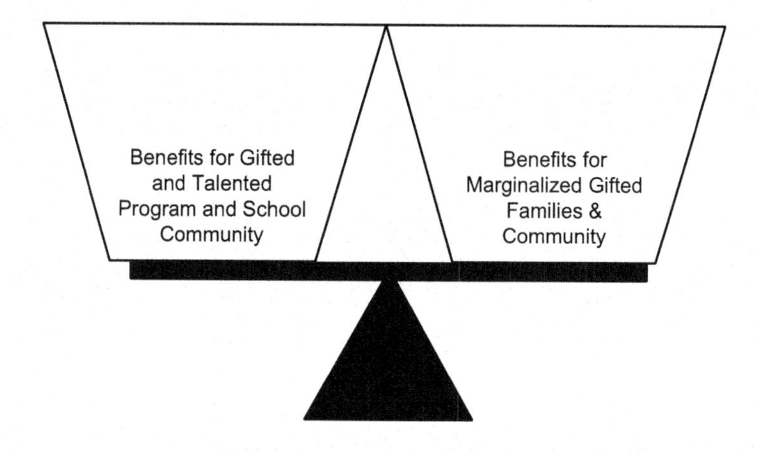

Reproducible 7.9: Checks and Balances

Checks and Balances: Evaluating the Alignment of the Gifted and Talented Families and Communities Engagement Activity with Program Goals		
Name of Activity	**Validity** In what ways does this event/activity meet (or not meet) the equity goals of the GT Program?	**Reliability** In what ways does this event/activity produce (or not produce) the same outcome every time with regards to the equity goals of the GT program?
	Proposed Improvements to Increase Validity*	**Proposed Improvements to Increase Reliability***

*Where the activity fails to meet validity or reliability, or is lower in either area, the next step is to explore options for increasing validity or reliability. For example, if the reliability is low because the event relies heavily on gifted and talented teachers creating new materials each time, consider creating activities which could be reused along with directions so that any gifted educator could run the event.

Notes

1 Haynes, C. C. (2016, June 8). "'I am America." *Freedom Forum Institute.* News & Commentary. Inside the First Amendment. https://www.freedomforuminstitute.org/2016/06/08/i-am-america/
2 Sutton, K. K., Lewis, K. D., & Beauchat, K. A. (2020). The role of teacher preparation programs in fostering preservice teachers' ability to effectively engage with families. *School Community Journal, 30*(2), 39–52.
3 PTA. (2009). PTA National standards for family-school partnerships: An implementation guide. PTA. https://www.pta.org/From_S3/National_Standards_Implementation_Guide_2009.pdf
4 Kaba, M. (2021). *We do this 'til we free us: Abolitionist organizing and transforming justice* (p. vxiii). Haymarket Books.
5 Lockhard, K., & Mun, R. U. (2020). Developing a strong home-school connection to better identify and serve culturally, linguistically, and economically diverse gifted and talented students. *Gifted Child Today, 43*(4), 231–238. doi: 10.1177/1076217520940743.
6 Novak, A.M. (2022). Not white saviors but critical scholars: The need for gifted critical race theory. In J. Nyberg & J. Manzone (Eds.), *Creating equitable services for the gifted: Protocols for identification, implementation, and evaluation* (pp. 246–262). IGI Global. https://doi.org/10.4018/978-1-7998-8153-7.ch016
7 Amanti, C. (2005). Beyond a beads and feathers approach. In N. González, L.C. Moll, C. Amanti (Eds.), *Funds of knowledge: Theorizing practices in households, communities, and classrooms* (pp. 131–142). Routledge.
8 Gorski, P.C. (2020). *Equity literacy principles.* EdChange and the Equity Literacy Institute. http://edchange.org/handouts/Equity-Literacy-Principles.pdf
9 Torrance's Creative Positives (1998), as adapted by Smutny, J. F., Bolaños, O., Haydon, K. P., Estrada Danley, G. (2012). *Discovering and developing talents in Spanish-speaking students.* Corwin.

8

Professional Learning is an Iterative Process

Lifelong learning is a catchphrase that is, perhaps, overused in the field of education, yet the message still rings true. The teachers who are recognized by their districts as Educator of the Year or Golden Apple Award winners are at the top of their field because they are continually refining their craft *through* learning. Champion tennis player Serena Williams says, "I really think a champion is defined not by their wins but by how they can recover when they fall."[1] Olympic athletes who bring home gold medals also are at the top of their game due to continual practice, modifying based on data, and ongoing learning. While the actual competition may be less than a minute long (Caeleb Dressel won the 100m butterfly with a record-setting time of 49.45 seconds!), the amount of time, effort and work put into preparing is measured in *years*. In the classroom, we only get a short period of time to work with our students and positively shape their future. Every moment counts! As professional learning facilitators, the same holds true; equity-driven professional learning is imperative to prepare gifted educators for the brief moments in time that they have gifted students in their classrooms, and the honor of impacting their lives.

Throughout this book, the tenets of professional learning were explored and applied through the Four Zones of Equity-Driven Professional Learning model. 4ZEPL provides a comprehensive research-based training plan which is ongoing, targeted, collaborative, reflective, and connects meaningfully to the classroom. We know that changing mindsets and practices is a challenging

DOI: 10.4324/9781003196204-9

task; yet change is not insurmountable. Equity within gifted education programs, policies and practices *is* possible.

We've all seen the inspirational teacher quotes; perhaps you even have some hanging in your classroom. A popular one says "Teachers change the world one child at a time." We know this *is* possible, and we all can probably share our own story of a child whose life has been positively impacted by a special teacher. We know firsthand the truth, the power, and the responsibility which rest in our hands. Former President Barack Obama shared,

> I will never forget that the only reason I'm standing here today is because somebody, somewhere stood up for me when it was risky. Stood up when it was hard. Stood up when it wasn't popular. And because that somebody stood up, a few more stood up. And then a few thousand stood up. And then a few million stood up. And standing up, with courage and clear purpose, they somehow managed to change the world.[2]

But what if we changed the quote to "Teachers, united, transform lives." Imagine the impact of a united team of gifted educators working as a team toward equity and creating avenues of engagement and success for marginalized gifted students. This is made possible through equity-driven professional learning. Consider these words from Dr. Theresa Perry:

> Few respectable people will publicly assert that Black people are intellectually inferior. The visible, in-your-face manifestations of oppression have been mostly eliminated. But you scarcely can find a Black student who cannot recall or give you a litany of instances when he or she was automatically assumed to be intellectually incompetent.[3]

Perry states that Black students will succeed when schools foster a leveling culture: one in which a culture of achievement is communicated by all educators and to the entire community, and where collectivism is appreciated. Moreover, Perry states that a united institution actively engaging in cultural responsiveness, while systematically affirming and basing instruction in the cultural formations of their community, will produce exceptional results.

Where do we begin? This question can be overwhelming at times; the 4ZEPL offers a concrete plan of action, integrated with the principles for equity-driven professional learning. We always suggest starting with data and the needs of the team. Just as a coach modifies the training plan based on the needs of the athletes, so too can the 4ZEPL be adapted for the gifted educators and tailored to the needs of the district or building. Equity work is not easy. It requires the learner to be reflective, honest with themselves, and willing to change what has always been done. Athletes who always train with the same workouts eventually find themselves stagnant and unable to move closer to their training goals. They must adjust their training plans to include workouts geared toward developing strength, endurance, flexibility, teamwork. As coaches in equity work, we must change our professional learning so that the learner can continue to grow. As PL facilitators, as educators of adult learners, we must remember to meet our educators in their zone of proximal development, differentiating the professional learning experience to meet participants where they are, and challenging them to grow.

Iterative cycles over time foster environments for continual development, allowing for the equity, diversity, social justice, inclusion, and belongingness work to take root.[4] We know the most impactful professional learning is when it is an iterative process, allowing for growth within and across concepts over time. Just like in the classroom, where mathematical concepts are introduced in elementary school, revisited in middle and then again secondary school, 4ZEPL spirals, allowing the learner to dive deeper into the complexity of giftedness, cultural awareness, equity, systemic and structural racism of understanding. The fluidity and flexibility of the 4ZEPL allow the facilitator and learner to move forward and backward through the zones as the learner grows or gaps in understanding arise. By monitoring understanding through informal checks for understanding, the coaches facilitate the growth of the gifted educators.

As your team of teachers experience success in the classroom and see a positive change in marginalized gifted populations, there will be a change in their perceptions of inequities.[5] Similarly, as educators' perceptions of inequities change, there will be a change in marginalization of gifted populations. Remember, lasting change takes time; there will be highs and lows as you work toward equity in gifted education. As facilitators in the PL process, we must continually embrace and celebrate the small victories; these lead to the big wins. Olympic gymnast Simone Biles said, "Don't wait until you've reached your goal to be proud of yourself. Be proud of every step you take toward reaching that goal." This is important; otherwise, one risks becoming too wrapped up in all the unaccomplished tasks and seemingly daunting work to be done. However, just like our athletes, we cannot be content only with small victories. Rather, we should view the small victories as checkpoints along the way to ensure that we are on the right path.

Put It in Play: Scope and Sequence

All these aspects are included in the following sample training scope and sequence. Figure 8.1 walks through the 4ZEPL over the span of a school year if PLCs or cohorts meet about twice a month (some months only once) but also have some "rest days" during which online activities or journaling can be completed. This is, of course, adaptable, and flexible for your particular use. Perhaps your PLCs can meet weekly. Or you might only meet once a month, but you can touch base online two additional times throughout the month. Note that there are suggestions for advance planning (don't forget the snacks!) and that the scope and sequence directly align and combine information from the Zones in Action planning charts in Chapters 2, 4, 5, 6, and 7 and the activities in the Professional Learning Playbooks in Chapters 4 to 7. And then on the pages that follow, you'll find our last thoughts to usher you out onto the field; our final words of wisdom as you put the zones into play.

Top Ten for Tips for Successful Coaches

Coach for Potential

The AppleTV (fictional) Coach Ted Lasso turns a new page in his career, coaching football (soccer) for the first time. He walks into the dressing room, turns to his fellow American coach and says, "I do love a locker room. It smells like potential." Just like giftedness is measured by achievement and potential, as facilitators, we can't expect all the educators in our PLCs to be "there" at the outset. And yes, this is hard. But every PLC, every training, every cohort, every faculty meeting—that's potential. Remember the ripple effect from the Scales activity in Chapter 4, Zone 1. You, the facilitator, are creating that ripple. Each of these educators is now in your sphere of influence. Angela sometimes jokes with one of her children, referencing the book *Artemis Fowl* by Eoin Colfer, "are we using our genius for good or evil today, my love?" Professional learning has great potential, and equity work is hard work; use it wisely.

Warm Up

Depending on the context of the PL, you may not go into the situation knowing your audience. Even if you are leading the PL at the school in which you are an administrator or gifted specialist, facilitating ongoing equity-driven professional learning (asking tough questions, and holding your peers' feet to the proverbial fire) is a different way of knowing your audience, and it is a different relationship. This takes a high degree of emotional intelligence, ongoing knowledge of your participants (*pulse-taking*), and flexibility. While

A Sample Training Scope and Sequence for Four Zone Equity Driven Professional Learning			
Summer Planning Time for the Facilitator of the 4ZEPL			
Backwards Planning: Identify your goals for the GT PL for the academic year; divide into sub goals per month. **Planning & Preparation:** Do your homework: using the 4ZEPL Playbook Activities identity areas where you need to brush on your content knowledge, gather any demographic or identification data, review your Gifted Educational Plan reach out to potential guest speakers **Take a Pulse:** Survey your teachers and create PLC groups. **Take Care of Logistics**: Reserve the meeting space and/or design the online modules, order any new materials for the PL, and don't forget the snacks! =)			
September & October PLC Focus: Zone 1: Increasing Educators' Understanding of Cultural Norms and Equity			
	Team Growth	Team Proficiency	Team Extension
Warm-Up Session (Work to be done before PLC meetings)	-Complete Cultural Awareness Surveys -Respond to any online PLC prompts Note: Team Extension reviews the expectations for serving as a PLC leader & agrees to take on leadership role		
September Session I	-Establish ground rules -Playbook Activities: Snowball Fight, What is Culture?, Caption This!	-Establish ground rules -Playbook Activities: Caption This! What is Racism?	-Establish ground rules -Serves as PLC leaders -Playbook Activities: What is Racism?
Rest Day Activities (Independent Practice Time for Reflection & Implementation of new ideas)	**-PLC Online Reflection Prompts** -Complete Identity Pie Chart → **Facilitator reflects on exit tickets & plans next PLC**		**-PLC Online Reflection Prompts** -Complete Implicit Bias Association -Prepare to assist in follow up session → **Facilitator reflects on exit tickets & plans next PLC**
September Session II	-Establish ground rules -Playbook Activities: What is Racism?, Scaffolded Notes	-Establish ground rules -Playbook Activities: Scales, Implicit Bias, Satellite Circles	-Serve as PLC leaders -Playbook Activities: Funds of Knowledge Activity
Rest Day Activities	**-PLC Online Reflection Prompts** -Connection to the Classroom Assignment: Bring back something to share about a topic covered in Z1 → **Facilitator reflects on exit tickets & plans next PLC: Evaluate if your PLC is ready to move forward or needs additional time**		**-PLC Online Reflection Prompts** -Complete Satellite Circles, Views from a Black Man -Prepare to assist in follow up session → **Facilitator reflects on exit tickets & plans next PLC**

Figure 8.1 A sample training scope and sequence for the Four Zone Equity-Driven Professional Learning Plan.

October Session I	-Playbook Activities: Implicit Bias Association, Introduction to FoK	-Playbook Activities:, Children's Literature Activities, Introduction to FoK	-Serve as PLC leaders -Connection to the Classroom Assignment: Bring back an example of how you recognized FoK in your gifted classroom Playbook Activities: Intersection of My Cultural Identity & My Students' Cultural Identities
Rest Day Activities:	**-PLC Online Reflection Prompts** -Connection to the Classroom Assignment: Bring back an example of how you recognized FoK in your gifted classroom and share a children's literature story with your students to raise cultural awareness → **Facilitator reflects on exit tickets & plans next PLC: Evaluate if your PLC is** ready to move forward or needs additional time		**-PLC Online Reflection Prompts** -Prepare to assist in follow up session → **Facilitator reflects on exit tickets & plans** next PLC
October Session II	-Debrief: Debrief: Team member share the children's literature story they used in the classroom & student reactions -Playbook Activities: Learning for Justice, Children's Literature Activities	-Debrief: Debrief: Team member share the children's literature story they used in the classroom & student reactions -Playbook Activities: Intersection of My Cultural Identity & My Students' Cultural Identities	-Serve as PLC leaders -Playbook Activities: Teaching Tolerance: Magic Carpet Ride Learning for Justice Activities
Rest Day Activities	**-PLC Online Reflection Prompts** -Connection to the Classroom Assignment: Look for examples of the inter-sectionality of cultures, bring an example back to share -Taking a Pulse Survey to prepare for Z2 PLC in November → **Facilitator reflects on exit tickets & plans next PLC: Evaluate if your PLC is** ready to move forward or needs additional time. As you begin Z2, you may need to adjust your PLC based on the Taking a Pulse surveys **Intersection of my cultural identity & my students' cultural identities as well as the FoK needs to be revisited as you move forward in the Zones.**		**-PLC Online Reflection Prompts** -Connection to the Classroom Assignment: Look for examples of the intersectionality of cultures, bring an example back to share -Taking a Pulse Survey to prepare for Z2 PLC in November -Prepare to assist in follow up session → **Facilitator reflects on exit tickets & plans** for the next PLC. As you begin Z2, you may need to adjust your PLC based on the Taking a Pulse surveys

Figure 8.1 (Continued)

November, December & January PLC Focus: Zone 2: Increasing Educators' Understanding of Characteristics of Gifted Marginalized Students			
November Session I	-Playbook Activities: Giftedness Jigsaw, Mythbusters	Playbook Activities: Myth or Fact Sort, Think-Pair-Share	-Serve as PLC leaders -Playbook Activities: District Data
Rest Day Activities	-PLC Online Reflection Prompts -**Connection to the Classroom Assignment: Look for unidentified students in** your grade level who may exhibit gifted characteristics → **Facilitator reflects on exit tickets & plans next PLC: Evaluate if your PLC is** ready to move forward or needs additional time ** Teachers who are new to gifted may need to spend more time on learning about gifted education in general before moving forward		-PLC Online Reflection Prompts -Connection to the Classroom: Look for uni-**dentified students in your grade level who may** exhibit gifted characteristics -Prepare to assist in follow up session → **Facilitator reflects on exit tickets & plans** next PLC
Iterative Insert	*There's only one planned session for November due to the break schedule. Circle back to Zone 1 with the Playbook Activity: Intersection of My Cultural Identity & My Students' Cultural Identities*		*Circle back to Zone 1 with the Playbook Activity: Scales*
December Session 1	-Debrief: Team member share their observations and discuss -Playbook Activities: Myth or Fact Sort, Equity Case Study, Think-Pair-Share	-Debrief: Team member share their observations and discuss -Playbook Activities: Equity Case Study, Hexagonal Thinking Activity: Equity	-Debrief: Team member share their observa-tions and discuss -Serve as PLC leaders **-Playbook activities: Identification Scenarios** Gallery Walk, Equity Case Study
Iterative Insert	*There's only one December meeting due to the break schedule. Bonus Online Activities! Circle back to Zone 2 with the Playbook Activity: Introduction to FoK*		*Circle back to Zone 2 with the Playbook Activity: Children's Literature Activities*
Rest Day Activities	-PLC Online Reflection Prompts -Connection to the Classroom Assignment: Select a gifted learner (current **or former) who didn't fit the traditional gifted child qualifications and write up their learning profile. Bring back to the next PLC session to share.** → **Facilitator reflects on exit tickets & plans next PLC: Evaluate if your PLC is** ready to move forward or needs additional time		PLC Online Reflection Prompts -Connection to the Classroom Assignment: Select a gifted learner (current or former) who **didn't fit the traditional gifted child qualifica-tions and write up their learning profile. Bring** back to the next PLC session to share. -Prepare to assist in follow up session → **Facilitator reflects on exit tickets & plans** next PLC

Figure 8.1 (Continued)

January Session 1	-Debrief: Team members share their learning profiles and workshop the gifted characteristics- be sure to change student names for confidentiality -Playbook Activities: Identification Scenarios Gallery Walk, Connecting to Current Profiles		-Debrief: Team members share their learning profiles and workshop the gifted characteristics- be sure to change student names for confidentiality -Serve as PLC leaders -Playbook Activities: Connecting to Current Profiles
Iterative Insert	*Just the one January meeting due to the break schedule. Bonus Online Activities!* *Circle back to Zone 1 with the Playbook Activities: Views from a Black Man, Scales*		
Rest Day Activities	**-PLC Online Reflection Prompts** -Connection to the Classroom Assignment: Evaluate your understanding of Z1 and Z2; What have you learned? What questions do you still have? What support do you need from your PLC team and coach? -Taking a Pulse Survey to prepare for Z3 PLC in November **→ Facilitator reflects on exit tickets & plans next PLC: Evaluate if your PLC is ready to move forward or needs additional time** * As you move through Z2, you will identify team members who need to spend more time training in Z1 before they are able to fully buy into Z2. This is normal and why this is an iterative process. Modify the training plan, strengthen areas of weakness- the time spent developing Z1 and Z2 understandings pays off exponentially as you move forward with Z3 & Z4. ***Plan for flexible PLC groups; adjust the team members based on their readiness profile before moving into Z3.**		
February & March PLC Focus: Zone 3: Increasing Classroom Support for Educators and Gifted Marginalized Students			
February Session 1	-Playbook Activities: Hexagonal Thinking: Giftedness & Identity, Fostering Growth through Mentorships	-Playbook Activities: Fostering Growth through Mentorships, This is Who I Am: A Photo Essay for Gifted Learners	-Serve as PLC leaders -Playbook Activities: Connecting Funds of Knowledge to Gifted Instructional Strategies
Rest Day Activities	**-PLC Online Reflection Prompts** -Connection to the Classroom Assignment: Select one of the two playbook activities from the session to teach in the gifted classroom, bring samples of student work back to share at the next PLC **→ Facilitator reflects on exit tickets & plans next PLC** ****You may find that in Z3, you only need two PLC groups as the instructional** strategies are new to most; we've adjusted based on our data, hence the change- **the key to grouping is that it always remains flexible!**		**-PLC Online Reflection Prompts** -Connection to the Classroom: Select one of the two playbook activities from the PLC session you helped to lead to teach in the gifted classroom, bring samples of student work back to share at the next PLC -Prepare to assist in follow up session **→ Facilitator reflects on exit tickets & plans next PLC**

Figure 8.1 (Continued)

Iterative Insert	*Ensure that you are connecting back to Zones 1 and 2 as needed. Revisit the Hexagonal Thinking Activity: Equity in the PLC, and encourage the use of the activity in revising lesson plans.*	*Circle back to Zone 2 with the Playbook **Activity: Identification Case Study***
February Session 2	-Debrief: Invite the PLC team to share their student work examples -Playbook Activities: Connecting Funds of Knowledge to Gifted Instructional Strategies	-Serve as PLC leaders -Playbook Activities: It Takes a Village: Engaging with Instructional Specialists
Rest Day Activities	**-PLC Online Reflection Prompts** -Connection to the Classroom Assignment: Take the Playbook Activity: Infusing Cultural Responsiveness back to the classroom, bring samples of student work back to share at the next PLC → **Facilitator reflects on exit tickets & plans next PLC**	**PLC Online Reflection Prompts** -Connection to the Classroom: Arrange a time for a demonstration lesson -Prepare to assist in follow up session → **Facilitator reflects on exit tickets & plans** next PLC
March Session 1	-Debrief: Invite the PLC team to share their student work examples -Playbook Activities: It takes a Village: Engaging with Instructional Specialists	-Serve as PLC leaders -Playbook Activities: Writing Culturally Responsive Enrichment Lessons and Curriculum Units
Rest Day Activities	**-PLC Online Reflection Prompts** -Connection to the Classroom Assignment: Reach out to at least one colleague about partnering to increase equity in your gifted lessons. Be prepared to share out at the next PLC meeting. → **Facilitator reflects on exit tickets & plans next PLC**	**PLC Online Reflection Prompts** -Connection to the Classroom: Implement a revised lesson plan, bring samples of student work and feedback to the next PLC meeting. -Prepare to assist in follow up session → **Facilitator reflects on exit tickets & plans** next PLC
March Session 2	-Debrief: Invite the PLC team to share their experiences reaching out to colleagues, troubleshoot any problems and share new ideas -Playbook Activities: Writing Culturally Responsive Enrichment Lessons and Curriculum Units	-Serve as PLC leaders -Share your experiences with revising curriculum and demonstration with the other PLC groups
Iterative Insert	*Circle back to Zone 2 with the Playbook Activity: Understanding the Culture of White Supremacy*	

Figure 8.1 (Continued)

Rest Day Activities	-PLC Online Reflection Prompts -Connection to the Classroom Assignment: Arrange a time for a demonstration teaching lesson. → **Facilitator reflects on exit tickets & plans next PLC** ** As you move through Z3, you will identify team members who need to spend more time training in Z2 & Z1 before they are able to fully buy into Z3. This is normal and why this is an iterative process. Continue to modify and strengthen areas of weakness by adjusting the training plan. **Plan for flexible PLC groups; adjust the team members based on their readiness profile before moving into Z4.**	PLC Online Reflection Prompts -Connection to the Classroom: Continue to revise and implement gifted curriculum, bring samples of student work and feedback to the next PLC meeting. -Prepare to assist in follow up session → **Facilitator reflects on exit tickets & plans next PLC**
April & May PLC Focus: Zone 4: Increasing and Developing Partnerships with Parents and the Community		
April Session 1	-Debrief: Invite the PLC team to share ways they are continuing to support **marginalized gifted learners beyond identification, address any ongoing** concerns -Playbook Activities: Get to Know Your Families, Keep it, Revise it, or Trash it. **You may find that in Z3, you only need two PLC groups as the instructional** strategies are new to most	-Serve as PLC leaders -Playbook Activities: Creating a GT Plan for Developing Community Partnerships
Rest Day Activities	-Debrief: Invite the PLC team to share what they learned from their conversations with families -Playbook Activities: Multilayer Communication with Gifted Families, Developing a GT Plan for Developing Community Partnerships **You may find that in Z3, you only need two PLC groups as the instructional** strategies are new to most -Building a Gifted Education Family, Community, and School Collaborative Council	-PLC Online Reflection Prompts -Connection to the Classroom: Continue drafting the GT Plan for Developing Community Partnerships with your PLC team -Prepare to assist in follow up session → **Facilitator reflects on exit tickets & plans** next PLC
Iterative Insert	*There's only one April session due to the break schedule. Bonus Online Activities! Circle back to Zone 3 with the Playbook Activity: Equity Detectives: Identifying Inequalities in K-12 Current Events, Making Your Presence Known*	
May Session 1	-Debrief: Invite the PLC team to share what they learned from their conversations with families -Playbook Activities: Multilayer Communication with Gifted Families, Developing a GT Plan for Developing Community Partnerships **You may find that in Z3, you only need two PLC groups as the instructional** strategies are new to most	-Serve as PLC leaders -Share out the draft of the GT Plan for Developing Community Partnerships with the other PLC teams -Playbook Activities: Families & Friends of the Gifted Booster Club Planning Organizer

Figure 8.1 (Continued)

<table>
<tr><td>Rest Day Activities</td><td colspan="2">-PLC Online Reflection Prompts
-Connection to the Classroom Assignment: Reach out to 3-5 of your gifted students in order to gather informal feedback about communication between families and school. Be prepared to share out at the next PLC meeting.
→ Facilitator reflects on exit tickets & plans next PLC</td><td>-PLC Online Reflection Prompts
-Connection to the Classroom: Continue drafting the Families & Friends of the Gifted Booster Club Planning Organizer with your PLC team
-Prepare to assist in follow up session
→ Facilitator reflects on exit tickets & plans next PLC</td></tr>
<tr><td>Iterative Insert</td><td>Circle back to Zones 2&3 with the Playbook Activities: This is Who I am: A Photo Essay for Gifted Learners; Identification Case Study</td><td>Circle back to Zones 2&3 with the Playbook Activities: Hexagonal thinking: Giftedness & Identity; Identification Case Study</td><td>Circle back to Zone 3 Playbook Activities: Hexagonal thinking: Giftedness & Identity; This is Who I am: A Photo Essay for Gifted Learners</td></tr>
<tr><td>May Session 2</td><td colspan="2">-Debrief: Invite the PLC team to share what they learned from their conversations with students
-Playbook Activities: Families & Friends of the Gifted Booster Club Planning Organizer, Equal Partnership Scales
**You may find that in Z3, you only need two PLC groups as the instructional strategies are new to most</td><td>-Serve as PLC leaders
-Share out the draft of the GT Plan for Developing Community Partnerships with the other PLC teams
-Playbook Activities: Checks & Balances</td></tr>
<tr><td>Rest Day Activities</td><td colspan="2">-PLC Online Reflection Prompts
-Connection to the Classroom Assignment: In PLC teams, review the draft of the GT Plan for Developing Community Partnerships and bring any modifications back to the next PLC meeting</td><td>-PLC Online Reflection Prompts
-Connection to the Classroom: Continue drafting the Families & Friends of the Gifted Booster Club Planning Organizer with your PLC team</td></tr>
<tr><td colspan="4">A Year in Review: Coach's Evaluation of the 4ZEPL Training Plan</td></tr>
<tr><td>June Session 1</td><td colspan="3">The last PL session of the year is reserved for the coach to review the progress made towards the goals established the previous summer.
-Review the goals & sub goals. Which ones did you meet? Which ones is your team still striving towards? Remember to celebrate the small wins--make sure to acknowledge the team's success.
-Assess the progress. Which PL sessions were most effective? Why? Which PL sessions need modification? How would you modify them? What factors influenced the implementation of the PL (weather cancellation, unexpected district policy changes, etc). Consider the growth of the individual players, where are they now compared to the beginning of the year?
-What's the plan for next year? Start planning and preparing for the upcoming academic year.</td></tr>
</table>

Figure 8.1 (Continued)

the *time is now* for equity, take the time (now) to build relationships and foster this new way of understanding your peers and/or faculty to ensure that the critical message is not lost in the urgency.

Stretch

4ZEPL is a multi-faceted approach to addressing inequities in gifted education. Systemic change is necessary for the field of gifted education to achieve equity, and this cannot be achieved by a one-person show. Do not be afraid to utilize your resources, ask the hard questions, and seek out practical solutions. As we tell our pre-service and in-service teachers, it is okay not to know, but it is not okay not to be willing to find out. We ask our participants to stretch during the PL process—but as the facilitator, you may also need to stretch.

Hydrate

You can't pour from an empty well. Take this literally (water and feed your body!) and figuratively: self-care is essential. Activist burnout is a significant detriment to not only the social justice activists themselves, but to the sustainability of the cause.[6] Burnout is both emotional and physical in nature, and *while it cannot be stemmed by self-care alone*, establishing healthy boundaries for work and home, adhering to schedules, meditation, routines, and yes, proper hydration, are helpful strategies to alleviating some of the stress placed on our individual bodies. Cheers!

Push to the Limits

One more from Coach Ted Lasso: "Taking on a challenge is a lot like riding a horse, isn't it? If you're comfortable while you're doing it, you're probably doing it wrong." We've talked about courageous conversations, brave spaces, and the pedagogy of discomfort; most of these have been from a participant perspective, and how you as the facilitator/coach need to be prepared to lead these discussions. You too may be pushed to the limits and may experience discomfort. Ideally, we recommend that gifted-equity facilitation be in pairs; there are great co-teaching models to follow. But we understand that gifted education is so often in a silo, and we are frequently sole practitioners in our field, whether at the school, district, state, or higher education level; combined with limited budgets, you may not have an option but to facilitate your professional learning on your own. Whenever possible, at conventions or through an online medium, make connections with others doing this work, so that you can have peer support to talk through issues. We are here for you too.

Take a Knee

NFL Player and activist Colin Kaepernick said, "I couldn't see another #SandraBland, #TamirRice, #WalterScott, #EricGarner. The list goes on and on and on. At what point do we do something about it?" Kaepernick began a silent and peaceful protest of racial injustice and police brutality, first by remaining sitting while the anthem played at the start of football games, and later by taking a knee. Fellow NFL player and author Michael Bennett remarked when he joined the protest, "By not standing, I wanted to honor the founding principles of this country—the freedom of self-expression, liberty, and the equal opportunity to pursue happiness—and challenge us to try to reach those goals."

Are we directing you to sit during the daily pledge to protest racial injustice? Well… no, but you are more than welcome to do so if you choose, per the Supreme Court in 1943 and a ruling in the case of the West Virginia School Board *vs.* Barnette. In Section 31 of the ruling on June 14, 1943, Justice Jackson wrote,

> Struggles to coerce uniformity of sentiment in support of some end thought essential to their time and country have been waged by many good as well as by evil men. Nationalism is a relatively recent phenomenon but at other times and places the ends have been racial or territorial security… Those who begin coercive elimination of dissent soon find themselves exterminating dissenters. Compulsory unification of opinion achieves only the unanimity of the graveyard.[7]

How strongly those words echo today, 60 years later. But again… no, we aren't asking you to take a knee, but saying that teachers are activists, engaged in transformative education. Activism is good teaching, and there is a pedagogy of teacher activism. How will you model antiracist or antibias teaching… or perhaps abolitionist teaching speaks to you? There is not only one way: www.rethinkingschools.org, www.teachingforjustice.org, and https://abolitionistteachingnetwork.org/ are great places to get started! As facilitators, model these approaches for the educators in your groups, and empower them to be change agents in the classrooms.

Empower Your Players

Elena Aguilar describes four phases of transformative coaching as action-oriented steps that coaches guide their clients through: *surfacing* the current reality (much like *taking a pulse*); *recognizing* the root causes of the of their problems and reflecting on their impacts; *exploring* emotions by naming, accepting, and understanding what they feel, thereby opening up a portal to deeper emotions of courage and commitment to the equity work and confidence in its pursuit; and *creating* new practices, beliefs and behaviors.[8] Recall from Chapter 1 that our overall goal is structural and systemic change within our spheres of influence. We are empowering change, coaching with research-based best practices, and then opening the doors to the field as the whistle blows!

Aguilar further describes five principles of transformative coaching: compassion, curiosity, connection, courage, and purpose. These principles help to inform the coaching process. Compassion centers the humanity of others and ourselves, while curiosity reminds us to suspend judgment and listen with open hearts and minds. Connection relates to the "both/and" rather than the "either/or" frame, reinforcing the importance of interrelatedness, and rejecting binary thinking. Courage provides the strength and urgency needed to action, even when risky. Purpose is fulfilled when we act with these four Cs: compassion, connection, curiosity, and courage. "Our purpose is to create a world characterized by justice, equity, and liberation. The journey is the destination."[9]

Feedback

"Game after game, year after year, you never stop thinking about the balls you get your hands on and don't catch." Football tight end Tony Gonzalez reflected on missing the passes, and what that taught him: "You learn a lot more about yourself and the opportunity for growth is so much greater when you lose." Feedback is an essential piece of the professional learning puzzle and part of your responsibility as a facilitator for your participants, but these tips are also designed for you! Consider how you can collect feedback to reflect on, to learn about yourself and provide opportunities for your own growth as a facilitator. This, again, is where having a professional learning partner is beneficial, to give each other feedback on presentation styles and facilitation practices. Reflecting upon body language and other nonverbal cues and *taking a pulse* throughout the PL experiences can provide you with valuable feedback as well. Ideally, you want to gather feedback early, continually, and often. Of course, one goal is to make improvements for the next group; but if you can make improvements for current participants, that's even better!

Cool Down

After a long, grueling day at work, don't you just love to relax in a nice ice-water bath? Wait, something seems off with that sentence! Angela likes her baths with bubbles and a book (and hot water, please!), but cooling down after exercise is essential to regulate body temperature, clean and repair muscles, and prevent blood from pooling in the veins—some athletes go straight for the polar plunge with an ice-water bath after a tough game. In the world of PL, this cool down is the closure, and it is what—all too often—we end up rushing through or even skipping altogether because we run out of time. But it is on this Top Ten list for a reason—it is imperative that we take time to regulate and reflect, clean and repair (mis)conceptions, and prevent (bad) blood from pooling in our hearts and minds. If you are running short on time (it happens to the best of us, ahem, Angela), take a polar plunge with a quick closure, but follow up with an online check-in, taking advantage of the digital world in which we live!

Coaching Hours

You didn't think we were *done*, did you? Coaches need professional learning and recertification hours, too! Never stop learning and engaging. Create new goals for yourself. Though she writes, researches, teaches, and presents in gifted education and equity, Angela regularly attends different equity, critical race theory (CRT) and ABAR-related training institutes, and is a repeat attendee at Abolitionist Teaching Network, Equity Literacy Institute, and CRT trainings and events, her grounding frameworks.

One of the biggest dangers in equity work can be the "woke White crew that thinks they're fine." This can be the toughest group to work with. Because we think we know it all, we aren't open to knowledge, listening to experiences, or engaging. Wait… did that say we? Yes, *we* can fall into the trap of what Layla Saad calls White exceptionalism.[10] While working on a chapter for this book, Angela was simultaneously attending an online institute, and she jokingly said to a few people, "I'll see you at the next session, though I'll probably only half listen to [name redacted so this person remains Angela's friend] because I've heard this talk before." Yes… *we*—what hubris, what White exceptionalism she exhibited! Ultimately, Angela *did* tune in, got caught up in the engaging presentation and closed down the chapter, and yes, she did learn something new.

One Last Pep Talk

Borrowing sage advice from President Obama, we leave you with these words of wisdom from his speech to the Howard graduating class of 2016:

> Now it's your turn. And the good news is, you're ready. And when your journey seems too hard, and when you run into a chorus of cynics who tell you that you're being foolish to keep believing or that you can't do something, or that you should just give up, or you should just settle—you might say to yourself a little phrase that I've found handy these last eight years: Yes, we can.[11]

Notes

1 Rizvi, A. (2012, Sept. 9). *The fall and rise of maturing Serena Williams.* The National. https://www.thenationalnews.com/sport/the-fall-and-rise-of-maturing-serena-williams-1.632294/
2 Obama, B. (2007, November 10). Speech at the Jefferson–Jackson Dinner.
3 Perry, T., Steele, C., & Hilliard, A. (2003). *Young, gifted and black: Promoting high achievement among African-American students.* Beacon Press.
4 Ayala, M. J., Carter, J. K., Fachon, A. S., Flaxman, S. M., Gil, M. A., Kenny, H. V., … & Volckens, J. (2021). Belonging in STEM: An interactive, iterative approach to create and maintain a diverse learning community. *Trends in Ecology & Evolution.* Advance online publication. doi: 10.1016/j.tree.2021.08.004.
5 Guskey, T. R. (2016). Gauge impact with 5 levels of data. *Learning Forward, 37*(1), 32–37.
6 Gorski, P. C. (2018). Racial battle fatigue and activist burnout in racial justice activists of color at predominately white colleges and universities. *Race Ethnicity and Education, 22*(1), 1–20. doi: 10.1080/13613324.2018.1497966
7 West Virginia State Board of Education et al. v. Barnette et al. https://www.law.cornell.edu/supremecourt/text/319/624 (section 31).
8 Aguilar, E. (2020). *Coaching for equity: Conversations that change practice.* Jossey-Bass.
9 Ibid., p. 46.
10 Saad, L. F. (2020). *Me and white supremacy: Combat racism, change the world, and become a good ancestor.* Sourcebooks.
11 Obama, B. (2016, May 7). Speech at Howard University.